# FinanciaLit™

Thomas J. Barrella

ISBN 978-1-7350069-0-1 pbk.
Abaco Press, Massapequa, NY.

*To the truest, toughest, most generous and supportive parents a person could wish for, Thomas C. and Sally Barrella*

## Acknowledgements

A world of thanks goes to my colleagues in the best business education department anywhere. The collaborative and collegial environment they've fostered have me arriving at school each day with the commitment to get after it. Their support of this project has given me that last bit of motivation needed to see it through to completion. These special people are Kathleen Goldin, Jason Muller, Diane Malley, Glenn Baumann, Matt Fiasconaro and Danielle Garrison.

I am grateful to our district administration for its extraordinary support of the business education program. Their interest in what we do and belief in how it benefits our students give us the confidence to shine. Thank you, Superintendent Dr. Tom Rogers and Assistant Superintendent Adele Bovard. Kudos to high school principal Dr. John Durante and assistant principals Ray Gessner, Chris Ruffini and Dave Steinberg. Special thanks to my direct supervisor, Maryanne Rinaudo-Concessi, who could not be more supportive.

For their fine stewardship of the district, I want to thank Board of Trustees President Tracy Frankel, Vice President Rob Gershon, and members Carol Cheng, Christopher DiFilippo, Andrew Feldman, Anna Levitan, Susan Parker, Thomas Rotolo and Chris Ulrich.

Much praise goes to our students, who are inquisitive, intelligent, motivated, mature, respectful and downright funny. It is you who make being an educator so rewarding.

Many thanks to my editor, Marianne Plunkert, whose keen insights helped refine the content, concepts and message. Thanks as well to Ryan Healey, Joe DeFino, James McGuire and Matt Csillag for critiquing various chapters.

# Foreword

## Don't be that guy

"I will work until I die." I read that in an article a few years back. How sad. Before you begin feeling sorry for the poor soul who said that, you might want to take a personal inventory of how much empathy you have to go around. This statement describes the *majority* of middle-class Americans.

"No way!" you protest. Yes way. A Wells Fargo survey of 1,000 people who earned between $25,000 and $100,000 annually showed that 37% of them planned to work until they were unable to or until they died.[i] "But 37% is not a majority!" you say. True, but the article goes on to state that another 34% expect to work until they are at least 80, a slightly less painful way of saying the same thing. Adding the two percentages together indicates that a staggering 71% of middle-class Americans are in a very bad way.

How can you avoid this fate? Become financially literate. Then, use your new skills to plan and live a more secure life. This book is for anyone who wants to come in out of the darkness and understand everything from the most basic financial concepts to a few quite sophisticated ones.

This is the book I've wanted to hand students who've told me that they couldn't fit our personal finance course into their schedules, so it covers a lot of ground.

More good news: I don't have an agenda. I'm sponsored by no one and have nothing to promote. Everything you'll read here is my own opinion, formed over decades as a student of business, government, society and life.

Regardless of how you happened on this book, welcome. I am committed to making it worth your while because the one thing that's more precious than your money is your time. Let's get started.

# Contents

# Chapter 1 What is wealth?

While money is critically important, it is but one of many pieces that must come together for us to have a life worth living. Let's begin with a broader look at life before turning our attention to finance.

One of the most enjoyable units in the personal finance course we offer is the one that explores wealth. If you were asked to list what you needed to live a happy life, how would you answer? Besides an ample amount of money, your thoughts may turn to your physical condition. "If you don't have your health, you don't have anything," the saying goes. Apple cofounder Steve Jobs appeared to be extremely wealthy, but in the end that didn't save him from failing health and eventual death.

We, as a society, are also turning much-needed attention to mental and emotional well-being. Deviating from the script, I characterize mental health as the ability to receive, ponder, remember, recall, process and synthesize information in a manner that allows a person to manage a modern life.

A person's emotional state, his or her ability to experience a range of feelings—from joy to sorrow and from anger to grief—is a reflection of the cumulative effects of life's positive and negative experiences. So impressionable are we humans that it's a rare person who arrives at adulthood without accumulating at least a carry-on-size piece of emotional baggage.

Summarizing the above, we can come up with a simple list of four aspects in which we may or may not be doing well. These are displayed in the table on the next page. It's difficult to imagine a person who is unable to check all four boxes being considered wealthy.

After exploring these ideas, I ask that students assign each aspect a weight commensurate with their assessment of its relative importance. It's my way of suggesting that perhaps the balance of a bank account isn't the only way to measure wealth. There's room for you to assign your percentages, so give it a try. But don't take the easy way out by assigning 25% to each!

| Type of wealth | Value to you (%) |
|---|---|
| Financial health | |
| Physical health | |
| Mental health | |
| Emotional health | |
| Total | 100% |

Over the years we've bandied about many additional ways in which a person can have a beneficial attribute that should be considered a form of wealth.

A select few people are acutely aware of what they were meant to do with their time on this earth. Their sense of *purpose* means they waste no time wandering around in search of a career they might be able to stomach. Their lack of self-doubt allows them to direct all of their energies toward the cause at hand. Not surprisingly, they have incredible *drive.* They can get where they're going by sheer force of will. They soldier on, going over, around and through roadblocks that leave mere mortals defeated. More often than not, however, they avoid having to roll up their sleeves. That's because their passion is so infectious that people usually give them what they came for!

Some people are so *gregarious* that they collect friends like lint. They maintain strong relationships. They're at ease approaching strangers. Name a city, and they've got a friend there. Ask them for a favor, and they know just who to call. How they stay so close with so many people so effortlessly is a mystery. Not surprisingly, when they have success, a crowd celebrates with them.

Let's give *intelligence* its due, and we're not just referring to book smarts. Howard Gardiner, in his 1983 book *Frames of Mind: The Theory of Multiple Intelligences,* identified eight! The point is that all of us are sharp in some way.

There are people whose insatiable *curiosity* allows them to find new intrigue by simply observing the world around them. They wonder, for example, why the letter *b* isn't swapped with *fl* in the word *butterfly,* resulting in a truly fitting name.

A select few people have a marketable *talent* that allows them to be paid handsomely for their artistry or athletic prowess. Does it get any better than that—being paid to do something one is passionate about? Even if a person's skills are not obviously marketable, possessing a knack for something can still make for a richer life. Great cooks whip up delectable meals out of whatever is in the fridge, while the rest of us stand there staring blankly as the cold air slips away.

If there's an aptitude that's hiding in the weeds, it's the ability for some people to go beyond just a garden-variety sense of well-being to reach a sublime sense of *acceptance.* Life can deal us any number of nasty cards, including the loss of a family member, the end of a significant relationship, loss of income and failing health. While some people never fully recover from these setbacks, others—often through their faith—are able to grieve what is lost and accept what is. They don't fear aging. They don't fear dying. Their ability to find peace, contentment and meaning no matter their circumstance might be characterized as maxing out their emotional health.

## Takeaways

#1: We are born with some forms of wealth, but we can (if we want) develop others.

#2: We can gain or lose one of more aspects of wealth over

the course of our lives. This is all the more reason to check in with ourselves from time to time to assess which are trending up, holding steady or trending down.

#3: Aggressive pursuit of one form of wealth usually comes at the expense of the others. Here is a great example:

A former student went to work for one of the Big Four accounting firms after college. During tax season he was working 80- to 100-hour weeks. So productive was he that the more he got done, the more work his boss directed his way. Although he was only in his mid-20s, his health was already being impacted by stress and lack of sleep. In the off-tax season he studied for and passed the four sections of the CPA exam. He stayed at the accounting firm just long enough to meet the CPA experience requirement. An avid runner, he went to work at a sneaker store in some earthy granola town.

#4: Rare is the person who has it all, despite outward appearances.

#5: Extreme wealth in one form does not inoculate a person from suffering a lack of other forms of wealth.

Earlier, we referred to Steve Jobs. Let's look at another personal profile:

James Simons is the brilliant mathematician who, in 1982, founded Renaissance Technologies. His ability to use mathematics to make sense of the ups and downs of financial markets allowed him to trade successfully, attract investor money and, over decades, accumulate a net worth in excess of $15 billion.[ii] That's wealthy. He is married with five kids, three with his first wife and two with his current wife. That's wealthier. In 1996, his son Paul was killed by a car while riding a bicycle near the Simons' Hamptons home. That's less wealthy. In 2003, his son Nick drowned while on a trip to Bali.[iii] That's even less wealthy. How much is a life worth? We would find out if we were able to offer Mr. Simons the ability to pay money to have his sons back.

Not 24 hours after the above was written, a story ran in the New York media about a man, a doctor, a surgeon—the chief thoracic surgeon, actually—at Hackensack University Medical Center. He was married to a renowned doctor, author and TV medical correspondent. They had two children. Two weeks ago, he and his wife got divorced. Yesterday, he jumped off the George Washington Bridge to his death.[iv] The good doctor had so much going for him, but his emotional wealth flat-lined.

#6: By far the biggest takeaway is that if we are honest with ourselves, we are much wealthier than we recognize. You are truly rich if:

- on a beautiful day you have the wherewithal to raise your gaze to the sky and feel the warmth of the sun on your face.
- you are not subject to abuse, neglect or ridicule. Instead of gnawing thoughts of inadequacy, brokenness and self-loathing, you are emotionally free to aspire to greater heights for yourself and those you love.
- you are not trapped in addiction, overwhelming debt, a serious illness or some other all-consuming trial you are fearful you won't survive.
- you have complete confidence in your economic value, and the idea that you will have difficulty earning a living never enters your mind.
- you are free to choose what to do with your time, even if it happens to be burning days binge-watching the latest series.
- there are people around you who love you and with whom you can be honest.
- you get up and going every day without giving a thought to your body because you are free from chronic illness

and physical limitations.[1]

To what do we owe our great fortune? The faithful say that it is simply God's grace. The secular say that it is pure chance to be born in our favorable time and place.

## Gratitude

No matter how we view our good fortune, our wealth is all for nought if we are unable to appreciate it. For those who don't wake up every day grateful for what they have, there is good news. Gratitude can be developed. Tonight at the dinner table, announce that every person present will identify three people or circumstances in their lives for which they are thankful. Keep that up for a month, and I'm guessing your perspective will begin to shift on a whole lot of levels. If you don't regularly eat dinner with friends or family, you should.

Unfortunately, achieving a state of gratitude is easier than keeping it. Modern life hurls at us a never-ending series of assaults that threaten to knock us out of the good place we work so diligently to inhabit.

Last week my wife returned home with a special surprise from the university where she's enrolled. It was a ticket. She had failed to maintain her license plate. Unbeknownst to us, a piece of paint had fallen off the plate, taking with it the contrast between the letters and the background. Should we get upset over it? The semester had just begun. She had her new parking authorization in the window. The authorities could have left her a note on the windshield. They knew she'd be returning.

Additionally, was the amount of the fine, $155, set to ensure

---

[1] Even if you are suffering under one of these unfortunate situations, there are resources available to address them. You probably realized, even if for just a moment, that you are not fated to be stuck in a bad situation and that with courage, perseverance and support, you can overcome these challenges and improve your life.

compliance with the law or punish us while generating revenue for the municipality? While standing in line at the DMV to get a new plate, we discussed whether to challenge the ticket, a proposition that would consume precious time and energy. In the end I checked the box marked "Guilty" and paid the fine. For a person with a strong righteous streak, it was difficult to check that box, but check it I did.

I am very grateful I'm able to afford the fine without having it derail our financial situation. I'm grateful we had nothing going on the afternoon we received the ticket, which allowed us to get new plates the same day. I'm grateful there was a DMV nearby that was open into the evening. I'm also grateful the DMV didn't charge us for the new plates and registration card.

The license plate ticket incident retreated from memory in the days that followed, which is a good thing because the very day I wrote about it, we received an envelope in the mail from EZ-Pass. A few weeks ago a family member (who shall remain nameless) drove through Delaware and failed to select the correct side at the point where the highway splits off. At that juncture, those with EZ-Pass sensors on their windshields go one way and those who do not go another way, since they have to stop at a booth and pay the toll. That section of road has a $4 toll that EZ-Pass holders pay while zooming past the overhead scanners at highway speed. This family member cruised past the scanner with no EZ-Pass sensor. The arrival of the envelope meant it was time to pay up. Opening it revealed the following:

| | |
|---|---|
| TOLL DUE | $ 4.00 |
| ADMINISTRATIVE FEE: | $ 25.00 |
| AMBULANCE CO. FUND: | $ 10.00 |
| COMBAT VIOLENT CRIMES: | $ 15.00 |
| BALANCE DUE: | $ 54.00 |

I called customer service just to make sure that we hadn't

missed an initial notice to pay without additional charges. The representative said that there was no prior notice. The $50 in additional fees, a 1,250%[2] penalty, is what the state believes is fair to extract from offenders like us.

Congratulations, Delaware, for you have gotten to us in a way that will rattle around in our psyches for a while and hamper our ability to get back to a place of gratitude.

Yet, get back we must. I should be grateful that, as was the case with the license plate fine, it's only money. Money can be replaced, which is more than can be said of lives and years. Most important, I am grateful that my family member made it back from the road trip safely.

Heck, I'm just grateful to be here. I've been fortunate with regard to financial, physical and mental health, but on the issue of emotional health, it's not exactly been a box of chocolates. In my youth I was (figuratively) pummelled so thoroughly that I could not get beyond introspection, beyond fear that my situation was terminal, that the burdens I was barely managing would eventually fell me. I took up long-term residence in very dark places where desperation and despair were the order of the day and each day seemed without end.[3] Yet I've always felt that life is a gift and known that I'm here for a reason. It is these beliefs that kept me putting one foot in front of the other, no matter how dire the situation. They say that if you're going through hell, keep going. I kept going.

While in my late teens, I'd founded a promising technology

---

[2] In Chapter 3 we will discuss how the penalty percentage was calculated.

[3] Psychologist John Bradshaw was a big help during those rough times, dropping some truth bombs that are still with me today. As an example, he cautioned against resorting to a recollection of all your accomplishments to affirm your self-worth. Bradshaw explained that we're called human beings, not human doings. It ought to be OK just to be.

company with three talented and motivated high school classmates. Single, young and driven, we worked so very hard, and basically ate up our 20s, for the cause.[4] The company would go on to an initial public offering and years later be bought by a competitor for over $1 billion. Prior to these milestones, however, a fateful encounter exposed my emotional deficit and blew my world to pieces. Not surprisingly, I did not participate in the windfall.

Some years later I'd accumulated enough money to build my dream house. That meant designing it and, with big assists from my brother Chris and my Dad, acting as the general contractor. It meant doing a significant amount of the carpentry and anything else necessary to clear the way for the next sub-contractor. We even sided the house ourselves, using a tricky but beautiful fibre-cement lap board. It took years to complete as we worked through every detail, but the house came out better than I could have dreamed. It is not the most grand or ornate. Its layout, proportions and mixture of textures, colors and materials just came together in a way that made it the nicest and most welcoming space in which I've ever been. It was with great pride that I gave family, friends and guests a tour of the *big blue house*. I would happily extend that offer to you, but it is no longer mine.

I've even had the good fortune to be invited on *The View*, only to have Joy Behar throw shade my way. Despite dreams dashed, every day I wake up determined to do and be my best as a husband, father, educator, family member and friend. It is gratitude that sustains me.

I graduated in the 1980s from a university in upstate New York, about 180 miles from where we lived on Long Island. A

---

[4] This is a perfect illustration of the distinction between mental health and emotional health. My brain worked just fine. By focusing on nothing but our company, I was able to avoid indefinitely acknowledging and dealing with my poor emotional state.

few years after graduation a college buddy named Paul, from a Detroit suburb, told me his employer, "Generous" Motors, was sending him back to school for a master's degree. My family and I invited him to spend Thanksgiving break with us, so he drove down in his new sports car, a Pontiac Fiero.

By that time, my aforementioned tech company partners and I were actively working on our business. One night we met for dinner at a local restaurant, after which we decided to go to one of my partner's parents' homes to continue the conversation. I sat shotgun in the low-slung two-seater while Paul showed it off by zipping around the area roads. Of course, the route from the restaurant to the home had to include a treacherous intersection. Ignoring the 20 MPH warning sign, Paul brought the Fiero toward the tight downhill right turn at too high a speed. By the time I realized that he had no idea what lay ahead, it was too late. The turn wound down around a hill and had a tightening radius, with a stop sign at the bottom for good measure. By mid-turn, the car was skidding sideways. A moment later, it moved in the direction it was pointed, nosing the front bumper into the hill. With its motion in that direction halted, the car began to roll. I leaned forward, grabbed the door handle and held on. There was a harrowing sound as the roof of car slammed the pavement. In the darkness, I saw a white flash as the back of my head hit the roof of the car.

My partners were following in another vehicle. They entered the turn to see the Fiero upside down. They rushed over just as Paul and I unbuckled our seat belts and crawled over shattered glass through the narrowed openings that the windows formerly occupied. Since the driver's side of the car was on the inside of the rotation, Paul was shaken but not hurt. I, on the other hand, stumbled around with blood streaming down my face. It was like a scene out of the horror movie *Carrie*.

A trip to the hospital for stitches to close a gash in my scalp and some precautionary tests was all that was necessary. So mortified was Paul that he flew home to Michigan the next day. I never heard from him again.

I've lost a friend, but am very grateful not to be dead, paralyzed or brain-injured. As my injury healed, I came to appreciate my good fortune more deeply, for such was the force of the blow that the area where my skull took the impact is slightly dented. I mean, you can't see it from across the street, but it's there. Could I be living these last 30-plus years on borrowed time? I believe so.[5]

My college days and fraternity experience produced some of my most cherished memories. The camaraderie developed with 30 brothers living together in the former town mayor's mansion was priceless. In my junior year I was elected chapter president. We threw epic parties. During one, several young women were gathered around one of their friends who was passed out on a couch. They tried to rouse her, but couldn't. To see the distress on their faces was sobering. Just as we were about to call 911, she came to. A potential tragedy, avoided. For that I am very grateful.

I used to drive home during breaks, carpooling with other students who lived on Long Island. It was raining on one return trip up the New York State Thruway. My car started hydroplaning. It began rotating, pointing in a direction that was slightly different from the direction the car was heading. I tried to correct gently. No dice. It swung as much to the other side, then completely around, eventually sliding down the embankment between the northbound and southbound lanes. After the car came to rest at the bottom of the collection area, we all got out to survey the damage. There was none. The only hint that something was amiss was shredded grass running up the side of the car. Within minutes, we were back on the road,

---

[5]Not long after the accident, the town completely reconfigured the intersection.

arriving at school as if nothing had happened. It was another tragedy avoided. I am grateful for New York State's civil engineers who elevated the travel lanes, thus separating them with a low gathering area that safely collected my car that evening.

Single into my early 40s, I was nonetheless able to find a lovely wife and gain two wonderful daughters at the same time. To be a part of their maturation from girls into fine young women has been priceless. The support of my wife has allowed us to overcome myriad challenges, including the flooding of our home during Hurricane Sandy and a botched house lift that actually made Sandy feel like a walk in the park. I admire her tenacity and am proud of how much she has accomplished. I am so grateful for the love and support of my wife and two daughters. On top of that, my parents are still alive and as engaged as ever. How fortunate am I?

Each year I have the awesome privilege of introducing sharp, inquisitive students to the world of money, finance and investing. In the classroom I am in my element. Both district and building leadership are confident that I know what I'm doing, and they give me the freedom to be my best.

Come holiday season, a handful of students (whose constituency cannot be predicted) will approach me after class with cards on which they express how much they enjoy being in my class. For them and their kind words I am grateful.

Besides building the aforementioned big blue house, I've renovated several others. No one has ever been injured working on these projects.

I have a slight build, so I gave away a lot in collisions along the boards of the rinks on which I played competitive ice hockey. A torn labrum in my left shoulder and another in my left hip portended a hobbled adulthood. Yet great health insurance provided access to talented surgeons who worked their arthroscopic magic and put me back together.

I am grateful for professional sports. Being a huge fan of

athletics played at high levels, I was fortunate to witness the hometown New York Islanders reel off four consecutive Stanley Cups. We moved our business to Atlanta in time to watch the Braves assemble a pitching line-up that featured future hall-of-famers Greg Maddux, Tom Glavine and John Smoltz. They put on a clinic nightly and helped propel the Braves to 14 straight division titles.

There are just too many compelling teams, players, story lines and epic matchups to fairly recount. But if I tried, I'd begin with the Bird–Magic rivalry and end with the emergence of Patrick Mahomes as magician. For being able to witness these players test their physical and mental limits in their quest for victory, I am grateful.

I'm also thankful that I can listen to any piece of music that ever gave me joy and learn about the amazing musicians and bands who create these treasures. A favorite diversion when listening to music on a computer is to read comments from other listeners as they attempt to put into words what the music means to them. A comment I especially liked was written by a guy talking about the Cars' music: "It's 40 years old, and it still sounds like it's coming from the future." I challenge you to fire up the song combination "Shoo Be Doo" and "Candy-O" and then refute his remark. It's never been easier to discover new music (and not-so-new music one has somehow missed). Like, where has Arcade Fire been hiding?

Just a few years ago my daughter was practicing driving in the neighborhood. She had been developing a bad habit of starting her turns late and wandering onto the far side of the street. I made the mistake of pointing this out mid-turn. She did a quick hand-over-hand maneuver, overcorrected and froze upon seeing that the car's tight turning radius had us heading for the curb. After jumping it, the car made a beeline for a power pole, which it proceeded to strike flush. We were shaken but not hurt. It was a nice fall evening. Had a neighbor and her dog been in our path, we surely would have run them over. Only, they weren't there. You get the idea. Gratitude. Develop it. Stay in it.

On a lighter note, I am pleased to announce after careful consideration that I have identified the wealthiest person in the world. He and his wife of 25+ years have two children. Tall and handsome, he sports a charming accent. He's hunky enough to play a superhero in the movies but has the depth to play Le Miserables' Jean Valjean! Following are reviews for his Broadway show from years back:

> *"The impossibly talented, impossibly energetic Mr. __________ is a glorious dinosaur among live entertainers of the 21st century: an honest-to-gosh old-fashioned matinee idol who connects to his audiences without a hint of contempt for them or for himself." –* ***The New York Times***[v]

> *"Whatever else he does, __________ brings joy to the stage. Comparisons are being offered to the deep impression made by a solo artist such as [Judy] Garland. But the rapturous emotional intensity that lingers is not what this performer provides. Garland left blood on the stage. __________ leaves sweat, and a smile." –* ***The Washington Post***[vi]

*People* magazine named him the year's "Sexiest Man Alive." Of course, all that talent has helped him accumulate a net worth in excess of $150 million.[vii] *Without cheating*, did you guess who it is? The answer is hidden in the middle of the book, so continue reading!

Before concluding this chapter, I'd like to introduce a feature we'll use throughout the book called *"Who is or was?"* Who doesn't like a good life story? Who hasn't learned something about themselves, others and humanity from them? When you see *"Who is or was?"*, please take a few minutes to learn the full stories of the people identified. Let's try it now:

*Who is or was?* Malala Yousafzai

So, what was the point of this little excursion? It's to help you develop perspective. It's about encouraging you to craft a well-rounded view of yourself. The financial dimension is only part of the whole you, and it's not nearly enough to make for a happy and rewarding life.[6]

## Exercises on wealth

1. Take the percentages of importance you assigned earlier to the different types of wealth and multiply each by a rating from 1 (lowest) to 5 (highest) that reflects how well you are doing in that wealth area. Adding up the results will tell you how wealthy you are. Compare with your classmates, friends and colleagues.

| Type of wealth | Value to you (%) | Your rating | Result |
|---|---|---|---|
| Financial health | | X | = |
| Physical health | | X | = |
| Mental health | | X | = |
| Emotional health | | X | = |
| Total | 100% | Total wealth | |

2. Identify one thing you can do in each of the four wealth areas to improve your standing.
3. Identify a well-known person who has one form of wealth in abundance but seems to be missing another

[6] Financial wealth will, however, allow you to choose your form of "misery."

in equal measure. Assess the person's overall wealth. Explain why you would or would not swap lives with the person.

4. Identify the person who you believe is the wealthiest in the world, supporting your answer with a discussion of the different ways he or she is wealthy.
5. Write down three current aspects of your life for which you are grateful. If they involve people, have you expressed your gratitude to them? Why or why not?
6. Describe an event in your past that could have ended very badly but didn't.

# Chapter 2 Are you ready?

It can happen at any moment. You can only hope that when it arrives, the judgment is not too harsh. Who or what is being judged? You. Who's doing the judging? That would be you as well.

For Buffalo Bills defensive player Vontae Davis, the moment arrived 47 seconds before the end of the first half of the Sunday, September 16, 2018, game against the Chargers. Mr. Davis explained in an interview a few days later:

> *"I went to the bench after that series, and it just hit me. I don't belong on that field anymore."* [viii]

Right there, right then, in the middle of the game, he retired! At rare points in our lives we are granted moments of stunning clarity about our place in the world. It might be realizing just how miserable you are dedicating your time and energy to an activity you're now doing to please others because you lost the passion for it a long time ago. For an aspiring athlete, it's the moment an opponent blows past him like he's standing still and he realizes he doesn't have what it takes to go pro. It might be the moment you realize a person you considered a peer has advanced far ahead of you in education, relationships, faith or career. It could be the moment you realize you're wasting your life and your gifts doing basically nothing.

The good news is that we don't have to wait for an "Aha!" moment or crisis to take action. A guy with a drug habit doesn't have to wake up in a hospital from a near overdose to realize he must turn his life around. A woman working a dead-end job doesn't have to let her debts become unmanageable before realizing she's headed for financial ruin.

All this is a roundabout way of saying that at any time you can sit down, take stock of your current situation and plan how to achieve the life you want for yourself. Planning, being proactive about your life, is so much better than always having life happen to you.

## Goals and plans

A plan is a series of coordinated goals. A goal is an attainable accomplishment or status you invest your time and energies to reach.

The following is not a goal: *I'm going to be mad rich.* A well-stated goal should:

- be reasonably attainable (i.e., realistic), or else it won't provide much motivation;
- be specific and measurable, or we won't know when we've achieved it;
- be time-bound, because a goal appropriate for one stage of life may not be for another;
- indicate the action that will lead to its attainment so that, in the unlikely instance you forget how you intended to reach the goal, you can look back and clue yourself in.

See if you can find the above elements in the following goals:

- For anyone: *By eliminating my sugary drink consumption, I will lose five pounds in the next 60 days.*
- For a teen: *By working 30 hours per week at my job, I will save $2,500 by the end of summer vacation.*

Long-term goals can be made more manageable if broken down into a series of medium-term goals that, in turn, can seem very attainable when further separated into short-term goals. For example, most people don't accumulate $25,000 in wealth without first reaching $2,500 in wealth. Therefore, establishing a series of connected, sequential goals will align your short, medium and long-term objectives.

## The arc of life

The mechanics of planning and goal setting are not really what this chapter is about, however. What's more important is that you fully appreciate that the decisions you make today will affect, often profoundly, where you will stand in the future.

And because the interests of Current You are often in conflict with those of Future You, those decisions can be very difficult. You can blow all your money living for today because tomorrow is not guaranteed. But it's more likely that you will escape tragedy and reach a point in your life where the body and/or mind slow down enough that you are no longer able to support yourself. Old and destitute is not a good look.

It might be really amazing to see the upcoming concert of your favorite singer from a pair of $500 floor seats (when $50 rafter seats might do), but investing the $900 difference will allow Future You to spend it on something even more satisfying.

Because marketers are really good at what they do, delaying gratification is a daily battle. We are bombarded at every turn with messages and images suggesting that we can essentially buy the happiness and elevated status we so justly deserve. It's likely to take all you've got to push back against the promotion of *consumerism* that permeates our lives.

## "Be yourself. Everyone else is taken."

I teach at a big, high-performing public high school. There are over 2,000 students enrolled in grades 9 through 12. Clubs often post affirmations and exhortations in the halls. One contained the above quote, which is profound. This is your life and you are the only person who can live it. Being your own person has special importance when it comes to financial planning because, as noted in the foreword of this book, the masses are living their lives in a manner that will leave them broke. If you don't want that to be you, then you'd better muster up the courage to go your own way.

As a teen, that might mean deciding not to keep up with the latest sneaker trends. Sure, you might be the object of snickering by your frenemies, but rest assured that you will have the last laugh. As an adult it might mean being looked down upon, literally, by a neighbor as his tricked-out $80,000 SUV rolls up alongside your not-so-boss Toyota Echo.

## Appearances can deceive

The crazy part of trying to "keep up with ~~Joneses~~ Kardashians" is that a lot of what you may be tempted to chase isn't even true. One day you are driving down the road and come upon two homes, A and B:

A

B

Which person is wealthier, the one who owns home A or the one who owns home B? What if you learned that home A is worth about $450,000 and home B about $350,000? That should pretty much end all discussion. The owner of home A is wealthier, at least from a financial standpoint, right?

Let's add a final bit of information: the mortgage on home A has a remaining balance of $300,000 while that on home B is

$100,000. Next is some simple math that incorporates this new information:

| | A | B |
|---|---|---|
| Market value of home | $ 450,000 | $ 350,000 |
| Loan remaining | - $ 300,000 | - $ 100,000 |
| Owner's worth in home | = $ 150,000 | = $ 250,000 |

Whoops. Appearances in this situation deceived. As we hinted at earlier, Americans regularly use debt (borrowed money), to purchase houses, cars and vacations they can't really afford and should not be buying. Thankfully, that's their problem, not yours.

Let's rewind and describe a different scenario regarding the two homes. Say you purchase home B with a reasonable *down payment* and a manageable monthly loan payment. Over time you get to know the couple who owns home A. It turns out they're a power couple, both earning salaries into the hundreds of thousands. They paid off their home loan years ago. Each winter they take a long ski trip to Aspen, Colorado. They have a winter home in Boca Raton, Florida. This family is living an epic life that they can afford. If you tried to keep up with them, it would lead to financial destruction, so you shouldn't even try. There will always be people richer, smarter, fitter, taller, younger, cooler, prettier and funnier than you. In our first chapter we talked a lot about gratitude. You may have forgotten that we also talked about acceptance.[7]

Now, none of this is to say that you cannot aspire higher, but you shouldn't live that higher lifestyle until you've got the income and financial resources to support it.

---

[7] I don't want to send you down a side road, but if you are throwing down with me hard, you must read the May 23, 2011 *BusinessWeek* cover article, "How Rajat Gupta Came Undone" because it describes one person's alleged inability to accept, and what it cost him. The article is available to *BusinessWeek* subscribers. Try your local library. It's worth the effort. Note: Mr. Gupta disputes the article's assertions.

## The interaction of the forms of wealth

Our earlier look at wealth discussed how the different forms interact and affect one another. For example, a person with significant physical limitations requires extensive assistance with regular life activities. The cost of this aid will make it more difficult to achieve financial well-being.

The lack of emotional well-being is squirrelly, manifesting itself in a variety of behaviors, all with the hope of feeling better. Drug use is common, as are compulsions. There's compulsive eating, compulsive cleaning and compulsive shopping. It is said that people who constantly buy shiny new things are doing so to fill a "hole in their souls." The fancy new object is able to take the focus off their bad feelings about themselves, if only for a while.

Hole-in-the-soulers may also turn to travel and adrenaline-inducing experiences such as sky diving and bungee jumping. As a person who has participated in many a shark dive, I can report that being 60 feet below the water's surface with sharks swimming in from every direction has a certain way of taking a person out of his or her head. I can also report that these distractions are not cheap. I'll save you the money by pointing out that it is literally impossible to outrun your demons because no matter how far or fast you travel, each morning you wake up with yourself.

The foregoing is to encourage you to acknowledge and tackle any emotional issues you may have because that will clear the way for you to achieve the overall wealth you deserve. If not addressed, these issues will likely sabotage your best laid plans.

## Winning the game

Gaming is a big thing. Consoles like Xbox and PlayStation sell in the millions. People of all ages eat up time playing games on their phones. Shows such as *Wheel of Fortune* and *Jeopardy* are going strong after decades. Esports is all the rage.

It might be beneficial to express our financial lives as a game and then explain what winning looks like.

Let's introduce Kayla. After completing her education, Kayla moves into the workforce. She establishes a living situation based on the level of compensation her job provides. That could mean a basement apartment. If she marries and starts a family, she'll need more living space. Thankfully, by that time her experience and credentials will allow her to earn the additional income needed to cover the higher cost of her nicer place. Alternatively, if she remains single, she might tire of the basement apartment at some point and feel a combination of relief and satisfaction by moving to a brighter apartment, perhaps with a view of the city.

As her income rises, Kayla goes from shopping at Kohl's to shopping at Macy's, or perhaps from Macy's to Nordstrom. She is making good money and should look the part. Similarly, after a decade of driving economy cars, she upgrades to a fine German-made automobile. Kayla has officially arrived.

She has also contracted an acute case of *lifestyle creep*, a stealth affliction that strikes most Americans. Kayla believes that as her income rises, so should her lifestyle. She has, after all, earned it. She naively assumes that because her income is rising, it will continue to go up. Kayla may believe she is just hitting her stride when in actuality she may be experiencing her peak earning years.

At some point Kayla is likely to realize that if she doesn't drag herself out of bed each morning, don her business armor and fight hard to earn that day's pay, all she has built will just disappear. Kayla doesn't own the apartment she's living in, nor the vehicle she's driving. The moment she's unable to pay, the sheriff and the repo man will dispossess her of them.

Kayla is the definition of a *wage slave*. How long must she continue slaving away? However long she wants to maintain her lifestyle. For middle-aged adults with 30 or more years of the grind under their belts, who are burnt toast both physically and mentally, it's a sobering awareness. This is not winning.

What does winning look like? The simple answer, which we'll explore later, is that Kayla manages to save and invest enough money over the course of her career that her accumulated investments produce the same annual income as she's earning at her job. When that threshold is reached, she is officially *financially independent.* She doesn't need her job anymore. She is free to drop out of the rat race, to walk into the office and address her colleagues with something understated like, "People, it's been real. Peace, I'm out."

*Who is or was?* Andy Gibb.

## Exercises to help you take stock of your life

1. Set a goal for yourself that meets all the requirements of a well-stated goal, which are that it be realistic, measurable, time-bound and descriptive of the action to be taken to achieve it.
2. Identify a sacrifice you've made that will set you up for a brighter future.
3. Describe a time when you decided to break off from a group and take your own path. What gave you the courage to do so?
4. List three measures you use when assessing how financially wealthy others are. Explain how your approach could lead to a faulty conclusion.
5. Identify how the lack of emotional well-being can derail a person's financial plans.
6. Describe how to win life's financial game.

# Chapter 3 Who's afraid of inflation?

A close friend of yours approaches with some news. Actually, it's two pieces of news, one good and one bad. We're going to assume you are the type of person who likes to receive, process and get the bad news out of the way first.

If it was easy to become financially independent, everyone would be. Everyone isn't. In fact, very few are. On the way to financial independence are a series of roadblocks, obstacles and gauntlets that can reduce even the most stout to tears. We'll discuss the first of these obstacles, inflation, in this chapter.

*A car sits on the side of a road while its occupants decide their next destination. A boat sits at rest on a lazy river while its passengers have lunch. While neither appear to be going anywhere, the water on which the boat sits is quietly moving down stream, taking the boat with it. If the goal of the boater is ultimately to reach a destination upriver, he is getting farther from it by sitting still.*

As consumers, we experience a similar phenomenon. Let's say you earn $250 in cash. You're spying new headphones that today can be purchased for $250. In an unusual move, you show restraint by stuffing the bills into an envelope that you place in the back of your bedroom dresser. A year later you retrieve the envelope because you're ready to purchase the headphones. Only, you can't because the price increased over the course of the year. By letting your money sit still, you actually fell behind.

## The many faces of inflation

Inflation is defined as "a general increase in price levels." There are at least three ways that inflation can affect us. First, as we just discussed, we have to pay a higher price for the goods we buy and services we consume.[8] Second, we pay the same price for less and less product. For example, a bag of chips in the vending machine at my school is puffed up as it's always been, but is practically devoid of chips.

Imagine you're the marketing manager of a snack food company whose sales and profits are no longer rising. Your most popular product is an individual package of bite-size cookies. Each bag is one ounce, has 111 calories and sells for $1.00. You feel constrained because you want to keep the nice round $1.00 price but don't want to be the first company to offer less than a one-ounce package. Then, it hits you. Knowing that calorie consumption and weight management are on many consumers' minds, you launch your new 0.90-ounce package with the bold new message "New 100-calorie size!" The price, of course, remains $1.00.

Let me give you another example. Say you're ready to give your apartment's ceiling a touch-up. The plan is to tape along the wall where it meets the ceiling, allowing you to paint the ceiling without worrying about getting white paint on the walls. You go to the home improvement store to buy the materials. There's one-inch wide tape available, but because you're not a pro, you grab the two-inch wide tape.

Standing in the checkout line, you're looking the roll over with a skeptical eye. Something is not right. It seems a little narrower than two inches. But it says right there on the shrink wrap that it's two-inch tape. Ah, then you see that, in parentheses, the label says it's really 1.88 inches wide. For what possible reason would the company short you 0.12 inches[9] of tape? Corporate profits must keep rising and this

---

[8] Some people view inflation from the perspective of the money it costs to purchase goods and services. If it now takes more dollars to purchase the same good or service, then the dollar must have lost value, suffering a loss of *purchasing power*.

[9] 2.00 inches minus 1.88 inches is 0.12 inches.

manufacturer made a calculated decision that the average consumer wouldn't notice or care about the missing tape. That may be, but the decrease in size, 0.12 inches, is 6% of the former width of two inches.[10] Congratulations, you've just been hit with 6% inflation. Thanks for playing.

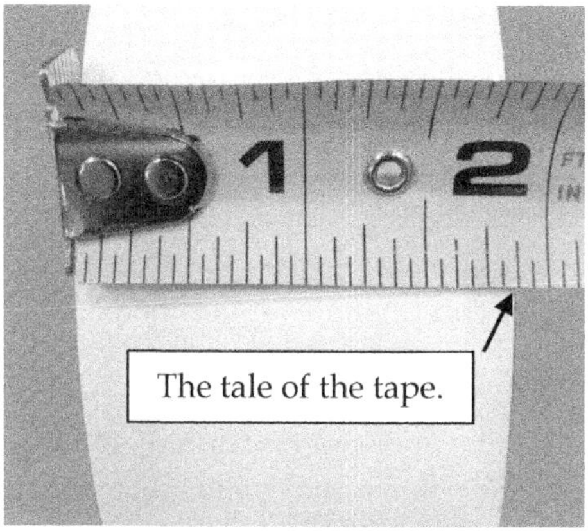


A third way inflation can affect us is that we end up paying the same price for a product of lesser quality. Time was when Swingline produced metal staplers as heavy as a brick. Decades later, the company is still going strong, but the staplers made today have a lot of plastic. They work fine. They'll last a long time. But they don't compare to their predecessors.

Quality degradation also occurs when companies replace some amount of what you think you're buying with inexpensive fillers or substitutes. Sometimes the entire product, like bacon bits, is a substitute.

My wife read an article a while ago on why you should buy whole bean coffee instead of ground coffee. Javaphiles among you are no doubt volunteering the answer: "So the aromatics

---

[10] 0.12 inches divided by 2.00 inches is 0.06, or 6%. The reduction in size is 6%.

released when grinding can be captured in the brewing that immediately follows!" Agreed. But the article indicated that a portion of ground coffee is ground twigs. It's harder to hide twigs among whole beans.[11]

## Back to school

In my foreword, I stated that this book is for everyone, which I really mean. To that end, I promise to do little more math than dividing one number by another. This allows us to calculate percentages, an important part of finance. If percentages aren't your thing, do not run away. This might be the moment when you finally conquer them!

### Percentages

Hold your hands and fingers out where you can count them. Hopefully, you have two hands and ten fingers. If you don't, imagine you do. One of your fingers represents one out of ten. Expressed as a fraction, it is 1 / 10, where the forward slash (/) means "out of." It also means "divide by." To translate the fraction to a decimal, you divide "1" by "10." Then, to translate the decimal into a percentage, you simply multiply by 100. The table on the next page displays all the fractions and percentages for finger counts.

---

*"I was reading in the paper today that Congress wants to replace the dollar bill with a coin. They've already done it. It's called a nickel."*
- Jay Leno

---

[11] Research pink slime when you get a moment.

| If you count this many fingers | The fraction of total fingers is | Calculating the fraction results in this decimal | Multiplying by 100 results in this percentage |
|---:|---:|---:|---:|
| 1 | 1/10 | 0.10 | 10% |
| 2 | 2/10 | 0.20 | 20% |
| 3 | 3/10 | 0.30 | 30% |
| 4 | 4/10 | 0.40 | 40% |
| 5 | 5/10 | 0.50 | 50% |
| 6 | 6/10 | 0.60 | 60% |
| 7 | 7/10 | 0.70 | 70% |
| 8 | 8/10 | 0.80 | 80% |
| 9 | 9/10 | 0.90 | 90% |
| 10 | 10/10 | 1.00 | 100% |

Question #1: What percentage of all your fingers does your right thumb represent? See the footnote below.[12]

Question #2: What percentage of your fingers do all the fingers on your left hand represent? See the footnote.[13]

Question #3: You and your friend start a corporation and have it issue you 50 shares of stock each. What percent of the total issued shares do you own? See the footnote.[14]

---

[12] Your right thumb is one out of your 10 fingers, so 1 / 10 is 0.10, which equals 10%.

[13] There are five fingers on your left hand. They are five out of your 10 total fingers, so 5 / 10 is 0.50, which equals 50%.

[14] You own 50 shares. The total number of shares issued is 100 (50 + 50). Dividing your shares by the total number of shares issued is 50 / 100 = 0.50, or 50%. Each of you owns 50% of the issued shares. Together you own 100%.

Remember that ticket from Delaware? The toll was $4 but the total bill was $54. We can calculate the penalty as a percentage of the toll as follows: ($54 - $4) / $4 = $50 / $4 = 12.5. The $50 fine is 12.50 times the $4 toll. Multiplying that figure by 100 makes it into a percentage: 12.50 times 100 = 1,250%.

## Rates of growth

There's a special kind of percentage that helps us keep score in finance called the *rate of growth*. Earlier, we said you earned $250, but in a fit of maturity set it aside instead of purchasing headphones. It is a year later, and your $250 can't buy them because the price has increased. Let's pick up that story and assume the price increased to $260. Subtracting $250 from $260, we see that this is a $10 price increase. No big deal. You'll just scrape up another $10 and make the purchase. But at some point, you should begin wondering what rate of increase the $10 price difference represents. Thankfully, calculating it is easy and builds on our discussion of percentages. Let's take a look:

Growth rate = (Price today – Price a year ago) / Price a year ago
Growth rate = ($260 – $250 ) / $250
Growth rate = $10 / $250
Growth rate = 0.04, or 4%

What did we just do? We expressed the price increase of $10 as a percentage of the original price of the headphones, $250. It turns out $10 is 4% of $250.[15] Who knew? Ten is the *dollar amount* of the price increase. Four percent is the *rate of growth* in the price.

The 4% increase in the price of $250 headphones was only $10. You can scrape it up pretty easily or simply decide not to

---

[15] Another way to look at percentages is to try to make a fraction, here 10 / 250, into a simpler one in which the denominator is 100. The 4% figure we calculated means that 10 / 250 is equivalent to 4 / 100.

purchase them. But, imagine that you just received a notice that the cost of your $2,500 auto insurance is going up 4%. You call other insurers but can't find a better rate. By multiplying $2,500 by 0.04 (the decimal equivalent of 4%) you realize that the cost is going up $100, a C-note. Not surprisingly, when you flip to the 2nd page of the notice, there's a bill for $2,600, the new cost to insure your vehicles for the coming year.

Now, imagine the rent on your nice two-bedroom apartment with a city view is $2,500 per month. Your rental agreement, better known as your *lease,* ends in one month. The area is becoming more popular and the few times you talked to the landlord she complained of rising property taxes and other costs. In your mailbox you find a letter from her saying that despite how much you remind her of her son and how nice it is to have you as a *tenant,* if you'd like to extend your lease and live there for another year, you must agree to a 4% rent increase. We just did this exact math. Four percent of $2,500 is $100. But instead of paying $100 extra per year, you'll be paying an extra $100 *per month.* A small number, just 4%, is starting to cause big problems.

## Measuring inflation ought to be easy

You make a shopping list, go to the supermarket and buy everything on the list. Upon returning home, you put the food away and set the shopping list and receipt (which totals $100) aside. A year later you go back to the store with the same shopping list and purchase the very same products. This time the receipt totals $103. We divide the $3 increase by the $100 prior cost to determine that the inflation rate was 3% last year. If it were only this easy.

### *Goods are put on sale*

At your local supermarket, the price of a single serving of Chobani Greek yogurt has ranged from the sale price of $1.00 all the way up to the regular price of $1.49. If the item was on sale when you initially purchased it, but not a year later, then the price will appear to have soared. Conversely, if you paid $1.49 initially but a year later it is on sale for $1.00, then the price will have plunged.

### *Price increases are not annual*

A small cup of American coffee at your favorite gourmet coffee shop has cost $2.20 for the few years you've been going there. One day you walk in and see that the price is now $2.50. That $0.30 increase is greater than 10%! True, but the preceding years saw a 0% rate of increase.

### *There is more than one price*

The Chobani yogurt is $1.49. You were hoping it would be on sale. Then, you realize it is, sort of, when you notice a promotion that reads "10/$10." You can buy 10 individual servings for $10, or one dollar each. That's a great deal, as long as you have room for them in your tiny apartment fridge.

### *The price changes, but so does the product*

Entering 2011, Netflix offered a $10 per month subscription that included movie DVDs by mail as well as movies served in a new way, streaming. That year it split the two services and set the price at $7.99 for each, as follows:

| | DVD by mail subscription | Streaming service | Total subscription cost |
|---|---|---|---|
| Before price | $10.00 for both | | $10.00 |
| After price | $7.99 | $7.99 | $15.98 |

To have both services would cost customers an extra $5.98, representing a whopping 59.8% price *increase*![16] With bandwidth getting better and its digital library growing, Netflix was basically telling its customers they'd be fine going

[16] ($15.98 - $10.00) / $10.00 = $5.98 / 10 = 0.598 = 59.8%.

with the streaming service only at a price of $7.99. The customers who went with that offer, paying $7.99 rather than $10 a month, experienced a 20.01% price *decrease*.[17]

We used to be able to pay a one-time fee for software such as Microsoft Office and Adobe Creative Suite. Now, these companies offer them using a *subscription model*. You pay a smaller yet never-ending monthly fee to use the software, but in return you receive support and are always able to use the most current version of the software. Good luck trying to calculate the rate of increase before and after subscription pricing was put in place.

Great news! The new generation of your favorite cell phone line is out. Last year's model was $800. The newest model is priced at $900, a 12.5% increase. [18] But upon reviewing the specs you learn that it is 15% faster, has a 20% longer battery life and features 15% higher camera resolution. Hmm.

## How the government estimates inflation

Inflation is officially measured by our Bureau of Labor Statistics (BLS) in Washington, D.C.[ix] BLS calls its shopping list a *market basket* of goods and services. Included in the basket are food, housing, clothing, transportation, medical care, recreation, education, communications, personal services and more.

The *consumer price index* (CPI) is the formal name for the average change in the price of this basket of goods over time. It is measured for different regions and the country as a whole. The CPI-U captures changes in a basket of goods and services tailored for *u*rban consumers.

---

[17] ($7.99 - $10.00) / $10.00 = -$2.01 / 10 = -0.201 = -20.1%.

[18] ($900 - $800) / $800 = $100 / $800 = 0.125 = 12.5%.

## What is the actual inflation rate?

Drum roll, please. The following table contains the official inflation rates over the last 10 years.[19]

| Year | Annual % change | Year | Annual % change |
|---|---|---|---|
| 2010 | 1.6% | 2015 | 0.1% |
| 2011 | 3.2% | 2016 | 1.3% |
| 2012 | 2.1% | 2017 | 2.1% |
| 2013 | 1.5% | 2018 | 2.4% |
| 2014 | 1.6% | 2019 | 1.8% |

This is mild inflation, averaging less than 2% per year. It is also the 10-year period following the Great Recession, wherein our economy had major trouble getting back on its feet.

Is overall inflation really that low? From 2003 to 2013, the cost of college tuition and fees rose 79.5%. The cost of medical care rose 43.1%.[x] Even if the annual rate of increase has moderated in recent years, that's cold comfort to those for whom prior cost escalation has nearly put college and health care out of reach.[20] Also according to BLS:

- the approximate official inflation rate during the decade from 1998 to 2008 was 2.5%.
- the approximate official inflation rate from 1913 (when the Federal Reserve was created) to 2013 was 3.2%.

---

[19] bls.gov. (accessed May 5, 2020)

[20] This paragraph was supposed to be followed with one about how personal observations are not very reliable and how we tend to complain about areas in which costs are soaring, while taking for granted areas in which prices have held steady (i.e., the rate of increase was 0%). I considered energy as a possible example of the latter. According to BLS, however, energy prices from 2003 to 2013 jumped 70.7%.

Now that inflation is top-of-mind, you may begin noticing it in the news. A year is too long to wait for this information, so BLS publishes inflation figures monthly. Odds are you will learn that inflation is "tame," coming in at an annualized rate of 1.-something percent, or perhaps even less than 1%. *Bloomberg BusinessWeek's* cover for the week of April 17, 2019 went so far as to ask, "Is Inflation Dead?" Um, no.

Imagine you have a small rash on your arm the size of a dime. It's barely noticeable and almost never itches. Out of an abundance of caution, you go to the dermatologist. She tells you that the rash is benign but it does spread at a rate of 1% to 2% per year. The next year when you visit the dermatologist, the rash is the size of quarter. It seems to be growing more rapidly than predicted, so your relief is palpable when the doctor assures you that this type of rash grows 1% to 2% per year. A year later, as the rash is enveloping your arm, you return to the dermatologist. Though you've been preparing for her response from the moment you made the appointment, you are nonetheless taken aback when the good doctor turns to you with a sympathetic smile and affirms once more that your rash grows at an annual rate of 1% to 2%.

The point of our story is that there is a significant disconnect between what we are being told by officials about inflation and what we are personally experiencing. It's not as though we can push back against the official inflation numbers because it would take a small army of economists to calculate our own rates. Going forward, we will assume that the average annual inflation rate will be 3%.

## Inflation is a bad man (or woman)

Now that we've got an inflation rate we can work with, let's put it into play. A year ago, the price of a six-pack of paper towels at the supermarket was $10. Now it's $10.30. The extra $0.30 is a 3% increase from last year's price.

Why do prices go up? There is a lot involved in manufacturing, packaging, shipping and stocking the towels. As costs along the way increase, they are passed on to consumers. A second reason is that most of the items we purchase are produced by corporations whose investors want them to achieve increasing profits each year. The supermarket itself is one such corporation. In addition to selling more of the product, increasing the price of the product will increase overall profits.[21]

An interesting exercise is to determine how long it will take for the price of the paper towels to double to $20. What percent growth does a doubling of the price represent? Let's calculate it. We're going to take the price increase and express it as a percent of the current $10 price: ($20 - $10) / $10 = $10 / $10 = 1.0 = 100%.

So, if inflation is 3% per year and we want to know how long it will take for the price to increase by 100%, we can divide 100% by 3%. Right? The result is 33.3 years. This analysis is straight-forward, but it is also incorrect.

If the price of the paper towels is $10.30 after a year, the following year's price increase will be $0.31. Why? The price isn't $10 anymore, it's $10.30. Three percent of a new, higher price will result in a greater price increase, as shown next:

| | Starting price | Inflation rate | Inflation amount | Ending price |
|---|---|---|---|---|
| First year | $10.00 | 3% | $0.30 | $10.30 |
| Year after | $10.30 | 3% | $0.31 | $10.61 |
| Two years after | $10.61 | 3% | $0.32 | $10.93 |

Note that we've added an arrow to show that the price at

[21] A strong counterbalance to the desire of corporations to raise prices is intense competition that may continue to hold price increases in check.

the end of one year is the same as the price going into the next year. We realize that the reason the price increase is growing larger is because we're paying inflation on prior inflation. How messed up is that? It gets worse. The increases accelerate because the price *compounds* on itself. The *exponential* growth in the price is illustrated below:[22]

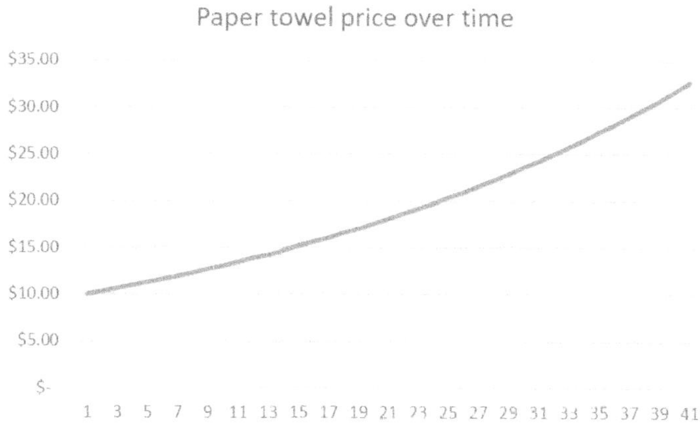


What's also interesting is that after three years, the paper towels can still be purchased for $10-something. For this reason, it's easy to miss the fact that the price is rising.[23]

In school, there was a formula for calculating exponential growth:

$$\text{Future price} = \text{Current price} \times (1 + \text{inflation rate})^{\text{number of years}}$$

We can calculate the future price in one year, then calculate the result for two years, and so on, as shown in three sets of columns in the table on the following page.

---

[22] The promised good news is that investments can also grow exponentially.

[23] Our exponential price curve isn't very dramatic because the rate of growth, in mathematical terms, is a modest 3%. For consumers however, 3% inflation is plenty insidious.

| Price of $10 paper towel pack growing at 3% per year | | | | | |
|---|---|---|---|---|---|
| Years from now | Price at year end | Years from now | Price at year end | Years from now | Price at year end |
| Today | $10.00 | | | | |
| 1 | $10.30 | 11 | $13.84 | 21 | $18.60 |
| 2 | $10.61 | 12 | $14.26 | 22 | $19.16 |
| 3 | $10.93 | 13 | $14.69 | 23 | $19.74 |
| 4 | $11.26 | 14 | $15.13 | 24 | $20.33 |
| 5 | $11.59 | 15 | $15.58 | 25 | $20.94 |
| 6 | $11.94 | 16 | $16.05 | 26 | $21.57 |
| 7 | $12.30 | 17 | $16.53 | 27 | $22.21 |
| 8 | $12.67 | 18 | $17.02 | 28 | $22.88 |
| 9 | $13.05 | 19 | $17.54 | 29 | $23.57 |
| 10 | $13.44 | 20 | $18.06 | 30 | $24.27 |

Now, look in the table to determine the first year the price is $20 or higher. What year is it? The 24th year. We can use the formula to confirm our answer:

Future price = Current price * (1 + inflation rate) $^{\text{number of years}}$
$20.33 = $10 * (1 + 0 .03) $^{24}$

Twenty-four years is much shorter than the 33 years we calculated with our faulty approach. Still, we're talking decades here, so why does it matter? Let's take the world's fastest look at the career of a woman we will call Gladys:

Age 22 Gladys was so excited to graduate college and begin her career. She had several job offers and agonized over which one to accept. Her decision was made easier by one offer that stood out due to its $60,000 starting salary, a full $5,000 more than all other offers.

Age 46  Gladys must have chosen well because at this mid-point in her career, she's found regular advancement at the same firm. Gladys has a spouse and three kids. It is now 24 years since she began her career.

Age 70  With an epic retirement party thrown by her co-workers to celebrate her amazing 48 years with the firm, Gladys calls it a career. It's tough to give up her $240,000 salary, but all things must come to an end. On her way home she stops at the supermarket to pick up a few things, including a six-pack of paper towels.

Gladys is a classic American success story. She walked into her office building for the first time earning $60,000 and walked out for the final time earning $240,000. What more need be said? A lot, actually.

The paper towels Gladys purchased on her final drive home from the office rang the register at $41.32, four times their initial price. Let's take another look at her final salary. At $240,000, it's four times her $60,000 starting salary. Her compensation has only kept pace with the rate of inflation. It's as if she spent her entire career at her starting salary. Sadly, "going nowhere fast" is what millions of hardworking Americans have been doing for the last 40 years![xi]

Colorless. Odorless. Rarely noticed. Inflation is the carbon monoxide of finance. It has killed many a financial dream. Let's make sure yours is not among them.

I ask a favor. Please listen to the song *Drive* by the Cars. Then, answer: *Who is or was?* Benjamin Orr.

## Exercises on inflation

1. Explain the different ways we can experience inflation.
2. Identify three reasons why it is difficult to accurately measure inflation.

3. Explain what role a "basket of goods" plays in the measurement of inflation.
4. Assuming an annual rate of inflation of 3%, determine how much a $20 haircut today will cost 40 years from now.
5. Explain why, if the price of a good is growing at an annual rate of 3% per year, it takes just 24 years for the price to double.
6. Research what government programs are "indexed" to the CPI, which means that payments made by the government will increase by the annual percentage change in the CPI.
7. Research the Boskin Commission. What the heck is Chained CPI? Why is or isn't it a fair measure of inflation?

# Chapter 4 Adventures in budgeting

To achieve financial independence we must spend less than we earn, allowing us to save the difference. There are several benefits of saving:

- If an emergency arises, we have the money needed to minimize its impact.
- There are things in life, such as higher education, a home and retirement, that are pricey.
- Knowing that we have a significant sum of money saved makes life so much less stressful than it can be if we have no idea how our bills will be paid. Why do you think the employees on *Undercover Boss* burst into tears when the boss declares she's giving them the not-exactly-life-changing sum of $10,000? They're stressed to the max!
- Having money saved gives us options. For example, when a neighbor makes available a lightly used car at an absurdly low price because he just wants it gone, we can seize the opportunity.
- Once money is saved, it can be placed into investments that themselves earn money.

How do we live our lives such that the money coming in is less than the money going out? The first step, as we explored earlier, is to make the personal commitment to doing so. The second is to create a budget that you will live by. A budget is a plan for earning money and then carefully allocating it to various types of spending and saving.

Most people don't budget. Who's got the time to sit down with their receipts, bills and bank statements to try making sense of them? Who's got the expertise to use an electronic spreadsheet to record and analyze spending? Not many. Great news, though. The cavalry has arrived in the form of budgeting apps for your smartphone that will do almost all of the work for you. That's the good news. The bad news is that now there's literally no excuse for not budgeting. More on budgeting apps later.

## Summer budget

Common living expenses are billed and paid monthly, so it's natural to use one month as our budgeting period.

Justine Brown is a college student. Spring semester is about to end and she's happy to have lined up a summer job. She will work 40 hours per week and earn $12 per hour. We can estimate that $2 per hour will be lost to taxes, resulting in a *take-home pay* of $10 per hour. Based on this rate, she will earn $400 per week and $1,600 per month.[24] She lives with her parents during the summer, relying on them for most of her meals and for a vehicle to get around. Her budget:

| Justine's Monthly Summer Budget | |
|---|---|
| **Category** / Description | Monthly |
| **Income** | $1,600 |
| **Expenses** | |
| Gas | $ 100 |
| Dining out | $ 100 |
| Clothing | $ 100 |
| Movies and entertainment | $ 100 |
| Total expenses | – $400 |
| **Available for saving** | = $1,200 |

← Justine plans on earning this. (Income)

} She plans to spend this. (Expenses)

← She will save this. (Available for saving)

By leaning on her parents, Justine's budget is a breeze. She's going to have fun but will also be able to sock away a few thousand dollars by summer's end.

---

[24] Dividing 52 weeks in a year by 12 months in a year reveals that there are actually 4.33 weeks in a month. If you can make your monthly budget work with two biweekly pay checks, then the extra 0.33 weeks of income you are not relying on acts as a cushion.

## Single budget

Let's look at Justine in her middle 20s. After school, she begins her professional career. Justine's annual salary is $66,000, which equates to $5,500 monthly. She loses $1,500 per month to various taxes, so her take-home pay is $5,500 minus $ 1,500, or $4,000. Justine and a sorority sister are sharing an apartment near mass transit. Because she can grab a subway train or a bus to the city, Justine doesn't own a vehicle.

Determined to stay in shape, she joined a nearby gym. She recently read that she should have an *emergency fund,* a cash account with three to six months of living expenses. Why? For an emergency! If she losses her job, is involved in an accident, or suffers an illness, she may go several months without income. The emergency fund, if adequately filled, will support her in these difficult situations.

Justine is a bit embarrassed because she's been on her own a few years and has never given a thought to building up this emergency cash cushion. Not wanting to tempt fate any longer, she's decided to prioritize it. Once it is adequately funded, once the balance has reached at least $16,000, she will direct the savings toward her retirement fund. In a similar manner, Justine is allocating money toward a *down payment* on a home. The down payment is the portion of a home's price that the buyer will pay in cash.

Justine's budget will also group expenses by category and provide more detail on the different objectives for which she is saving. We also added a column to express her spending as a percent of her take-home pay.[25]

---

[25] Comparing individual spending to take-home pay and not salary is a departure from most discussions of budgeting. It simplifies the concept because money lost to taxes is not available to spend or save. In addition, the percentage of tax owed changes as a person's income level changes, making the comparison of spending to salary inconsistent.

| Justine's Monthly Budget | | |
|---|---|---|
| **Category** / Description | Budgeted | % of take- home |
| **Income** | | |
| Salary | $ 5,500 | |
| – Income taxes | $1,500 | |
| = Take home pay | $ 4,000 | 100.00% |
| **Expenses / spending** | | |
| **Housing** | | |
| Apartment rent | $ 1,200 | |
| Gas / Electric / Water | $ 75 | |
| Renter's insurance | $ 25 | |
| Total housing | $ 1,300 | 32.50% |
| **Food** | | |
| Groceries | $ 400 | |
| Dining out | $ 200 | |
| Total food | $ 600 | 15.00% |
| **Healthcare** | | |
| Health insurance | $ 425 | |
| Doctor visits | $35 | |
| Dentist visits | $25 | |
| Prescriptions and medications | $ 15 | |
| Total healthcare | $ 500 | 12.50% |
| **Transportation** | | |
| Public transit monthly ticket | $ 200 | 5.00 % |
| Ride sharing | $ 100 | 2.50 % |
| Total transportation | $ 300 | 7.50 % |
| Student loan | $ 200 | 5.00 % |
| Clothing / footwear | $ 100 | 2.50 % |
| Home internet / streaming | $ 50 | 1.25 % |
| Cellular service / phones | $ 50 | 1.25 % |
| Entertainment | $ 150 | 3.75 % |
| Recreation & hobbies | $ 50 | 1.25 % |
| Gym & classes | $ 50 | 1.25 % |
| Total expenses | – $ 3,350 | 83.75 % |
| **Available for saving** | = $ 650 | 16.25 % |
| Emergency fund | $ 350 | 8.75 % |
| Retirement saving / investing | $ 0 | 0.00 % |
| Home down payment | $ 200 | 5.00 % |
| Annual vacation | $ 100 | 2.50 % |
| Total savings | – $ 650 | 16.25 % |
| **Budget surplus or (deficit)** | = $ 0 | 0.00 % |

The most valuable number in the percentage column is her housing cost. At 32.50%, she spends a little less than one-third of her take-home pay for her place.

A year ago, Justine had been struggling mightily to make ends meet. No matter what she did to conserve cash, she was always behind. The culprit, however, was right there in plain sight. Justine had rented a two-bedroom apartment by herself. She figured she could set up a home office in the 2nd bedroom and use its closet for storage. There was also her alternate vision of hosting out-of-town friends in style in their very own guest bedroom.

Two years ago, Justine's monthly rent was not $1,200, but $2,300. When it rose to $2,400 she realized that her housing costs, which were already high, were breaking her budget. By taking on a roommate, she halved her housing expenses and was finally able to create a workable budget. Unfortunately, housing costs have inflated to the point that millions of American are spending at least 50% of their income on it![xii]

Justine has no dental insurance and is budgeting $25 per month ($300 per year) for a visit or two. She'd better brush well and remember to floss.

Another percentage that's important to consider is how much a person is able to commit to saving. In Justine's case, she is distributing a substantial 15% of her take-home pay among all forms of savings.

As a renter, Justine does not own her apartment. The maintenance costs to repair things that break fall on the *landlord*. Under the terms of the lease, she and her roommate are responsible for their *utilities*. If she and her roommate want to keep the temperature a toasty 75 degrees in winter, it is at their expense. If Justine's roommate is partial to 30-minute showers, besides being shut out of the bathroom for long stretches, Justine is on the hook for half of the water used and the energy consumed to heat it.

Justine is young and healthy and is budgeting only $35 per

month for doctor visits. That equates to $420 for the year, which she hopes will cover a few visits and routine tests. Her employer is small and is not obligated to offer health insurance. So, Justine has enrolled in an individual healthcare plan. Unfortunately, these plans do little more than keep people from going bankrupt in the event of a serious accident or injury. Justine must pay the full cost of the first $4,000 of any medical care she may need before the insurance begins paying. It will be costly for Justine to suffer a serious injury or illness. Come to think of it, now might be a good time to raise her emergency fund target to $20,000.

Justine's doctor-visit budget line item provides an illustration of the difference between a budgeted expenditure and actual *cash flow*. Justine won't be spending $35 each month on medical care. If she makes two doctor visits six months apart, spending a total of $420, that leaves 10 other months in which she will spend $0. This, dear reader, is the limitation of making a *uniform* monthly budget. If you want to take the next step, develop a budget for each month of the year. This will allow you to capture each month's unique characteristics and cash flows, such as cash outlays for college tuition just before spring and fall semesters begin.

Finally, after college Justine began paying off her student loan at a rate of $200 per month.[26]

## Family budget

Let's now fast-forward another 10 years. Justine has been lured away from her former employer to take a better job with higher pay and better benefits. She has gotten married and now has two young kids. Falling prey to the lure of better schools and a backyard where the kids can play, Justine and her husband Alberto bought a home in the suburbs. With her

---

26 The $200 per month budgeted (for 10 years) is sufficient to pay a $19,750 loan that incurs a 4% annual rate of interest.

earning prospects better than his, they decided that Alberto would be the children's primary caregiver.

Their home is within walking distance of the commuter rail station that will get Justine into the city in just under an hour. What else has changed? Justine's student loans are paid off, and her emergency account is fully funded. With the kids in grade school, Alberto has begun taking on consulting jobs that allow him to work when the kids are in school.

Their budget on the next page shows Justine earning $100,000 per year. Alberto is earning $26,000, for a combined family income of $126,000 per year. This equates to $10,500 per month. After losing $2,500 to taxes, their combined after-tax monthly take-home pay is $8,000. The family's income is higher than the national average household income, so why are we not using numbers closer to the national averages?

- It is amazing how easily even a six-figure (i.e., $ 100,000 or higher) income can evaporate across a plethora of living expenses. Lifestyle creep is a cautionary tale if ever there was one and we're about to demonstrate it. So, ahem, is inflation.
- There are tens of millions of people on the west coast and in the northeast for whom this is an average wage. Due to the high cost of living in these areas, this level of income may barely support a middle-class lifestyle.
- When incomes in an area are lower, so are the costs of living. People with incomes less than we've shown may be able to scale the budget down proportionately.

---

*"Someone is sitting in the shade today because someone planted a tree a long time ago.*
- Warren Buffett

---

| Justine and Alberto's Family Monthly Budget | | | | |
|---|---|---|---|---|
| **Category** / Description | Budgeted | % of take home | Actual spending / saving | Variance % |
| **Income** | | | | |
| Salary | $ 10,500 | | | |
| – Income taxes | $ 2,500 | | | |
| = Take home pay | $ 8,000 | 100.00 % | | |
| **Expenses / spending** | | | | |
| **Housing** | | | | |
| Mortgage payment | $1,800 | | | |
| Property tax | $ 500 | | | |
| Gas / Electric / Water | $ 400 | | | |
| Homeowners insurance | $ 100 | | | |
| Total housing | $ 2,800 | 35.00 % | | |
| **Food** | | | | |
| Groceries | $ 1,200 | | | |
| Dining out | $ 300 | | | |
| Total food | $ 1,500 | 18.75 % | | |
| **Healthcare** | | | | |
| Health insurance | $ 450 | | | |
| Doctor visit co-pays | $ 25 | | | |
| Dentist visits | $100 | | | |
| Prescriptions / medications | $ 25 | | | |
| Total healthcare | $ 600 | 7.50 % | | |
| **Transportation** | | | | |
| Auto payment | $ 300 | | | |
| Auto insurance | $ 100 | | | |
| Fuel | $ 100 | | | |
| Maintenance (wipers, filters) | $ 25 | | | |
| Rail / subway monthly ticket | $ 275 | | | |
| Total transportation | $ 800 | 10.00 % | | |
| **Child care** | | | | |
| School supplies / tech / fees | $ 50 | | | |
| Sports equip / apparel / fees | $ 50 | | | |
| Babysitting | $ 100 | | | |
| Total child care | $ 200 | 2.50 % | | |

| Justine and Alberto's Family Budget (continued) | | | | |
|---|---|---|---|---|
| **Category**/ Description | Budgeted | % of take home | Actual spending / saving | Variance % |
| **Expenses / spending (cont.)** | | | | |
| Clothing / footwear | $ 100 | 1.25 % | | |
| Home internet / streaming | $ 100 | 1.25 % | | |
| Cellular service / phones | $ 100 | 1.25 % | | |
| Entertainment | $ 200 | 2.50 % | | |
| Recreation / hobbies | $ 50 | 0.625 % | | |
| Life insurance | $ 100 | 1.25 % | | |
| Lawn care / landscaping | $ 100 | 1.25 % | | |
| Home maintenance / repair | $ 50 | 0.625 % | | |
| Other: | | | | |
| Other | | | | |
| Other: | | | | |
| Total expenses / spending | – $ 6,700 | 83.75 % | | |
| **Available for saving / giving** | = $ 1,300 | 16.25 % | | |
| Emergency fund | $ 0 | 0.00 % | | |
| Retirement saving / investing | $ 600 | 7.50 % | | |
| College funds | $ 300 | 3.75 % | | |
| Annual vacation | $ 200 | 2.50 % | | |
| Charitable giving / donations | $ 200 | 2.50 % | | |
| Total intended saving / giving. | - $ 1,300 | 16.25 % | | |
| **Budget surplus or (deficit)** | = $ 0 | 0.00 % | | |

As the smooth speakers at your local TED talk like to say, there's a lot to unpack. Let's get to it.

**Housing** Justine and her husband are no longer renters. They're owners. They took out a *mortgage*, a loan to purchase their home. Now that they own their house and the land on which it sits, they owe property taxes to their local government. The $1,800 mortgage payment is the result of purchasing a $400,000 home with a $50,000 down payment and $350,000 borrowed at a 4.625% annual interest rate, to be paid over 30 years.

The bigger a home gets, the bigger everything connected to it gets. The price is higher because there's more house to enjoy. Property taxes are usually a percentage of the value of the home, so they go up as well. The bigger the space, the more energy is needed to heat and cool it, which drives up the utility bills. The bigger it is, the more likely it is to be filled with appliances and gadgets that can break down, which means more maintenance and repair bills. Finally, the bigger and more valuable the home is, the more it costs to insure. For these reasons it's not a good idea to buy more home than needed.

**Food** You might be spying that $1,200 grocery budget and believe the couple can pare it down to free up more money for savings. But it's not as big as it seems. There is an average of 30 days in a month, so let's divide $1,200 by 30. We get $40 per day. There are four people in the household. Let's divide $40 per day by four people. We get $10. We're not done. There are three meals in a day, so let's divide $10 by 3 meals. We get $3.33. Justine's budget allows her to spend $3.33 per meal per person. Unfortunately, good food, the food around the outside of the supermarket, the food that doesn't come in a box, is not cheap.

Justine has budgeted $300 for dining out with the family. However, if she and Alberto are like the average couple, half of that is at risk of being eaten up by $5 Starbucks lattes.

**Healthcare** One of the major benefits Justine is enjoying is the health insurance offered by her employer. You may have noticed that the family's $450 health insurance *premium* is only slightly higher than she paid for a single plan. The reason is that while the family insurance plan is much more expensive, Justine's employer is paying 75% of premium. This is basically additional compensation in the vicinity of $15,000 per year that's being paid directly to the health insurance company on her family's behalf.

A *co-payment* or *co-pay* is the dollar amount the patient is required to pay for a doctor's visit. The co-pay under Justine's health insurance plan is $25 per visit, so by budgeting $25 Justine is expecting one family member to make a visit to the doctor each month.

Like her old employer, her new employer does not provide dental insurance. Justine and Alberto must pay for the cost of all cleanings and procedures.

**Transportation** Because their home is within walking distance of the commuter train station, the family is able to meet its needs with one automobile. While personal finance life hackers may talk about buying a beater car with change you find in the couch, not everyone is comfortable driving an aging vehicle around. Older vehicles are more likely to need repairs. They may also lack current safety features and be less fuel efficient. A reasonable option is to purchase a gently-used vehicle using a loan, with reasonable payments, that will end in five years. The footnote below shows what $300 per month gets them.[27]

**Entertainment** You can get a lot of bang for your buck with a Netflix subscription, but it might be nice to take in a ball game or concert every now and then. The cost of four tickets, transportation to the stadium and food can easily exceed the family's $200 budget. A strategy that can work here is to take in a game every few months.

**Saving** With the emergency fund at an adequate level, Justine is no longer adding to it. Is the $600 designated for retirement savings enough? We'll look into this later.

At $200 per month, she's allocating $2,400 for the family's

---

[27] Let's say that the family can pay $1,000 in cash toward the purchase of a $16,000 automobile that is lightly used. Assuming a sales tax rate of 6.5% (which adds $1,040), a 4.5% interest rate and a loan paid over five years, the monthly payment is $299.03. Rounding up, we see that $300 paid monthly for five years is the cost of borrowing $16,040.

annual vacation. That's weak! Heck, if airline travel is in high demand and the tickets are $600 each, multiplying that fare by the four family members eats up the entire vacation budget! Looks like they'll be driving to Florida again this year.

We are introducing the idea of charitable giving. God commanded the Israelites to contribute a *tithe,* which translates to 10%. In reality, Americans give about 2% to 3% of their income to charity.[xiii] Your thoughts about giving and how much you are able to give are likely to change over the course of your life. One thing is undeniably true, however: to be able to give, to be charitable, to help others, is a blessing.

The infamous **"Other"** It looks like Justine and Alberto have it all under control. Did you actually think they'd get off so easily? We call your attention to those suspicious blank lines that are just hanging out, passive-aggressive style. This budget is, in fact, not as comprehensive as it appears because there are more things that the average family spends money on than the couple has considered. Take another look at the list of budgeted expenses and then think about other things on which people regularly spend their money.

For example, unless Justine and Alberto put a bowl over their kids' heads every two weeks and carefully cut the hair descending below the rim, the family will spend money on haircuts. More broadly, all the things that Justine, Alberto and their family do to maintain a nice appearance can fall under a category called "Personal grooming."

It's on these little-thought-of expenses that the budgeting app comes into play. When they pay for the first haircut after beginning to use the app, it will ask "What is this?" The couple will realize it does not fit under any of the previous categories they've set up, so they will quickly assign the cost of the haircut to a new "Personal grooming" category. Now that the new category has been created, it's time to budget some money for it. Let's say they're going to budget $100 monthly. Something's gotta give. Look again through the budget and think about where you would advise the couple to cut spending and/or saving by a total of $100. It's not so easy. We've identified several more commonly overlooked expenditures in the footnote below, so when you are stumped, have a look.[28]

## Houston, we have a variance

We've made Justine's family budget more insightful than her single budget by adding two more columns: her actual spending and the *variance*. A month after the budget was created, the results are in! We can examine the family's actual spending. Following is a portion of the couple's budget with their actual spending written in the appropriate column:

| **Expenses / spending (cont.)** | Budgeted | % of take home | Actual spending / saving | Variance % |
|---|---|---|---|---|
| Clothing and footwear | $ 100 | 1.25 % | $ 80 | |
| Home internet / streaming | $ 100 | 1.25 % | $ 115 | |
| Cellular service / phones | $ 100 | 1.25 % | $ 100 | |

One item was under budget, one was over budget and one was right on the number. Determining what's over and under is useful. But we can easily take this further and determine by how much (not just in dollar terms, but in relative terms).

We do this by calculating how much we were over or under budget and determining the percent of the budgeted amount the difference represents. For "Clothing and footwear":

Variance = ($ actual spent – $ budgeted) / $ budgeted
Variance = ($ 80 – $ 100 ) / $ 100
Variance = –$ 20 / $ 100
Variance = –.20, which multiplied by 100, is – 20%.

[28] Common spending categories not in the budget include pet care, sporting goods, school supplies, field trips, gifts and subscriptions (to publications, computer applications, etc.).

Spending on clothing was 20% under budget this month. Pound it! Performing the same calculation with the other spending areas results in the following:

| **Expenses / spending (cont.)** | Budgeted | % of take home | Actual spending / saving | Variance % |
|---|---|---|---|---|
| Clothing and footwear | $ 100 | 1.25 % | $ 80 | - 20% |
| Home internet / streaming | $ 100 | 1.25 % | $ 115 | + 15% |
| Cellular service / phones | $ 100 | 1.25 % | $ 100 | 0 % |

Keep in mind that your budgeting app will do all of this in an instant. What we're doing here is illustrating the principle. Now, let's say that the family is tracking its budget over time and realizes that internet/streaming spending is consistently $115. It's always over budget. Looking into this, Justine realizes that when she and Alberto budgeted this category, they did not take into consideration taxes and fees. The actual bill is $115 every month. What to do? Revise the budget for the category to $115.

Notice that there is no expected expense for banking services or to maintain a credit card because there are many banks that offer these services for free. There is no reason why we should incur fees for messing up because we're using technology that will provide notifications and make automatic payments.

Thankfully, this family is intact. Otherwise there would be significant line items for *alimony* (i.e., the cost of supporting one's former spouse) and *child support,* either being paid or received. Divorce can be extremely stressful because where there was formerly one cost for housing, after the divorce there are two.[29]

---

[29] If you search the Internet you will find a slew of articles about how unhappy couples literally cannot afford to divorce. Or, if they divorce, they continue to live in the same home. Awkward!

More on budgeting:

- Many people approach budgeting by separating fixed expenses from variable expenses. Fixed expenses, like the rent, are the same every month. How much you spend on clothing can vary from month to month. Ultimately though, all expenses are variable. When your lease is up you can move to an apartment with a lower rent. We chose instead to organize Justine and Alberto's budget around expense categories.
- A person who earns a steady salary has a much easier time budgeting income than a person, such as a real estate agent, who works on commission and whose earnings may vary significantly from month to month.
- The most common span between paydays for salaried employees is two weeks. An example is a firm that pays its employees every other Friday. This frequency is known as *biweekly*.

## There's an app for that

Earlier we discussed how a free budgeting app for your phone will make constructing a budget a breeze. Check out these amazing features you can have working for you, many for free:

- You can see your entire financial picture in one place, including the balances of your bank, investment, credit card and loan accounts.
- By requiring you to set goals that are dollar-based and time-bound, things start getting real—real fast. Let's say you want to have $4,800 two years from now so you can purchase your first car. That's only 24 months away. You better figure out how to earn and save 1/24th of $4,800 (which is $200) per month or it's just not going to happen.
- You can literally look at a single day in your financial life. Given that the average number of days in a month is 30, if

your take-home pay is $3,000 per month, then you take home $100 each day. If your car payment is $300 per month, that's $10 per day. You've got $90 per day left after making your car payment. Breaking your finances down in this way is illuminating.

- The apps let you know how you're doing in real time so you can throttle back on areas where you're going over budget and even guiltlessly indulge in categories where you are under budget.
- They can also keep track of your cash flow, which, as we discussed earlier, can differ greatly from the number you see on your uniform monthly budget.
- You can coordinate your personal finances with your significant other when you both interact with the budgeting app.
- You can compare your spending by category to the average percentages of other people using the app.
- Spending that's most difficult to track is that which is paid with cash. Some apps allow you to take a photo of the cash receipt you receive after making a purchase. They analyze what's on it, conveniently bringing it into your digital budgeting realm.
- They can help you avoid costly mistakes. We'll talk later about the use of credit cards, but for now we'll just say that it's easy to mess up when using them. This can result in substantial fees. An app that ensures you pay your credit card bill on time (and more importantly ensures you have the funds to pay it) is priceless.
- The apps can analyze the details of your various accounts and propose alternatives that will earn you more money. For example, if you have $10,000 in your emergency fund bank account that pays you 0.5% annual interest, the app may identify and suggest that you move your money to a

bank that offers 1% interest.

- o Similarly, they can identify discounts and subscriptions that can save you money on services you use regularly.

Because personal finance apps are a relatively new field, there are literally dozens of companies trying to grab a piece of the market. To find an app that best meets your needs, do an internet search for the best budgeting apps and invest time learning about each. It is best to go with an app that has a large user base because this makes it more likely to be around for the long term.

## The student comment that hung in the air

It was 2008. I was teaching one of the sections of our investing course. The stock market was melting down and financial firms were falling like dominos. Monthly job losses numbered in the hundreds of thousands. Home foreclosures were soaring. We were holding a discussion of the latest news and its implications. A student raised his hand and remarked, "Mr. Barrella, we've been talking for a while about how bad things are, but I just don't see it." Wow. I was so glad he identified the disconnect he was feeling.

The most obvious explanation is that he lives in a middle- to upper-middle-class community. Perhaps no businesses in the area failed and no families on his block lost their homes.

But there could be another reason. Let's place Justine and Alberto in 2008. The family has grown to love their neighborhood. Families on both sides of their home have children the same ages as theirs. One neighbor has a pool. The other, a trampoline. The kids are always in each other's homes and their parents couldn't be happier. Alberto takes part in planning the annual block party that has quickly grown into the big event of the summer.

Justine watches the financial news nervously because her firm provides technology to banks. It's concerning any time her firm's clients are under stress. Reeling from billions in losses, the banks quietly cut back on technology spending. One day, the unthinkable happens. Justine is called into the office of the human resources manager and given the bad news. Her position is being eliminated as part of the firm's effort to downsize and survive the crisis. The firm will pay her six months of salary as *severance.* At least Justine and Alberto will have months before needing to think about tapping into their emergency fund. The severance period is also long enough for Justine to undertake a thorough search for a new position.

A few months later Justine lands a new position at a great company with similar medical benefits, but that pays an annual salary of $87,000. Her former position paid $100,000. Justine hopes that if she works hard she can demonstrate her value and earn salary increases that will get her income back up near her former salary. For the foreseeable future, however, the family's take-home pay is $7,200, down from $8,000. That's $800 less per month. Given that their expenses and spending still total $6,700 per month, they are left with just $500 for saving and giving instead of the $1,300 they previously had available.

The couple that felt so blessed is now reeling. The $500 they've got left can't be adequately distributed across the saving and giving categories. Their hopes and dreams have suffered a serious blow. They debate, even argue, about the best way to respond. Having just begun giving to charity, they'd feel embarrassed to pull the plug so quickly after times got tough. Should they eliminate all non-essential spending and be miserable living under *austerity*? Should Alberto get a night job? Should they sell the house? Let's not even go there.

Next, we illustrate how the couple distributed their $500 in the month after Justine began her new job.

| Justine and Alberto's Family Budget (continued) | | | | |
|---|---|---|---|---|
| **Category**/ Description | Monthly budget | % of Take home | Actual spending / saving | Variance % |
| **Expenses / spending (cont.)** | | | | |
| ... | | | | |
| Total expenses / spending | – $ 6,700 | 93.06 % | – $ 6,700 | |
| **Available for saving / giving** | = $ 500 | 6.94 % | = $ 500 | |
| Emergency fund | $ 0 | 0.00 % | $ 0 | 0 % |
| Retirement saving / investing | $ 600 | 7.50 % | $ 100 | – 83 % |
| College funds | $ 300 | 8.33 % | $ 100 | – 67 % |
| Annual vacation | $ 200 | 2.78 % | $ 200 | 0 % |
| Charitable giving / donations | $ 200 | 2.78 % | $100 | – 50 % |
| Total intended saving / giving. | $ 1,300 | 18.06 % | | |
| **Budget surplus or (deficit)** | = ($ 800) | 11.11 % | | |

As we can see, the numbers just don't work. They slashed retirement saving from $600 per month to $100 per month. They reduced their college savings by two-thirds. Crazy thing is, as neighbors pass the couple's house they have no idea of the turmoil going on inside the hearts and minds of Justine and Alberto. Passersby have no reason to think anything is amiss. The house looks great. The yard is tidy. With the couple continuing to fund the annual vacation, even the kids are unaware. There is simply no way to know that Justine and Alberto have suffered a significant financial setback.

Imagine if Justine had only been able to find another job that paid $75,000 per year. We'd be talking about $25,000 less in annual income and the need to make even more painful decisions. This is the picture I painted for the students that day.

## Inflation's ongoing squeeze

Above is a scenario that involves a dramatic and hopefully rare job loss. Due to inflation, however, we all experience a persistent budget challenge.

Justine and Alberto have total monthly spending of $6,700. Their $1,800 monthly mortgage payment and $300 auto loan payment are fixed and not subject to inflation. The same goes for their $100 per month life insurance payment. These fixed payments total $2,200. Subtracting this amount from the $6,700 in monthly spending results in $4,500 in spending that is subject to inflation. Let's use this figure to calculate the inflation Justine and Alberto will experience this year:

$ 4,500 x 0.03 = $ 135

Their $4,500 of expenses this year will be $4,635 next year, a $135 increase. Take another look at the couple's budget. Can you find places to cut $135 from spending? Maybe you can work it out this year, but how about next year? Next year's increase will be:

$ 4,635 x 0.03 = $ 139

Remember, inflation is building on itself. After last year's belt tightening, can you find another $139 in reduced spending for the couple? Having difficulty? Now you know the challenge faced each year by families across America.

Is there an escape? We must look to the income side of the budget. It is essential that the couple's income increases each year at least by the rate at which prices are rising. Otherwise inflation, the carbon monoxide of personal finance, will eventually overwhelm them.

## Debt is a four-letter word

*Debt,* whose b is silent when pronounced, is borrowed money. We've had Justine taking on at least three types of debt as she progressed through her life. Can you identify them? She borrowed money to go to college. She and Alberto borrowed money to purchase a car. Finally, the couple borrowed money to purchase a home.

Justin and Alberto have been successful at using debt to

achieve the life they have. However, debt can be extremely dangerous. Not all expensive degrees lead to high-paying careers. There's no guarantee that a person embarking on a college education will complete it. Injury, illness, job dislocation, a novel virus or other event can deal a serious blow to our income. Unfortunately, our debts remain, unperturbed and expecting to be paid.

While their use of debt is not unusual, just a few generations ago any use of debt was taboo. If people did not have the cash to purchase something they wanted, they simply waited, worked and saved until they accumulated the necessary funds. Nothing is stopping you from living a debt-free life. In Chapter 2 we explained that how fast you achieve financial independence is determined by how strong your desire is. The more modest a life Current You is willing to live, the more (and sooner) Future You will benefit.

## Omg, we forgot the first rule of budgeting

It seems that I failed to remember the first rule of budgeting until this very moment. I beg your forgiveness as I try to figure out a way not to have to rewrite this chapter. OK, I think I've got it. Let's have another look at our general approach to budgeting:

Income – Spending = Money available for saving

That is, you earn money, spend some of it and save the rest. Under this approach, if one spending category this month is higher than we budgeted, there's less money available for saving. Next month, if some other spending category "blows up," we'll again have less money available for saving. Before we know it we'll be chronically saving less than planned and our financial dreams, like a mirage, will evaporate before our eyes. Is there a better way? What if we were to reverse our approach by swapping the positions of saving and spending, as shown next.

Income – Saving = Money available for spending

By first squirreling away the dollars we've budgeted for savings each month, we can be sure we're on track to meet our financial goals. The dollars left after we save are those available for spending. What happens if a spending category blows up, as we just alluded to? Other spending categories must suffer. Say you are invited to a $500-per-couple fundraiser for a local politician to whose agency you've submitted a proposal. You simply can't turn down the opportunity to show support and make other contacts that may help you win the business. That's going to mean a month during which there will be no dining out, no clothing purchases and no haircuts for the family. There will, however, be plenty of ramen noodles.

This approach will ensure your savings stay on track. Whether you can stomach it goes right back to a previous question we asked: how badly do you want financial independence? This tactic, by the way, is called *Pay yourself first.*

*Who is or was?* Richard Jewell.

## Exercises on budgeting

1. Identify how a budgeter knows when his or her emergency fund has enough cash in it.
2. Explain why a person's salary is different from his or her take-home pay.
3. Identify the largest expense category and explain how a single person can keep it manageable.
4. Describe how a budget changes as a person progresses from being single to being married with children.
5. Explain lifestyle creep and describe why it stands in the way of achieving financial independence.
6. Calculate the variance of the "Entertainment" category

for which the family budget is $200 per month and actual spending during the month was $260.

7. Research and identify three leading budget apps. What is the greatest strength of each?
8. Research and list five tips for getting the most for your money when purchasing things you need.
9. Explain how the actual cash spent in a category may be different from the dollar amount budgeted, yet not be a variance. Instead, it is an illumination of the difference between a budget amount and actual cash flow. How can this limitation of a standardized monthly budget be overcome?
10. Identify the instances where Justine took on debt, explaining why they were or weren't good decisions.
11. We described a scenario where Justine lost her job and was only able to find a replacement that paid her $13,000 per year less than the old one. The budget the family had under her old job was no longer workable. What path would you advise the family to take?
12. Let's say the family insists on staying in place. Please revise the budget to most equitably reflect the drop of $800 in monthly take-home pay.
13. Explain the philosophy behind the *Pay yourself first* approach, also discussing why you do or don't agree with it.

# Chapter 5 Bank on it

In our last chapter we stated that one of the most important steps a person can take to begin building financial security is to establish and build an emergency fund. What form should this fund take? You might suspect that putting cash in a shoe box under your bed is not a great idea, and you would be correct. Better to open a bank account and place your money in it. Banks serve basic, but important functions, including:

- safeguarding our money
- receiving money that others direct our way
- paying our money to others at our direction, and
- paying us interest on money we have there.[30]

The good news about putting money in the bank is that it is safe. The Federal Deposit Insurance Corporation (FDIC) insures individual accounts up to $250,000.

## Do your job

All else equal, you should put your money where it will earn the highest rate of interest. The internet allows you to conveniently research which banks offer the best rates. Your aspirations must be modest because money in the bank is not a classic investment, as we'll explain later. The principal role of a bank, its job, is to hold your money safely and make it available to you the moment you need it.

An *asset*, something of value that you own, is *liquid* when it can be converted to cash quickly with little or no loss in value. In other words, you would not have to drop the price to get someone to buy it from you. Money in the bank is as liquid as

[30] Why would a bank pay you interest on your money? To incent you to place it with the bank. Once there, the bank can lend a portion of it out to others at a higher rate, earning a profit.

it gets. That makes it a perfect place to keep your emergency fund. Why? Well, what's most important about responding to an emergency? The ability to act quickly. Having money readily available enables you to do just that.

## Types of bank accounts

In your research you will come across several types of bank accounts. Let's briefly discuss the most important:

### Checking account

Back in the day, a person paid another person by sending him or her a *check*. A check is a written order from you to your bank to pay your money to the person or organization whose name you wrote on the check.

A checking account is the type you open when you expect your money to fly out the door frequently to cover the planned expenditures in your budget. All this activity costs the bank. You will use its ATMs, website and phone app. You will make a phone call or chat with customer service when a problem arises. The bank may be required to print and mail you any number of paper statements and notices. The more activity you have with your account, the more it costs the bank. Over time an unwritten compromise has emerged: you conduct all the transactions you wish and it'll all be free. But in return, the bank won't pay you interest on the money you have in your checking account.[31]

On the other hand, a bank is a business and competition is intense. Promotions can take the form of special above-market checking account rates designed to attract new money—like yours. *Promotional rates* usually specify an upper limit on the

---

[31] A common tweak to the compromise is that you get free checking as long as you keep a certain minimum balance in your account, such as $1,000. If your average daily balance falls below the minimum during the month, there is a fee, such as $5 or $10.

balance on which it will be paid, such as 1.5% interest on the first $10,000 in the account. Unfortunately, promotional rates can be watered down or eliminated at any time. If you manage to find a bank that pays an interest rate that is close to the inflation rate, you will be preserving the purchasing power of your money and should consider that a victory.

As a form of payment, checks are going the way of the Dodo bird. But for hundreds of years they were the go-to means by which payments were made.[32] Given this age of cyber theft, which you risk when paying electronically, rumors of their demise may be premature. Even if you don't write checks, you are likely to receive them. Let's have a look at one that Justine has recently written:

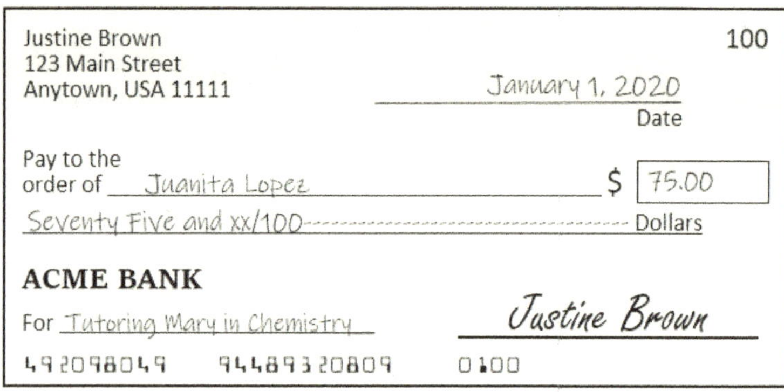
Justine Brown
123 Main Street
Anytown, USA 11111
100
January 1, 2020
Date
Pay to the order of Juanita Lopez $ 75.00
Seventy Five and xx/100 Dollars
ACME BANK
For Tutoring Mary in Chemistry
Justine Brown
492098049 944893 20809 0100

Justine (who has an account at Acme Bank) is paying Juanita Lopez for tutoring her daughter Mary in chemistry.

What's to stop an unscrupulous person from taking a black pen and rounding out the 7 in "75" to make it look like a 9, thereby making the check worth $95? It wouldn't agree with

---

32 Each year at the end of our personal finance class, I ask students to identify the subject area that they found most valuable. A student recently wrote that he enjoyed learning how to write checks because it made him feel like a boss! Indeed, in millions of small businesses, the person who signs the checks to pay employees, landlords, suppliers and the like, is truly the boss.

the dollar amount that is spelled out on the line below for backup.

What's to stop a person who managed to steal one or more of Justine's checks from spending her money? A decidedly low-tech device: her signature. The ability of one person to mimic another's signature is practically nil.

True story: When I lived in the ATL, I hired a husband and wife team to restore the window moldings in my old house. Restoring meant removing the layer upon layer of paint that had been applied over decades. It can be melted off with a torch. It can be softened up with a slather of gel that needs time to work its magic. Either way, it's slow work. The couple asked if they could bring by a guy who was new in town and who they were trying to help get work. I agreed. Big mistake. The guy was around just long enough to see what he could lift from my house, including several checks. I didn't know anything was amiss for a while since the guy took the checks from the back of the book, which meant it could take weeks before I noticed they were missing. This was not his first rodeo.

Back in the day, when your bank statement arrived in the mail, the envelope also contained the checks you'd written that had made it to the people and organizations you paid. After the funds were deposited in the recipients' banks, the checks were sent back to your bank and were stuffed into the envelope with your statement. What a journey![33]

Thumbing through the stack of *cleared* checks one day, I saw a few written in big bubbly letters, with a signature that looked nothing like my own. These were the stolen checks. I brought them to my bank, which compared the signature on them to mine and promptly put the amount of the checks back into my account.

---

[33] Now you don't get the original check back with your statement, only a miniaturized picture of the front and back.

When a person writes a check for more money than is actually in his or her account, the bank may pay the amount of the check, even knowing that it will result in a negative account balance. This is called *overdraft* protection. In such an instance, the bank will notify the account holder to quickly deposit or transfer enough cash to cover the deficit. The bank isn't actually being kind. It's taking advantage of an opportunity to earn money. It charges a hefty fee for covering an overdrawn check. The alternative is not very appealing. If a person's bank doesn't make good on an overdrawn check, then the recipient's bank will *bounce* it back to him or her. Then, both banks will assess fees. Next, the receiver of the overdrawn check will chase down the check writer, demanding an explanation, reimbursement of his or her bank's fees, and of course, payment by some other means. It's not pretty. Let's identify everything of import on a check:

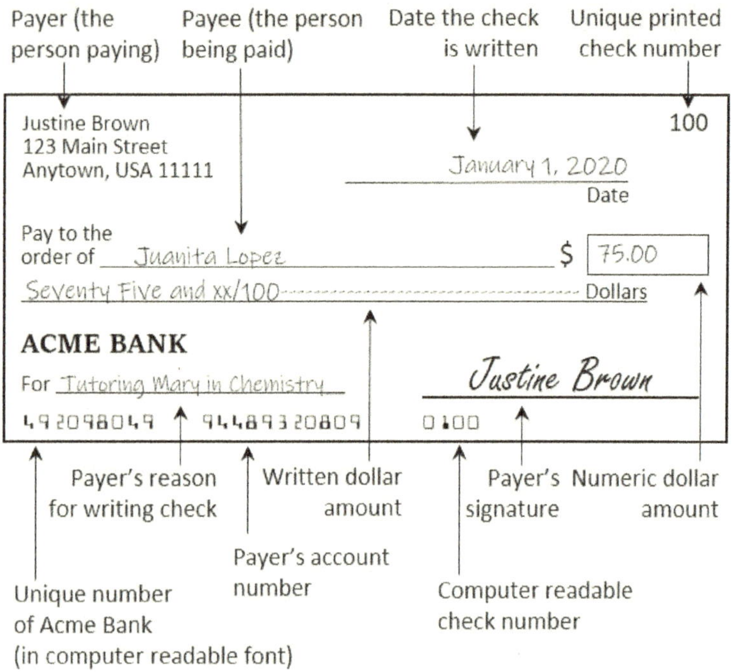

As we've noted in one of the callouts, every bank has a unique identifier in our banking system. That number, shown in the lower left of the check, is known as the *routing number* or *ABA number* (wherein ABA is short for "American Bankers Association," the entity that originally assigned the numbers). The routing number for each bank is publicly available information and can be found online.

The next number that's kind of a big deal is your unique account number at the bank. You are assigned this number when you open your account. It's the number to the right of the routing number on the check.

You will need these two numbers any time you want to move money in or out of your account electronically because, together, they identify your exclusive bank account in the United States. You should never give your account number to any party you don't know because this may enable an unscrupulous actor to transfer money *out* of your account.

Now, back to our story. As Juanita is leaving Justine and Alberto's home, Justine thanks her for helping Mary and then hands her the check. Juanita thanks Justine as she places it into her bag. What does she do next? How does Juanita get the money she's earned into her account? She has to *endorse* the check by signing the back.

A *blank* endorsement is risky because it makes the check a free agent. If Juanita loses it before depositing it at her bank, whoever finds it can deposit it into his or her own account.

A safer approach is the *restrictive* endorsement because it indicates a specific destination for the funds. In the illustration to the left, the destination is Juanita's account, with the number 34683362696.

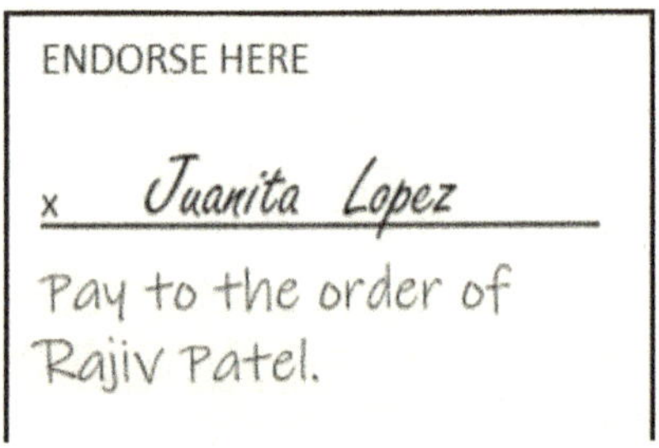


Let's say that by some strange confluence of events, Juanita's friend Rajiv bought two $75 concert tickets to ensure he secured seats before they sold out. Juanita can pay Rajiv for her ticket by signing the check over to him with this *full* endorsement.

With the first two endorsement examples above, the final step is for Juanita to deposit the check by taking it to her bank. More recently, we've seen that checks can be deposited using the bank's mobile app by taking a photo of the front and back of the check. In this case, the restrictive endorsement Juanita would write is "For mobile deposit to," followed by her account number.

## Savings account

As Justine and Alberto follow their budget and build up cash each month, they will eventually accumulate more money than they need to cover their expenses. One year ago, Justine had an average balance of about $5,000 in her checking account. Now, her average balance is in excess of $10,000. It's much more than she needs to manage the family's daily personal finances. After all, a year ago she had an average account balance of $5,000 and had no cash flow problems.

So, Justine talks to her banker and learns that she can take the excess $5,000 and put it into a savings account. In return for her agreement to limit the number of deposits and withdrawals, the bank will pay her a higher rate of interest (as compared to her checking account).

What makes a savings account for excess cash a no-brainer is her ability to link her savings and checking accounts electronically and move money painlessly between them, as needed. In the unlikely event that she spends more money than she has in her checking account, she can cover it with cash she transfers from her savings account. Her bank may even offer to do this automatically.

## Certificate of Deposit (abbreviated CD)

Eventually, Justine's saving account reaches a balance of $10,000. Now what? She sits down with her banker again and reviews the family's current situation with him. It includes the little morsel that her son is finishing his junior year of high school and that college is just a little more than a year away.

She bounces an idea off the banker., having overheard that now might be a good time to throw some cash into the stock market. The banker points out that if the market goes down over the course of the next year, she will suffer a loss when she sells her stocks to contribute to her son's first-year tuition. Better, the banker says, to purchase a *Certificate of Deposit (CD)* with the bank.[34]

A CD ratchets up the obligations of both you and your bank. You make a commitment to leave your money with the bank for a specified period of time, and it agrees to pay you an interest rate that is in excess of what your cash can earn in a savings account. Your time commitment enables the bank to

---

[34] Another option is a money market account, which has some of the features of a checking account and sometimes pays a higher rate of interest than a regular savings account.

better estimate how much money it will have on hand to lend to others.

Common CD terms range from one month to sixty months (i.e., five years). The longer the term of the CD, the higher the rate of interest paid. A reasonable move by Justine at this point is to take $5,000 from her savings account and purchase a 12-month, $5,000 CD.

What's her downside? As long as she purchases the CD with what is truly excess cash, there shouldn't be any downside. She has agreed to use some of her highly *liquid* (remember that term?) savings account funds to buy a certificate that she must hold for one year, but that will earn her a higher rate of interest. When the CD matures at the end of the 12 months, she will get her $5,000 back, along with the interest it earned.

The great news about CDs is that because banks half-expect their depositors to need to get at the cash used to purchase the CD before it *matures*, "breaking" the CD is not too painful. If something comes up during the 12-month period such that Justine decides she needs the money in the CD, the penalty will be a few months of interest. In this instance, she may wind up earning less than if she'd left the money in her savings account, but that's the cost of breaking the agreement.

Think of the progression of accumulated cash through the three types of accounts we just introduced as the cascading fountain shown on the next page.

---

*Our character is basically a composite of our habits. Because they are consistent, often unconscious patterns, they constantly, daily, express our character.*

\- Stephen Covey

---

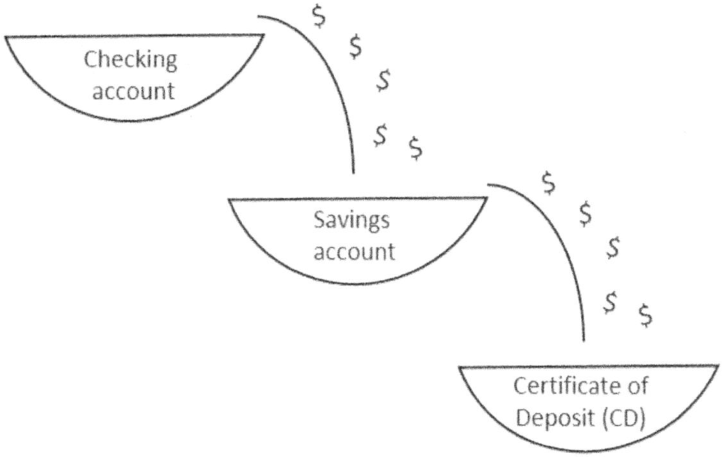


Because the money you have in your checking account supports your daily financial activities, money in it shouldn't be considered part of your emergency fund. Money in your savings account does qualify as emergency funding. At the risk of upsetting some unknown purist who might be reading intently, money in your CDs, as long it can be accessed quickly and at a modest penalty, qualifies as well.

## The saga of APR versus APY

You are cruising past a bank and see a banner in the window proclaiming:

# EARN 2.427% APY WITH OUR SAVINGS ACCOUNT!

You hit the brakes on your bicycle (that you ride not just to lower your carbon footprint, but also to get in some exercise) and take a closer look. In smaller writing, a footnote states, "APR 2.4%." You are confused.

Please sit down. It's time for the talk. APR stands for Annual Percentage Rate. APY stands for Annual Percentage Yield. I know, this is not helping. Bear with me.

The annual rate of interest the bank is offering on savings

accounts is 2.4%. We will earn 2.4% on money we place into the saving account after it is there for one year. From time immemorial, we've been receiving monthly bank statements. We can look forward to opening them if we know we'll find a line showing us the interest we earned. For this to happen, the bank must calculate and pay interest monthly. How can we earn interest on a monthly basis when the rate of interest applies to a whole year? The bank will calculate monthly interest as follows:

Monthly interest rate % = Annual interest rate % / 12 months
Monthly interest rate % = 2.4% / 12 months
Monthly interest rate % = 0.2%

Instead of paying us 2.4% only at the end of the year, the bank will instead pay 0.2% per month. Assume that we deposit $1,000 on January 1st into this savings account. The table below illustrates how the balance grows each month.

| | Starting balance | Interest rate | Interest earned | Ending balance |
|---|---|---|---|---|
| January | $ 1,000.00 | 0.2% | $ 2.00 | $ 1,002.00 |
| February | $ 1,002.00 | 0.2% | $ 2.00 | $ 1,004.00 |
| March | $ 1,004.00 | 0.2% | $ 2.01 | $ 1,006.01 |
| April | $ 1,006.01 | 0.2% | $ 2.01 | $ 1,008.02 |
| May | $ 1,008.02 | 0.2% | $ 2.02 | $ 1,010.04 |
| June | $ 1,010.04 | 0.2% | $ 2.02 | $ 1,012.06 |
| July | $ 1,012.06 | 0.2% | $ 2.02 | $ 1,014.08 |
| August | $ 1,014.08 | 0.2% | $ 2.03 | $ 1,016.11 |
| September | $ 1,016.11 | 0.2% | $ 2.03 | $ 1,018.14 |
| October | $ 1,018.14 | 0.2% | $ 2.04 | $ 1,020.18 |
| November | $ 1,020.18 | 0.2% | $ 2.04 | $ 1,022.22 |
| December | $ 1,022.22 | 0.2% | $ 2.04 | $ 1,024.27 |

As in previous examples, the arrow illustrates that the balance in the account at the end of a period—in this case, a month—is the starting balance of the next period. Had we been paid 2.4% interest only at the very end of the year, we would have earned 2.4% of $1,000.00, or $24 in interest. Our account balance would be $1,000.00 plus the $24 in interest, or $1,024.00. As we can see by examining the figure at the bottom right of the table, we actually have $1,024.27. Why the extra 27 cents?

This table should look familiar. It illustrates compound, or exponential, growth. In January, we earned $2.00 in interest. Okay, so it's not a big number. But our account has $2.00 more in it that can earn interest for the rest of the year. The extra $0.27 is the interest we earned on prior interest because the 2.4% annual rate was calculated and paid monthly. Let's look at the two ways of calculating interest side by side:

| | APY (interest applied monthly) | | | APR (interest applied once at the end of the year) | | |
|---|---|---|---|---|---|---|
| | Interest rate | Interest earned | Ending balance | Interest rate | Interest earned | Ending balance |
| January | 0.2% | $ 2.00 | $ 1,002.00 | 0.0% | $ 0.00 | $ 1,000.00 |
| February | 0.2% | $ 2.00 | $ 1,004.00 | 0.0% | $ 0.00 | $ 1,000.00 |
| March | 0.2% | $ 2.01 | $ 1,006.01 | 0.0% | $ 0.00 | $ 1,000.00 |
| April | 0.2% | $ 2.01 | $ 1,008.02 | 0.0% | $ 0.00 | $ 1,000.00 |
| May | 0.2% | $ 2.02 | $ 1,010.04 | 0.0% | $ 0.00 | $ 1,000.00 |
| June | 0.2% | $ 2.02 | $ 1,012.06 | 0.0% | $ 0.00 | $ 1,000.00 |
| July | 0.2% | $ 2.02 | $ 1,014.08 | 0.0% | $ 0.00 | $ 1,000.00 |
| August | 0.2% | $ 2.03 | $ 1,016.11 | 0.0% | $ 0.00 | $ 1,000.00 |
| September | 0.2% | $ 2.03 | $ 1,018.14 | 0.0% | $ 0.00 | $ 1,000.00 |
| October | 0.2% | $ 2.04 | $ 1,020.18 | 0.0% | $ 0.00 | $ 1,000.00 |
| November | 0.2% | $ 2.04 | $ 1,022.22 | 0.0% | $ 0.00 | $ 1,000.00 |
| December | 0.2% | $ 2.04 | **$ 1,024.27** | 2.4% | $ 24.00 | **$ 1,024.00** |

As we can see, it's better to earn 0.2% per month than 2.4% once at the end of the year. The formula for converting the Annual Percentage Rate (APR) to Annual Percentage Yield (APY), as well as the application of the formula using this example, is provided in the next footnote.[35]

Why should you care about the difference between APY and APR? After all, we just calculated a ridiculously small difference of $0.27. This is true, but it is also true that our $1,000 in savings is not a lot of money. Moreover, there have been times in our nation's past wherein the difference between APR and APY was a big deal. In 1984, you could get a one-year CD that paid 11% APR (again, annual percentage rate).[xiv] When interest is paid monthly, that translates to an annual percentage yield (APY) of 11.57%.[36] Unless you just signed a Max contract in a professional sport, you shouldn't dismiss the opportunity to earn a half-percent extra.

We will revisit APY and APR in our discussion on credit and credit cards. Bear in mind that we're not the ones earning interest when we use a credit card. We're paying it. To make matters worse, the rates and the balances are often high.

## Welcome to the revolution

One of the amazing aspects about teaching business is its dynamic nature. The advancements we observe all around us result from *creative destruction,* where *creative* developments lead to the demise of something else. One such example is the development of movie streaming, which led to the *destruction*

---

[35] $APY = (1 + APR / \# \text{ of times compounded})^{\# \text{ of periods in a year}} - 1$

$APY = (1 + 0.024) /12 \quad )^{12} \quad - 1$

$APY = (1 + .002)^{12} - 1$

$APY = 1.02427 - 1$

$APY = 0.02427 = 2.427\%$

[36] $APY = (1+.11/12)^{12} - 1 = 1.0092^{12} - 1 = 1.1157 - 1 = 0.1157 = 11.57\%.$

of video rental stores.

Technological advancement is behind much of this destruction. Using the example above, if telecom companies hadn't built high-speed networks across the land, it wouldn't be feasible to offer movie streaming.

Earlier, we discussed how using checks is a tried and true way for people to pay each other. Let's say that Jada wants to pay $50 to her Aunt Toni, who lives in another state. A few decades ago Jada would do so by sending a check to Aunt Toni. She would write the check and put it in the mail. A few days later, it would arrive at Aunt Toni's residence. Her aunt might be on vacation, in which case a neighbor would gather her mail. After returning home, it might take Aunt Toni a few days to sift through the mail. When she does get to Jada's check, she might set it aside until the next time she intends to run errands around town. The point is that it could literally take weeks for money to pass from Jada to Aunt Toni. In the interim, Jada would have recorded that she paid her aunt $50, but her aunt would not have recorded the receipt of $50.

The revolution in banking is that money is being moved in *real time*. You press the "Send" button on a phone app and it's done. If you were to check your account balance moments later, the payment would be visible, and your account balance reduced by the amount of the payment. Truly amazing. Of course, you and the recipient must have the phone app installed and set up beforehand. But that one-time setup literally ushers in a lifetime of frictionless money movement for you.

## The debit / ATM card

Real-time banking also enables us to pay for the goods and services we consume at local businesses electronically with funds in our bank account by using a *debit card* that is linked to our account. We swipe, insert or tap the card to pay, and the money is zipped from our account to that of the store.

Besides checks, another bridge to old-school banking is actual U.S. currency, the bills we put in our wallet. Some businesses and people want to be paid only in cash.

There are several ways to convert the money we hold in electronic form to cash-in-hand. The easiest of these is to withdraw it using an Automated Teller Machine (ATM). Our debit card doubles as our ATM card. Put it in the machine and then enter a password and the amount you want to withdraw. Out spits the money. Most ATMs are accessible 24 hours per day.[37]

Another method you can use to withdraw cash from your account is to visit a branch,[38] where you will fill out a *withdrawal slip* with your account number, the amount of cash you want to withdraw and your signature. You will hand the slip to the bank teller, who will hand over your cash. Of course, any time you convert your electronic money to paper money your account is updated in real time.

## I have what the bank says I have

We're almost there, almost at a post-check world where all transfers of money are electronic and thus, all banking is real time. In this new world, what you have in your account is what your banking app says is in your account.

Let's step back in time to just a few years ago, a time when a staple of every person's handbag or briefcase was a check book. In addition to a small stack of checks, the check book contained a folded-over booklet in which we could record to whom we were writing checks, on what dates, and in what dollar amounts.

---

37 Most banks place a limit on the amount of cash that can be withdrawn from an ATM in a day. Five hundred dollars is a common limit.

38 Bank locations are known as branches, although at least one bank—TD Bank—refers to them as stores.

This document is called a *register* or *ledger*. Its purpose is to record transaction details and maintain a *running balance* of the account. A blank register is illustrated next:

| Check No. | Date | Description | Check / Charge / Withdrawal $ | √ | Deposit $ | Balance $ |
|---|---|---|---|---|---|---|
| | | | | | | |
| | | | | | | |
| | | | | | | |
| | | | | | | |

Let's take it for a spin. Feng just opened his first checking account with a $100 cash deposit. Two days later, he used his debit card to buy a $15 lunch at Panera. Three days after that, he visited an ATM machine to withdraw $10 so he would be ready to tip a guy who is about to install internet service. The next day, he writes his first check, number 001, for $25 to his friend Esther as a birthday gift. These four activities are recorded as follows:

| Check No. | Date | Description | Check / Charge / Withdrawal $ | √ | Deposit $ | Balance $ |
|---|---|---|---|---|---|---|
| | 1/1/XX | Open account | | | $ 100 | $100 |
| Debit | 1/3/XX | Lunch at Panera | $ 15 | | | $ 85 |
| ATM | 1/6/XX | Installer tip | $ 10 | | | $ 75 |
| 001 | 1/7/XX | B'day – Esther C. | $ 25 | | | $ 50 |

The balance is tallied in the right-most column of the table. If you ever become the treasurer of a club, association or condo board, you will use a register to track the money that moves in and out of your organization's account.

Feng's register has separate columns for activities that lower the account balance (Check/Charge/Withdrawal $) and those that add to it (Deposit $). We can take up less space by consolidating these two columns into one as follows:

| Check No. | Date | Description | √ | Transaction $ | Balance $ |
|---|---|---|---|---|---|
| | 1/1/XX | Open account | √ | $ 100 | $100 |
| Debit | 1/3/XX | Lunch at Panera | √ | - $ 15 | $ 85 |
| ATM | 1/6/XX | Installer tip | √ | - $ 10 | $ 75 |
| 001 | 1/7/XX | B'day – Esther C. | | - $ 25 | $ 50 |

Looking down the "Transaction $" column, we see that transactions that subtract from the account have a minus sign in front of the dollar amount. We should also quickly explain the purpose of the check (√) column. When Feng looks at his banking app, it says he has $75 in his account. However, Feng's handwritten register is showing $50. The reason, of course, is that Feng has recorded the check he gave to Esther Chu, but Esther has yet to deposit it into her bank account.

Banks have no idea what people do with their checks until the recipients deposit them into their accounts. We enter a check mark for a transaction when it has cleared the bank. Feng can access his banking app in the days following Esther's party and enter a check mark in his register when the $25 check clears and has been deducted from his account.

Of course, if Feng never uses checks all of his banking will be real time. He can theoretically get rid of the √ column. Heck, because the banking app keeps a real-time register that is right there in his pocket where he keeps his phone, there's really no point in Feng spending the time and energy to keep his own record of his banking activity. Or is there?

True story: Years back, I had to get some cash before driving to the city. I stopped at the closest ATM along my route. After placing my card in the machine and entering my password, I punched in that I wanted to withdraw $100. Then I waited, and waited, and waited. After five minutes, I hit the cancel button. Thankfully, the machine regurgitated my card. Off I went to the next closest bank branch. The same thing happened at its ATM. Time to proceed to a third branch. That

ATM cooperated by producing five $20 bills. I didn't give it another thought until my next bank statement arrived, showing that I had made three ATM withdrawals, each for $100! Your bank and its systems are not infallible. If you don't keep a separate register of your banking activity, you may be less likely to catch a mistake.

The reason for that squishy phrase *"may be less likely"* is that, given the literal real-time command that you can have of your bank account (complete with the ability to set up notification of all activity), you can watch your account like a hawk and make sure it is accurate and correct. Had my ATM adventure happened today and the app notified me of not one, not two, but three ATM withdrawals for $100, I could have marched into the nearest branch much sooner and ~~given them a piece of my mind~~ politely discussed the problem with a representative.

On the other hand, life can become hectic, notifications don't always come through and, even if they do, you might simply miss them. The bottom line is that if you don't keep a separate register to track your account activity and balance, you are at the mercy of the bank to do it accurately for you.

## A check-free, real-time banking life

A quick canvassing of former students who are now young adults revealed that not one of them has ever written a check. They admitted that they may have needed to write one, but don't remember because that's where their parents would have stepped in. These discussions make it clear, however, that check-free banking is here.

What is important to know is that even if you never ordered blank checks for your account when you opened it, and you do not have a suitable check-writing family member to help, you can still come up with a check if necessary.

**Bank check** One day you walk into your nearest bank branch and take a seat at the desk of a representative. You provide some ID, which she uses to look up your account.

Let's say that you have $2,000 in the account. You're there because you need a $500 check to rent a party tent. You suggest to the banker that she take $500 out of your account and put it into one of the bank's own accounts.[39] Now that the bank has $500 of your money in its account, you can request that it write a $500 check to the tent supplier. Not surprisingly, this is known as a *bank check* or a *cashier's check.* A bank check is actually preferred by recipients over a personal check because it is basically assured to be paid.[40]

**Certified check** Another twist on this approach is for the bank to set aside $500 electronically in your account so that it can't be withdrawn and then write a *certified check* to be paid from your account.

To compensate it for the time and effort it takes to write a check to the party you need to pay in the amount you are paying, the bank will charge you a nominal fee, such as $10.

**Money order** A final solution to paying another party in a secure way is to buy a *money order.* Money orders can be purchased at your bank, local post office, and even at select big businesses such as Walmart. You simply show up with $500 in cash and exchange it for a $500 money order on which you identify your intended recipient as the payee (remember that term from our discussion of checks?). The money order is "drawn" on the entity from which you purchased it, so you are not the payer on the order. Instead, the payer is your bank, the U.S. Postal Service or Walmart.

Generally speaking, money orders are available in amounts up to $1,000. Because they are less expensive than a bank or certified check, money orders are popular for small

---

[39] It is interesting to consider that a bank can have accounts with itself.

[40] That word *basically* is used here because, despite enhanced security features on the bank's check, it can still be forged. If someone ever wants to pay you for your car with a bank check, call the bank and make sure the check is legit before handing over the keys.

transactions wherein an assured form of non-cash payment is required.

## Banks in other flavors

Most of us are familiar with large banks such as Chase, Citibank and Bank of America. They blanket their service area with convenient locations and vast networks of ATMs. This is important because your use of an ATM machine may only be free if it is one that your bank owns. ATM fees can be very steep, too. That's because if you don't have an account with it, the bank whose ATM you used charges a fee and your bank piles on by charging you one as well.

Let's say you pull into a rest stop on the interstate highway and realize you are out of cash. There are about $20 in cash tolls between your location and home. So, you use the ATM there, which does not belong to your bank. You only need $20, but the fees total $5. Ouch.[41] This is an example of an unforced error, the type of which we should do our best to avoid.

### Virtual banks

It is very expensive for a bank to maintain branches in convenient locations all over town. For many people, this investment is greatly appreciated. Our financial lives can be complicated, and it is awfully nice to be able to stop in, sit down and discuss our situation with a banker.

Still, what if you have your banking life so tricked out that everything is done electronically? Your pay is *direct-deposited* from your employer's account to yours every payday. You pay your bills using your banking app. You make quick work of the occasional check you do receive, depositing it electronically using your mobile device.

---

41 If you think that $5 is no big deal, then please put this book down now and send me as many $5 bills as will fit into an envelope.

One day you realize that while you regularly use the ATMs located in the lobbies of your bank's branches, you haven't stepped inside the bank for years. The bank's employees are ready to serve you, but you never need assistance.

The economist in you might begin wondering if you are somehow paying for a service you don't use. Then you see an online ad for a virtual bank. It has no branches and exists only online. How can that be? Well, as was just pointed out, if you can do your banking electronically, you can go years without ever needing to go inside a branch. They must not need to be there. Without an array of expensive branches to support, the costs of a virtual bank are much lower than that of a conventional bank. This enables the virtual bank to pay you higher rates of interest on your deposits.

But wait. If the bank has no branches, then it also has no ATMs. How will you access cash? The virtual bank has an elegant solution that turns a weakness into a strength. Knowing that it doesn't have any ATMs, it invites you to use any bank's ATM. We're talking hundreds of thousands of machines if we add up all the ones owned by different banks. You will, of course, incur a fee for which the virtual bank will pay you back. Problem solved.

What are the drawbacks of a virtual bank? As mentioned earlier, banks usually put a limit of a few hundred dollars on the amount of cash that you can withdraw from an ATM in a day. As the customer of a conventional bank, you can walk into one of its branches and walk out a little while later with thousands in cash. So, if you frequently need access to significant amounts of cash, a virtual bank may not be your cup of tea.

We also discussed visiting a branch and walking out with a bank check or certified check. That's also not going to be as easy for a customer of a virtual bank. You can get one of them from your virtual bank, but it has to be delivered.

Another issue that seems like it's from a bygone era is that some important information, such as a birth certificate, exists only in document form. Many banks offer *safe deposit boxes* in their branch locations. You can use a safe deposit box to protect critical documents from loss by fire or theft. Jewelry and other small valuables can also be stored in your box. A virtual bank has no branches within which safe deposits boxes can be rented.

## Credit unions

Imagine that you are the pastor of a megachurch with 10,000 members. In your ongoing discussions with your members you learn that some of them are flush with cash they want to put to good use, while other members could benefit from being able to borrow money at reasonable interest rates.

This is a perfect situation for the formation of a *credit union*. A credit union accepts the deposits of those with excess cash and lends it out to those who need cash. Unlike a bank, which is available to anyone who wants to use its services, your credit union would be open only to members of your church. Instead of being operated to earn a profit as banks are, your credit union would be run for the benefit of church members who deposit or borrow money.

Besides houses of worship, credit unions are also commonly formed for employees of specific businesses, governments and schools. For example, as an educator at a school in Nassau County, I was able to join the Nassau Educators Federal Credit Union (NEFCU).[42]

Because they are not run to maximize profits, credit unions pay depositors higher rates of interest than the average bank, and the interest rates they charge on loans is typically lower. Therefore, it's a good idea to do some research to determine if you qualify to be a member of one. It helps that many credit unions extend membership to entire families and even

---

42 NEFCU recently rebranded itself Jovia, a derivation of jovial.

extended families. For example, you may be allowed to open an account at a credit union for teachers if a parent is one.

Following is a table of approximate interest rates offered by the types of institutions we discussed. Where the traditional banks are concerned, New York area rates are cited. There are a variety of terms and conditions that must be met to receive these rates, which are subject to change at any time. The terms and conditions vary by financial institution, so the following is not an apples-to-apples comparison. Generally, the rates are for accounts with no minimum balance requirements. When you are ready to open an account, do your own research to learn the best offers available.

| **Regular bank** | Checking APY | Savings APY | 12-month CD APY |
|---|---|---|---|
| Citibank | [A] 0.00% | Up to 0.15% | Up to 0.30% |
| Chase | 0.01% | Up to 0.03% | [B] 0.20% |
| Bank of America | 0.01% | Up to 0.06% | [C] 0.20% |
| **Virtual bank** | | | |
| Discover | [D] 1.00% | 1.25% | 1.35% |
| Ally | 0.10% | 1.25% | 1.35% |
| Axos | [E] Up to 1.25% | 1.30% | 0.40% |
| **Credit union** | | | |
| State Employees | 0.25% | 0.40% | 0.80% |
| Navy | 0.05% | 0.25% | 1.35% |
| Alliant | 0.25% | 1.20% | 1.30% |
| [A] Interest is not available on Basic and Access Account checking. | | | |
| [B] CD is for 11 months. | | | |
| [C] CD is for 13 months. | | | |
| [D] 1% is paid on purchases up to $3,000 per month made using the debit card. | | | |
| [E] Requires use of debit card 15 times per month. | | | |

No single institution may offer the best rates across the board. However, a common requirement to qualify for the rates shown is that you open and link both checking and savings accounts with the same institution. Therefore, you should consider going with one that has the best rates overall.

Just as with any business, banks sometimes make special offers that are available for a limited time, such as an especially high rate on a CD of a certain term. Again, it pays to shop around.

## Blurring the banking lines

Earlier, we discussed banking apps in a general sense, explaining that they help you move money from one party's bank account to another's. However, some of these services are more than just go-betweens.

Let's say that you set up both a PayPal account and an eBay account. Next, you list a lightly used juicer for sale on eBay. A few days later it sells for $100 and the buyer sends $100 to your PayPal account. You haven't linked your PayPal account to a bank account, so PayPal doesn't pass your money along. Instead, your money is kept in your PayPal account. In this way, PayPal is acting as a bank. The same is true for Venmo and Cash App. No doubt that as "FinTech" continues to evolve, so too will banking.

*Who is or was?* Michael Schumacher.

## Exercises on banking

1. Explain the important role that a bank plays in your financial planning and why this role can be critical.
2. Explain the general progression of bank account types that people advance to as they accumulate more and more money.
3. Our chapter on budgeting discusses the importance of having an emergency fund. Does the money held in a checking account, a savings account, and/or a CD count as emergency funds? Why or why not?

4. Calculate the APY of a savings account that has an APR of 1.2% with interest calculated and paid monthly.
5. Identify one feature of a check that is interesting, explaining why.
6. Explain what real-time banking is and why using checks mucks up the works.
7. Explain the risk you run by not keeping your own bank account register.
8. Identify three ways that even a person who has never written a check can nevertheless pay an organization which requires payment in check form.
9. Compare and contrast conventional banks, virtual banks and credit unions.
10. Identify one way that advancements in technology are making it easier for us to meet our banking needs.

# Chapter 6 You deserve credit

We just discussed the ins and outs of banking, along with the services banks provide. You may have noticed that we skipped over one of them: making loans. Borrowing money falls under the broader topic of *credit*, which we're going to discuss in this chapter.

Regardless of how you feel or what you know about credit, you should read this chapter. For, while it must be respected, credit can be very useful in select situations.

*Credit* refers to your acquisition of a good, a service or even cash before paying for it. You purchase a mountain bike from the outdoor store where you work. The boss says that you can pay for it through deductions he'll take from your future paychecks. The mountain bike is a *good*, a physical item that you can move around. The boss has granted you credit in the amount of the cost of the bike.

After getting your haircut at the local barber, you are aghast after reaching into your wallet and finding no greenbacks. It's near closing time. You apologize profusely and promise that you will return in the morning to pay for the *service*. You've just been granted credit for the value of the haircut.

Our definition of credit ended with the indication that you can even receive *cash* before paying for it. This is a way of saying that a person can receive money that is expected to be paid back at some point in the future, which describes a *loan*.

## Warning! Warning! Warning!

Hold on while I search for a public domain image of a skull and crossbones, or maybe a hazardous materials warning sign, in an attempt to convey the gravity of the topic. It's difficult to begin discussing credit because it is akin to dynamite. Come Independence Day you can make some loud sounds that elicit oohs and aahs from your neighbors, but there's a good chance you will eventually pay a high price for messing with it.

Why is credit dangerous? Let's start with the obvious. The amount of any money borrowed must be paid back, usually with interest. Interest raises the stakes because you will have to pay more, often much more, than you borrowed. Once you're in debt, there is no easy way out. There are no smart bombs or do-overs. There's no waking up from the nightmare, not even an *Inception*-style waking up from a dream within a dream. You bought it. You spent it. You owe it. You are obligated to pay it.

Second, we have a positive image of the word *credit*. The title of this chapter is a compliment. You must have done something admirable to be held in such high regard. When a bank proclaims that you are creditworthy, that you are qualified to borrow significant sums of money just by signing on the dotted line, you have officially arrived. Of course, we are conflating the goodwill that comes from being a good person with handling one's financial affairs in a responsible manner. But it's too easy to do so because they both speak to a person's trustworthiness.

A third reason that it is too easy to fall into a trap is that credit is marketed to us in a manner similar to that of the next great smart phone. We're told about its great features, such as repayment flexibility. We're sold on its benefits, like the fact that it will enable us to pay off other high interest rate debts, renovate our kitchens or make that long overdue vacation a reality.

It's not just banks that sing the praises of credit. Respected economists have been known to utter the phrase, "Credit is the lifeblood of the economy." Huh? What? Why are these people saying this? The short explanation is that for a long time, people and businesses have used borrowed money to make purchases of everything from equipment to buildings to vehicles to components to materials. If they were suddenly to decide that borrowing money is too risky and vow not to purchase these big-ticket items until they've saved up enough to pay cash, the economy would crash. For example, how long does it take to save up enough money to purchase a new car? Five years? If every consumer decided today to begin saving the full purchase price of a new car, then no cars would be bought for the next five years. This, of course, would devastate the auto industry and the people who work in it. The sad truth is that the health of an economy whose participants are accustomed to ample use of credit to make purchases relies on their continuing to use it.

A final reason that credit is so dangerous is that when we take on debt, there is a lot of paper shuffling and button clicking, but no receipt of actual green U.S. currency. This can make the experience feel completely unreal. How much difference is there between $5,000.00 and $50,000.00? It's just a bunch of zeroes. At some level we know we are going into debt, but because no one is stacking a never-ending stream of C-notes in the palm of our hand, it is all too easy to miss the gravity of our obligation to pay it all back, with interest. Even if we do understand the magnitude of the situation, we may consider some borrowing "good" debt, such as a loan for the purpose of getting a college education. I mean, we have to spend money to make money, no?

It's been suggested that if you want to take control of your spending, simply pay for every purchase with cash. Those classy Maui Jim sunglasses you adore were just put on sale for $200? A steal. But if you reached into your wallet and began peeling off a series of $20 bills, at some point you might realize that it takes a lot of hard work to earn $200. As perfect a look as they help you achieve, you may acknowledge that you already own several pairs of other perfectly fine glasses. You might put the bills back in your wallet, put the wallet back in your pocket and walk out of the store.

## Types of credit

There are a million ways from Sunday to get yourself into debt but, thankfully, they can be herded into three major forms that we will explain next.

### 1. Term loan

Stan walks into a Chevrolet dealer. As a lifelong Corvette fan who has owned several, he is especially excited to learn that the 2020 Stingray has finally arrived. Having reached the limits of performance that a front-engine, rear-wheel-drive setup allows, Chevrolet undertook a complete redesign that has the engine *behind* the driver, super-car style.

At $75,000, it offers the performance of famous European brands for half the price. With sales tax, the total cost comes to $80,000. Stan tells the dealer that he can put $10,000 down. He wonders out loud if he will qualify to borrow the $70,000 difference. "This is America," the dealer replies, adding, "I've never had a customer for whom I couldn't get a loan, and I'm not going to let you be the first."

After gathering several pieces of Stan's personal information and punching some numbers into the computer, the dealer wheels around to give Stan the good news. He's been approved for a $70,000 loan at a low annual interest rate of 4.5%. He will pay it back at a rate of $1,305.01 per month over five years. The *term* of this loan is 5 years, which means that Stan will have to make 60 total payments.[43] As with all *term loans,* the same payment is made at equal intervals (usually monthly) over the loan's life. Each payment that Stan will make is called an *installment,* so this is also known as an *installment loan*. The more expensive the item being purchased, the more likely it is to be financed by a term loan.

Stan isn't as excited as the dealer and mumbles about how

---

[43] 60 = 12 months x 5 years.

the monthly payment is as high as a mortgage payment. Before Stan's second thoughts can gather steam, the dealer reels him back in by asking, "What monthly payment did you have in mind?" Stan replies, "It has to be less than $1,000." After another turn at the computer, the dealer offers even better news. By extending the term to seven years, Stan's monthly payment will drop to $973.01. Another problem solved by finance. Another American out the door with way more debt than he walked in with.

### *Secured by collateral*

The interest rate we quoted on the car loan above, 4.5%, is low for a reason. The Corvette that is being financed via the term loan is *collateral*. It *secures* the loan. If Stan doesn't keep up with his payments, the repo (short for *repossession*) man will take the car away. It will then be sold, and the proceeds used to pay off Stan's loan.[44] The presence of collateral lessens the risk for the lender, which allows it to charge a low rate of interest.

It is always better for the lender and borrower to decide on a loan term that is well short of the useful life of the good being purchased. Otherwise, there's a chance that as it ages, its market value will drop below the amount of the loan remaining. This is called being *upside-down* on the loan, and it's no fun.

Imagine selling your used car (on which there is a loan in the amount of $13,000) for only $11,000 because that's all it's worth. On the day of the sale, the buyer will pay the bank, not you, $11,000. Then, you will write a check to the bank for an additional $2,000 in order to pay off the loan in full. You're out the car and $2,000. Some sale.

---

[44] In the case of a house that cannot simply be hauled away, the borrower will be forced to leave the home. The process begins with *foreclosure* and ends with *eviction*.

### *Breaking down a term loan*

Let's introduce video-editing freelancer Isabella. She's ready to spend $9,000 on a new system of hardware and software. The new platform should allow her to get work done faster and even tackle more ambitious projects. She conservatively estimates that the new system will allow her to earn $1,000 per month in additional income.

Isabella will pay $4,000 in cash and borrow $5,000 (for a total of $9,000), using a one-year, 6% term loan. That is, a bank will lend her $5,000 at an APR of 6%. She will pay off the loan by making 12 equal monthly payments.

As we've seen before, however, the payment isn't the only thing that will be happening monthly. Interest will also be computed and charged monthly. The monthly rate is the annual 6% rate divided by 12 months, which equates to 0.5%, or one-half of one percent per month. It's actually more accurate to describe this as a 12-month loan with a monthly interest rate of 0.5%, because that's what it really is.

The big question: how much will Isabella have to pay each month? You had to go on faith that the monthly payment amounts we provided for Stan's Corvette loan were accurate. There is a formula that can be used to calculate the payment on a term loan. It is given in the next footnote.[45] Using the formula, we calculate that Isabella must make 12 monthly payments of $430.33 to pay off her loan and the associated interest in full. We stated earlier that she believed the new equipment would allow her to generate an additional $1,000 of income per month, so this payment should not be a challenge.

Let's now look at the "internals" of the loan by examining a table showing how her payments fully pay off the loan. We're going to assume that Isabella took out the loan on January 1

---

[45] $\$\text{ pmt} = \$\text{ borrowed} \times \text{monthly rate} / [1 - (1 + \text{monthly rate})^{-\#\text{ of months}}]$

and that she makes her first payment at the end of January. This means that one month of interest on the full loan amount of the $5,000 loan is also owed by the end of January. Five thousand dollars x 0.50% is $25. At the end of the month, the bank adds the $25 in interest, subtracts her $430.33 payment and arrives at an ending balance of $4,594.67. This process repeats until the end of the term of the loan.

Examining the following table, how can we be sure that $430.33 is the correct monthly payment? The ending loan balance at the bottom right of the table is $0.00.

| | A | B | C= A x B | D | A+C-D |
|---|---|---|---|---|---|
| | Starting loan balance | Monthly interest rate | Monthly interest amount | Month-end payment | Ending loan balance |
| January | $ 5,000.00 | 0.5% | $ 25.00 | $ 430.33 | $ 4,594.67 |
| February | $ 4,594.67 | 0.5% | $ 22.97 | $ 430.33 | $ 4,187.31 |
| March | $ 4,187.31 | 0.5% | $ 20.94 | $ 430.33 | $ 3,777.91 |
| April | $ 3,777.91 | 0.5% | $ 18.89 | $ 430.33 | $ 3,366.47 |
| May | $ 3,366.47 | 0.5% | $ 16.83 | $ 430.33 | $ 2,952.97 |
| June | $ 2,952.97 | 0.5% | $ 14.76 | $ 430.33 | $ 2,537.40 |
| July | $ 2,537.40 | 0.5% | $ 12.69 | $ 430.33 | $ 2,119.76 |
| August | $ 2,119.76 | 0.5% | $ 10.60 | $ 430.33 | $ 1,700.03 |
| September | $ 1,700.03 | 0.5% | $ 8.50 | $ 430.33 | $ 1,278.19 |
| October | $ 1,278.19 | 0.5% | $ 6.39 | $ 430.33 | $ 854.25 |
| November | $ 854.25 | 0.5% | $ 4.27 | $ 430.33 | $ 428.19 |
| December | $ 428.19 | 0.5% | $ 2.14 | $ 430.33 | $ 0.00 |
| Totals | | 6.0% | $ 163.99 | $ 5,163.99 | |

In looking down the "Monthly interest amount" column, you may have noticed that the amount of the interest owed decreases each month. The reason? Isabella owes less and less on the loan itself with each passing month. In fact, the monthly installment can be viewed as having two parts: i) a portion that pays the current month's interest, and ii) a portion that pays off some of the loan (i.e., reduces the loan *principal)*. We home in on this using the following *amortization table*:

| | A | B | C | A – C |
|---|---|---|---|---|
| | | Portion of $430.33 payment that... | | |
| | Starting loan balance | pays this month's interest | pays off the loan principal | Ending loan balance |
| January | $ 5,000.00 | $ 25.00 | $ 405.33 | $ 4,594.67 |
| February | $ 4,594.67 | $ 22.97 | $ 407.36 | $ 4,187.31 |
| March | $ 4,187.31 | $ 20.94 | $ 409.40 | $ 3,777.91 |
| April | $ 3,777.91 | $ 18.89 | $ 411.44 | $ 3,366.47 |
| May | $ 3,366.47 | $ 16.83 | $ 413.50 | $ 2,952.97 |
| June | $ 2,952.97 | $ 14.76 | $ 415.57 | $ 2,537.40 |
| July | $ 2,537.40 | $ 12.69 | $ 417.65 | $ 2,119.76 |
| August | $ 2,119.76 | $ 10.60 | $ 419.73 | $ 1,700.03 |
| September | $ 1,700.03 | $ 8.50 | $ 421.83 | $ 1,278.19 |
| October | $ 1,278.19 | $ 6.39 | $ 423.94 | $ 854.25 |
| November | $ 854.25 | $ 4.27 | $ 426.06 | $ 428.19 |
| December | $ 428.19 | $ 2.14 | $ 428.19 | $ 0.00 |

Notice that as the amount of interest due decreases, more of each month's payment is available to reduce the loan. This decrease in the amount owed results in an even lower interest figure the next month. If we were to chart it, we'd see that the interest amount accelerates downward as the payment portion that goes toward reducing the principal accelerates upward.

Before we move on, we should note that the first table shows that Isabella paid a total of $163.99 in interest. Why is it such a small fraction of the money borrowed? For one thing, the interest rate is reasonably low. More importantly, with a loan term of only one year, she began repaying a significant amount of the principal starting just one month after taking the loan.

### Buying a home

Let's revisit Justine and Alberto from our budgeting chapter. Instead of buying a home with a mortgage as they started their family, they contemplate toughing it out in their apartment while dutifully saving to purchase a home with cash. Their two kids could room together in the apartment's second bedroom. As the children grew and matured, they'd lobby unsuccessfully for their own space, with frustration and fights being the order of the day. There'd be scant space to store sports gear, bicycles, offseason clothes and holiday decorations, let alone host a get-together. Sleepovers would be out of the question. Eventually, the kids would move on to college and then start their careers in other cities. At some point they'd get a call from their excited parents. "What are we celebrating?" the children would ask. Their parents' reply: "We finally saved up enough money to buy a home!" Such is the alternative to not taking out a mortgage to house a growing family.

A critical distinction between taking out a mortgage to purchase a home versus getting a loan to finance another big-ticket item, like a Corvette or an SUV, is that a home is generally an *appreciating* asset. Its value usually rises over time. This isn't the case for ordinary cars and SUVs, which are *depreciating assets.* We hinted at this reality earlier when we explained that the term a lender will offer to the purchaser of a depreciating asset will, in part, be determined by how quickly the asset's value is expected to drop.

Thankfully, depreciating collateral isn't an issue that typically pertains to home loans. Add in the desire for affordable payments and we arrive at the standard mortgage term in America: 30 years! That's a mighty long time. Add 30 years to your age. Think about what your life may be like 30 years from today, and you'll get some sense of the length of time we're talking about.

However, no one is stopping you from making your payments sooner than they're owed in an effort to pay off the mortgage early. One well-known strategy is to take out a 30-year loan and then make one extra payment each year. Instead of 12 payments in one year, the borrower will make 13. Another is to walk boldly into the bank and request a 15-year mortgage for the home you're buying. With this strategy, each monthly payment over the 15 years will be higher than it would be with a 30-year mortgage because you are paying the loan off in half the time. If the term of the loan is halved, then it follows that the monthly payment will double. Or does it? We're about to find out.

Let's review Justine and Alberto's mortgage. They borrowed $350,000 at a 4.625% annual interest rate, to be repaid over 30 years. The monthly payment is $1,800. If they can eke out one extra payment per year, how much would that shorten their loan's term? How much more is the monthly payment on a 15-year mortgage? We've laid out the results on the next page, so have a look.

What have we learned? If the couple can consistently throw down one extra payment each year, they can cut four years and seven months off the term of their mortgage. The reason is that every penny of an extra payment reduces the principal of the loan. With this approach they will make 25 of these extra payments, which equates to two years and one month of additional payments, yet shorten the term of the loan by more than twice that.

Did halving the term of the loan to 15 years double the current $1,800 payment? Not even close. At $2,700, it is only

50% higher.[46] How can that be? As we learned early on, interest accumulates on prior interest. If the couple can pay an extra $900 ($2,700 minus $1,800) every month to reduce the loan principal, they will significantly short-circuit the interest compounding process.

| | Justine and Alberto's current 30-year mortgage | Their 30-yr mortgage with one extra payment yearly * | Their opting for a 15-year mortgage |
|---|---|---|---|
| Amount borrowed | $ 350,000 | $ 350,000 | $ 350,000 |
| Annual int. rate | 4.625% | 4.625% | 4.625% |
| Monthly payment | $ 1,800 | $ 1,800 | $ 2,700 |
| Extra payment / year | None | 1 | None |
| Total interest paid | $ 297,816 | $ 244,895 | $ 135,981 |
| Total amount paid | $ 647,816 | $ 594,895 | $ 485,981 |
| Amount saved | | $ 52,921 | $ 161,935 |
| Term | 30 years | 25 years, 5 months | 15 years |
| * Extra monthly payment is to be made at the beginning of each year. | | | |
| All dollar amounts are rounded up. | | | |

Would it have been realistic for Justine and Alberto to take out a 15-year mortgage? Could the couple have managed to make a mortgage payment that was $900 higher than the 30-year mortgage payment?

Prior to the scenario in which Justine lost her higher-paying job, the couple was setting aside $1,300 per month for various forms of saving, as repeated next:

46 ($2,700 - $1,800) / $1,800 = $900 / $1,800 = 0.50 = 50%.

| Justine and Alberto's Family Budget | | | | |
|---|---|---|---|---|
| **Category**/ Description | Monthly budget | % of Take-home | Actual spending / saving | Variance % |
| **Expenses / spending (cont.)** | | | | |
| … | | | | |
| Total expenses / spending | – $ 6,700 | 83.75 % | | |
| **Available for saving / giving** | = $ 1,300 | 16.25 % | | |
| Emergency fund | $ 0 | 0.00 % | | |
| Retirement saving / investing | $ 600 | 7.50 % | | |
| College funds | $ 300 | 3.75 % | | |
| Annual vacation | $ 200 | 2.50 % | | |
| Charitable giving / donations | $ 200 | 2.50 % | | |
| Total intended saving / giving. | $ 1,300 | 16.25 % | | |
| **Budget surplus or (deficit)** | = $ 0 | 0.00 % | | |

The largest savings component was the $600 being directed to the "Retirement saving / investing" category. Paying off a mortgage is a form of saving, so all $600 of it could have been repurposed toward the higher mortgage payment. That would have left the couple needing to find an additional $300 of lower spending, lower saving and/or additional income to fully accommodate the $900 higher mortgage payment. It would not have been easy, but it was within the realm of possibility to take on the 15-year mortgage.

The big benefit to a 15-year mortgage, of course, is that it is paid and gone in only 15 years. At that point, the tens of thousands of dollars per year that were formerly directed to the bank can flood into the couple's retirement saving and investing accounts.

Finally, don't snooze on the "Amount saved" row in our mortgage comparison. The reason that cutting the mortgage term in half resulted in the payment increasing by only 50% is that a staggering $161,935 less interest is incurred (compared to the 30-year mortgage).

### *Student loans*

Student loans are generally term loans. Federally provided loans have a standard 10-year term that can be extended up to 25 years.[xv] Hopefully at this point you understand the mechanics of term loans and are equipped to evaluate the numerous loan offers that will surely come your way when you apply to college.

The bigger issue, the elephant in the room, is that the ready availability of student loans, combined with the exorbitant costs of many colleges, has created a disaster of a magnitude that is difficult to fathom. Student loan debt, which seemed to have reached the ignominious milestone of $1 trillion only recently, now exceeds $1.5 trillion. The average student debt exceeds $36,000.[xvi]

Let's work with this figure. We're going to say that Yusuf graduates from college with $36,000 in debt. Further, he gets a job in his field that pays $25 per hour. The standard workday is eight hours. The standard work week is five days. This means the standard work week is eight times five, or 40 hours. There are 52 weeks in a year, of which we'll say Yusuf will work 50 and take two as unpaid vacation. Forty hours times 50 weeks is 2,000 hours. There are approximately 2,000 regular work hours in a year. If we multiply 2,000 by $25 per hour, we realize that Yusuf is knocking down $50,000 per year. Not bad.

Yusuf loses $5 of his $25 per hour to various taxes, so his take-home pay is $20 per hour. Not counting his student loan debt, his normal expenditures amount to about $16 per hour. This means that $4 per hour is left to cover both his student loan payments and desired savings. Dividing $4 into $36,000, we get 9,000. This is the number of hours Yusuf will have to work to pay off his student loan debt. Since there are 2,000 work hours in a year, and 9,000 hours divided by 2,000 hours is 4.5, Yusuf will have to dedicate the next 4.5 years to paying this debt, to the exclusion of all savings.[47]

This is scary stuff. As an educator who celebrates a 500-student, college-bound graduating class each June, I think about it constantly. The question I always come back to is this: what, exactly, educational advances justify the rapid cost increases in the last several decades? Are students being plugged in, *Matrix*-style, so that knowledge can be directly downloaded into their brains? If not—if a college education is still mostly chalk-talk—then it reflects poorly on the stewards of higher education.

To be sure, there are a number of justifiable reasons for the rise in costs, including significant reductions in state aid (which mostly affect state universities) and increased construction spending to address the disrepair of buildings of a certain era.[xvii] But when we learn that a textbook can cost over $250 and that some universities are indulging their students with lazy rivers, only the most saintly among us can hold cynicism at bay.

## *Buying vs. leasing*

Earlier in this chapter we learned about Stan and his affinity for Corvettes. Let's say that even if the dealer gets the monthly payment below $1,000, his significant other balks at the purchase. What now? Could the dealer have one more card up his sleeve? Please.

"Look, Stan, I understand you've got to keep the peace in your relationship, so why don't we consider a lease? With a standard *closed-end* lease, you drive the 'Vette for three years. At that point, you can either purchase it by paying us its depreciated value, or you can return it to us. You are basically

---

[47] We didn't include interest on the debt, which would make the situation worse. On the other hand, we also haven't considered any pay increases Yusuf may be able to achieve, which would make it better.

renting the vehicle and enjoying the best three years of its life—the first three. Is this something you would consider?" Not wanting to give up on his dream, Sam responds, "I would absolutely consider it."

Returning to the computer, the dealer explores the lease option. Before he can make his seat warm, the dealer pops back up. "Stan," he says with a wry smile. "I have incredible news. If you decide on the lease, your payment will be only $779.52. That's nearly $200 less than the payment would be on the 7-year loan! It gets better. Instead of paying $10,000 up front, you'll only need to put up $8,000. My friend, are you ready to put your John Hancock on a few papers and drive out of here in that shimmering Long-Beach-Red Metallic beauty?"

Regardless of whether Sam decides to seek approval from his sweetie or make the decision himself and deal with the fallout later, he should at least ask some questions. It would be wise for him to reach for his waders first.

The money men have taken the straight-forward interest rate being assessed and divided it by 24. The result is what they've named the *money factor*. So much for transparency. You might wonder why interest is involved in a vehicle rental. This is one of the details that the dealer would rather avoid reviewing with Stan. After all, if the payment is acceptable and Stan knows his options three years out, what does it matter?

OK, so Stan leases the vehicle and is blown away by its performance and practicality. What other car has the grip to pull more than 1.0g on the skid pad while sauntering down the highway achieving 25+ miles per gallon? Neighbors observe Stan garaging the beast, washing it regularly and otherwise babying it.

At the end of three years, his ride has been driven 35,000 miles. Why would he purchase what is, after all, a used car? The most important reason is that he is intimately familiar with the person who was behind the wheel for all 35,000 miles of the highways and byways over which it's been driven. It is him.

The next reason that he would purchase it is that the *residual value* (i.e., depreciated value) that was stated when the lease was originated, is reasonable. The new Corvette's purchase price was $75,000, against which Stan paid $5,000[48] when he signed the lease. The residual (aka buyout) value stated right there on the lease paperwork, is $50,000.

What it boils down to is that a bank lent Stan $70,000 three years ago at a rate of 4.5%.[49] The monthly payments he was required to make were set such that they would reduce the loan principal to $50,000 after three years.

Although the bank that financed the lease was happy to collect Stan's payments for three years, its specialty is leases. It wants out of the deal now, so someone better step up and pay it $50,000. If Stan was to turn the vehicle in, the dealer would sell it and use the proceeds to pay the $50,000 owed. If Stan wants to keep it, he will have to take out a term loan with another bank and use the proceeds to pay off the current loan.

We'll be here for a month of Sundays if we continue down this worm hole, but I cannot resist a few more paces. Ready? Vehicles that hold their value, which don't depreciate so much over the first three years of their life, are less expensive to lease than vehicles that do not. For example, if the Corvette's residual value was $55,000 instead of $50,000, this would mean $5,000 less that the loan would have to be paid down

---

[48] Five thousand dollars of the down payment will reduce the loan, effectively acting as a prepayment of the monthly installments. Most of the remaining money will be considered a prepayment of the sales tax that will be applied to each monthly payment.

[49] $70,000 = $75,000 new vehicle value - $5,000 down payment.

over the three-year lease. As a result, the monthly payment would drop tremendously, from $779.52 to $650.02.

The buyout value stated at the time of the lease is basically an estimate of the market value the vehicle will have in three years. It is not, however, in either the dealer's or the lender's best interest to overestimate it. Imagine that everyone thought that the first year of the new-generation Corvette would hold its value very well, leading the bank to set the buyout value at $55,000. Stan would benefit from the lower payments that such a high residual allows. At lease-end, if Stan looks on line and sees that used Corvettes similar to his are selling for just $50,000, he will surrender his vehicle, buy one of the better used ones on the market, and save $5,000.

Besides having a fair buyout value, the vehicle being returned must be in good condition and have been driven a reasonable number of miles for a lease to work for all parties. Otherwise, it won't fetch enough in the resale market for the dealer to fully repay the loan principal.

We would be remiss to close this subject without considering the role of leasing in our personal finances. Debt, as we've discussed, can be dangerous. Nevertheless, if a term loan is used to purchase a gently used vehicle that will provide many years of service beyond the loan's end, this is a defensible use of debt. With a lease, yes, the monthly payments are lower. But that's because the payment is only providing use of the vehicle, not ownership. The point is that if a person must resort to leasing in order to drive off the lot in a vehicle he really wants, he cannot afford that vehicle.

If you need another reason to be wary of leasing, it's that there are so many moving parts it's very difficult to understand what you are really paying. Let's say you see an advertisement promising that in return for $199 per month you can lease your dream car. When you arrive at the dealership, you learn that it's an *ultra-low mileage* lease, meaning that if you drive it more than 7,500 miles per year (the national average is 13,476 miles[xviii]), you will be on the hook for $0.25 to $0.50 for each additional mile. On top of that, there is the *capital cost reduction*, the large payment the dealer collects up front to make this amazing deal possible.[50] If the dealer collects $3,600 from you, that is basically $100 per each of the 36 monthly payments to be made over the course of a 3-year lease. You can boast to your friends that you leased your ride for only $199 per month, but you would not be straight with them or yourself. The monthly cost is $299. You just happened to pay $100 of it up front.[51]

I ask another favor. Watch the documentary *The Best That Never Was*. Then answer: *Who is or was?* Marcus Dupree.

## 2. Revolving credit

Young Timmy's yellow bucket holds one gallon of sand. Yet, after a morning at the beach, Timmy has made a sand pile that must be 50 gallons in size! How can that be? He did it, of course, with a "revolving" routine of filling and emptying his bucket.

*Revolving credit* is credit you use by making purchases, paying off those purchases, and then making subsequent purchases. The most common form of revolving credit is a *credit card*. How do credit cards work? By using the fateful triangle on the following page, we'll follow Zainab's purchase of a $1,000 refrigerator from a local appliance retailer (we'll call Repliance) that she pays for with her bank credit card.

FYI, a *retailer* is a business that sells products to consumers (as opposed to other businesses). A *merchant* is a business that accepts credit cards (as opposed to requiring customers to pay in cash or by some other means).

---

[50] In Stan's case the capital cost reduction was $5,000.

[51] The true cost is even higher because when you prepay you lose the opportunity for your money to earn interest over the lease term.

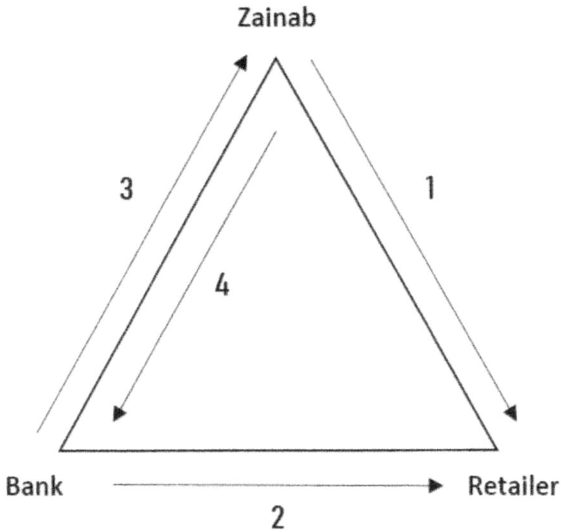


1. Zainab appears to pay Repliance $1,000 as she stands at the register, uses her credit card and is handed a printed receipt for $1,000. However, nobody's actually getting paid anything.
2. The next day Zainab's bank pays Repliance $975 for her purchase.[52]
3. At month-end, the bank sends Zainab a statement showing all the purchases she's made using her card, including the $1,000 fridge.
4. By the due date, Zainab sends her payment to the bank.

As you can see, the merchant pays a heavy price for accepting credit cards because the bank takes a piece of the purchase.[53] In our example, the fee is 2.5% of $1,000, or $25. As

---

[52] The merchant is usually paid from one to three days after purchase.

[53] This is an over-simplification, as this fee is shared among several entities: the bank; the payment association, such as Visa or Mastercard; the payment service provider; and other parties. This

a result, instead of Repliance receiving $1,000, it is paid only $975.

You might be wondering why Repliance would accept credit cards if it has to take this hit. Does it have a choice? Consumers expect it. They don't carry around large amounts of cash. If Repliance won't take her credit card, Zainab will just drive down the road to an appliance retailer that will. In addition, a business assigns tremendous value to getting paid via an assured form of payment that is received quickly. Instead of taking a $1,000 personal check from Zainab and waiting days to learn if it will clear or bounce, Repliance prefers knowing it will receive $975 the next day.

However, some businesses do push back. The *profit margin* of a business is the percentage of profit earned from each sale. If a company sells for $10 a product that has a total cost of $9.00 (including not only the cost of the product but the other expenses of running the business), its profit is only $1.00, or 10%. Such a business may look upon the 2.5% fee, essentially a quarter of its profit,[54] and realize that it cannot afford to accept credit cards. It will buck convention, posting prominently signs declaring that customers must pay with cash. Trendy restaurants may be able to get away with this but the average business risks turning customers off.

An alternative, which we see frequently at gas stations, is for the merchant to set one price for the product if the customer pays with cash and a higher price when the customer pays with a credit card. This passes on the cost of credit card payments to the customers who use them.

But our focus is on personal financial literacy, so let's return our attention there. Zainab's credit card statement will contain

---

make the processing of a credit card seem effortless to the consumer but opaque to the merchant.

[54] A 2.5 % fee / 10% profit = 0.25 = 25%.

a list of her purchases in chronological order. A sample from one of my own statements follows:

| | | |
|---|---|---|
| 12/16 | BURGER BAR MASSAPEQUE PA NY | 50.00 |
| 12/17 | WINTERS BROS WASTE SYSTEM 631-2447272 NY | 53.28 |
| 12/17 | EXXONMOBIL 48289276 SEAFORD NY | 32.44 |
| 12/19 | STAPLES 00101469 MASSAPEQUA NY | 45.60 |
| 12/20 | PANERA BREAD #204072 MASSAPEQUA NY | 15.59 |
| 12/20 | NEW YORK STATE DMV 518-4740904 NY | 135.00 |
| 12/21 | SPOTHERO 844-356-8054 8443568054 IL | 25.00 |

An exercise I ask my students to do is to sit down with their parents and make a list of items on which it's easy to spend $50. Dinner out? Of course. A new garment? Yes. A concert ticket? That will usually cost more. A new cell phone case? Affirmative. A parking ticket? Unfortunately. The point here is that if you make just one random and unbudgeted $50 purchase per day, the total at the bottom of that list will be $1,500. It's simple math. There are 30 days in the average month. Spending $50 each of those 30 days will result in credit card debt of $1,500. How much of a problem this represents depends on how many of the purchases were not budgeted.

The monthly credit card statement has an account summary, as shown below:

| | |
|---|---|
| Previous Balance | $2,411.84 |
| Payment, Credits | -$2,411.84 |
| Purchases | +$4,516.05 |
| Cash Advances | $0.00 |
| Balance Transfers | $0.00 |
| Fees Charged | $0.00 |
| Interest Charged | $0.00 |
| **New Balance** | **$4,516.05** |

Now, it looks like I've lost my mind by spending thousands more than I did the previous month. But this extra spending could be on airfares and other travel arrangements to solidify a budgeted family vacation, meaning that nothing is amiss.

This jump in spending again illustrates the difference

between a budgeted monthly figure and actual cash flowing in and out. Let's revisit this issue with a brief example. If a family expects to spend $3,600 on a year-end family vacation, that amounts to $300 per month ($3,600 divided by 12 months). But airlines and hotels don't provide a monthly payment plan. The airline tickets will be purchased on a day in one specific month, and there will be a day in one month on which the hotel will be booked. By the end of the year, the actual spending will equal the budgeted amount, but it won't on a month-by-month basis. We mentioned earlier that if we wanted to take our budgeting to the next level, we should create an individual plan for each calendar month that will allow us to budget actual cash flow.

Credit card users know that there is a *grace period,* a minimum three-week window, after the bill is generated and mailed, in which it must be paid.[xix] The following will help us determine what to pay:

| | |
|---|---|
| **Payment Due Date:** | **02/10/20** |
| **New Balance:** | **$4,516.05** |
| **Minimum Payment:** | **$90.00** |

The hope of the bank is that you will not be able to pay the amount you owe by the date it is owed. The first month that this occurs, you are officially in debt. The bank has won an important battle. To make it much easier for you to rationalize paying less—much less—than you owe, the bank calculates and shows you a *minimum payment.* This is the smallest sum you can pay and still preserve the normal interest rate you were offered when you applied for the card. "Normal" in the world of credit cards is around 12% to 18% per year. Because interest is calculated and charged monthly, it is more accurate to state that the normal rate is 1% per month (12% divided by 12 months) to 1.5% per month (18% divided by 12 months).

In our example, if you divide the minimum payment shown ($90) by the amount owed ($4,516.05), you will find that it is roughly 2%. Imagine, the bank tells you that it's all good, that you can continue to make purchases using the card and "enjoy" the normal interest rate on your balance as long as you pay at least 2% of what you owe. Hello? If you pay only 2% of your balance, you'll owe 98% of what you've previously bought with the card, plus 98% of your new purchases! Keep that up and you will accumulate debt rapidly. At some point, you will bump up against your *credit limit*, the maximum amount the bank permits you to owe on the card. The average credit limit on U.S. credit cards is about $8,000.[xx] For the purpose of discussion, let's say that the limit on your card is $10,000.

During your descent into indebtedness you may make the mistake of sending in a payment late. This will cost you a *late payment fee* of, say, $39. More importantly, when you make a mistake such as this, when you trigger the trip wire, the interest rate charged on future purchases will escalate to the *penalty rate*. Now we're talking annual interest rates of 24% or higher. Folks, that's 2% per month. Do you remember the rate of interest we said your money could earn in a bank? You'd be lucky to earn 2% on money you leave with the bank for 12 months, a full year. Here, you are being charged 2% interest in a *single month*. Think about that for a minute. It will take you an entire year to earn the same interest that you will be charged in one month if you have debt at the penalty rate.

You may have noticed that when we were comparing the Annual Percentage Rate (APR) a bank pays us on money deposited with it to the Annual Percentage Yield (APY), the APY wasn't much higher. For example, we found that an APR of 2.4% translates to only a slightly higher APY of 2.427%.

Let's try this exercise with $1,000 of debt incurring interest at the 24% penalty rate. That's the APR, the annual interest rate the bank is earning from you. But as we've just noted, you are really being charged 2% per month, not 24% at the end of the year.

| | APY (interest compounded monthly) | | | APR (interest applied once at the end of the year) | | |
|---|---|---|---|---|---|---|
| | Interest rate | Interest owed | Ending balance | Interest rate | Interest owed | Ending balance |
| January | 2.0% | $ 20.00 | $ 1,020.00 | 0.0% | $ 0.00 | $ 1,000.00 |
| February | 2.0% | $ 20.40 | $ 1,040.40 | 0.0% | $ 0.00 | $ 1,000.00 |
| March | 2.0% | $ 20.81 | $ 1,061.21 | 0.0% | $ 0.00 | $ 1,000.00 |
| April | 2.0% | $ 21.22 | $ 1,082.43 | 0.0% | $ 0.00 | $ 1,000.00 |
| May | 2.0% | $ 21.65 | $ 1,104.08 | 0.0% | $ 0.00 | $ 1,000.00 |
| June | 2.0% | $ 22.08 | $ 1,126.16 | 0.0% | $ 0.00 | $ 1,000.00 |
| July | 2.0% | $ 22.52 | $ 1,148.69 | 0.0% | $ 0.00 | $ 1,000.00 |
| August | 2.0% | $ 22.97 | $ 1,171.66 | 0.0% | $ 0.00 | $ 1,000.00 |
| September | 2.0% | $ 23.43 | $ 1,195.09 | 0.0% | $ 0.00 | $ 1,000.00 |
| October | 2.0% | $ 23.90 | $ 1,218.99 | 0.0% | $ 0.00 | $ 1,000.00 |
| November | 2.0% | $ 24.38 | $ 1,243.37 | 0.0% | $ 0.00 | $ 1,000.00 |
| December | 2.0% | $ 24.87 | **$ 1,268.24** | 24.0% | $240.00 | **$ 1,240.00** |

Total interest of $268.24 (i.e., the amount above the initial $1,000 debt) means that the APY is 26.824%, significantly higher than the APR of 24%.[55] Some credit cards have penalty rates that scoot right up to 30% annually but to avoid reaching that threshold, are set at "only" 29.99%. The APY for that rate is 34.5%![56] Notice that the higher the APR, the bigger the difference between it and the APY.

When your card is in the penalty box, it is basically toxic. You'd be crazy to use it again. Not to worry, though, as you are sure to receive a steady stream of new card offers delivered right to your mailbox. Let's say that you sign one of these pre-approved applications, send it back and receive another card a week later. You promise yourself to be more

---

[55] APY = $(1+0.24/12)^{12} - 1 = 1.02^{12} - 1 = 1.26824 - 1 = 0.26824 = 26.824\%$.

[56] APY = $(1+0.2999/12)^{12} - 1 = 1.02499^{12} - 1 = 1.345 - 1 = 0.345 = 34.5\%$.

responsible with it and you deliver on your promise. Instead of reaching this card's $10,000 credit limit in one year as you did with your first card, this time it takes two years. You now have $20,000 in credit card debt. Thankfully, none of your debt was incurred under a penalty rate. It's all 12% debt.

A family member sees an infomercial on TV and demands that you be the subject of an intervention. You see the error of your ways and cut up your two cards. Next, you tighten your belt, carving out $200 in your monthly budget to pay off your debt. At that pace, how long will it take you? Take a minute to think about the scenario: $20,000 of 1% per month debt that you will pay off at a clip of $200 per month. Will it take five years? Ten years? The answer is that there is no payback period. One percent of $20,000 is $200. You are paying only the interest. The debt is still there, generating $200 in interest each and every month, forever.

And that, dear reader, is exactly where the bank wants you. If your debt is too high, you might do something drastic, like declare personal bankruptcy. If your debt is not so big, if it's only a few thousand, then you might resolve to put in some overtime at work or sell your beloved sneaker collection and pay it off. In neither of these cases is the bank collecting interest from you.

In our scenario, wherein your $20,000 of debt is too high to pay off but not so high that you can't pay the interest, you are officially a *financial zombie*. For your sins you will pay the bank interest on your debt for the rest of your life. At least you won't be lonely. Total credit card debt in the United States is in the vicinity of $1 trillion.[xxi]

But instead of breaking out the violins at your pity party, a better move would be to tap into the mojo of personal finance guru Dave Ramsey. Dave plays the role of drill instructor for his fans, the guy who kicks them in the pants. You can't b.s. your parents, and people in debt can't b.s. Dave. He tells them to stop feeling sorry for themselves, to get an extra job, to buy mass quantities of rice and beans, and to show the debt who is boss by paying it off. Any questions?

*Who is or was?* Riley Howell.

## *Required disclosures*

Look, people drowning in credit card debt can't say they weren't warned. The law requires credit card issuers to disclose all the fees and interest charges associated with their cards. Following is a sample of disclosures that are impossible to miss:

| **Interest Rates and Interest Charges** | |
|---|---|
| **Annual Percentage Rate (APR) for Purchases** | **13.99%**<br>This APR will vary with the market based on the Prime Rate. |
| **APR for Introductory Purchases** | **0%**<br>This APR will apply to purchases made in the first 12 billing cycles |
| **APR for Balance Transfers** | **0%**<br>This APR will apply for the first 12 billing cycles on transfers made in the first 60 days. |
| **APR for Cash Advances** | **27.49%**<br>This APR will vary with the market based on the Prime Rate. |
| **Penalty APR and When it Applies** | **29.99%**<br>This APR will vary with the market based on the Prime Rate.<br>This APR may be applied to new transactions on your account if:<br>1) you make one or more late payments, or<br>2) your payment is returned by your bank.<br>We may also consider your creditworthiness in determining whether or not to apply the penalty APR to your Account.<br>How Long Will the Penalty APR Apply? If the |

| | |
|---|---|
| | Penalty APR is applied, it will apply for at least 6 months. We review your account every 6 months after the Penalty APR is applied. The Penalty APR will continue to apply until after you have made timely payments, with no returned payments during the 6 months being reviewed. |
| **Paying Interest** | Your due date is at least 25 days after the close of the billing period. We will not charge you interest on purchases if you pay each month your entire balance by the due date. We will begin charging interest on cash advances and balance transfers on the transaction date. |
| **For Credit Card Tips from the Consumer Financial Protection Bureau** | **To learn more about factors to consider when applying for or using a credit card, visit the website of the Consumer Financial Protection Bureau at http://www.consumerfinance.gov/learnmore** |

| **Fees** | |
|---|---|
| **Annual Membership Fee** | $0. |
| **Transaction Fees** | |
| • **Balance Transfer** | Either **$5** or **3%** of the amount of each transfer, whichever is greater. |
| • **Cash advance** | Either **$10** or **5%** of the amount of the advance, whichever is greater. |
| • **Foreign transaction** | **None** |
| **Penalty fees** | |
| • **Late Payment** | Up to **$39** |
| • **Returned payment** | Up to **$39** |
| • **Over limit** | **None** |

Just as it seemed we had completed our discussion of credit cards, the information in these tables drags us back in! Banks have to compete with each other. To entice you to choose its card, a bank may offer a low, or even 0%, *Introductory APR,* which will last for a certain number of billing cycles (aka months). In the 2nd row of the first table above, we see that any purchases made but not paid for will incur no interest for one whole year. The bank hopes that because you're getting something for free, you'll use the card frequently. Besides, what is the point of paying the whole balance owed when it's not costing you to have a balance? There isn't any. However, if you continue to make purchases with the card, one year will fly by faster than you can imagine and you'll owe thousands you're unlikely to be able to pay. The bank can then begin charging you interest.

When competition is intense, banks may even attempt to take each other's customers. This is done by offering a low, or even 0%, *Balance transfer APR* for a certain number of months. Let's assume Destiny owes $10,000 on a credit card and the balance is subject to interest at a 24% APR. She gets a credit card offer in the mail that provides 12 months of 0% interest on balances she transfers for a low, low one-time transfer fee of 4%. Destiny applies for and receives the new card. Next, she fills out a balance transfer form that directs the new bank to pay the old bank $10,000. With the 4% fee added, Destiny now owes the new bank $10,400. Yes, she's in more debt. But, by taking a $400 hit up front, the $200 per month in interest on her old card goes bye-bye for one year. Destiny has just gained a reprieve during which she should get her act together and pay off every penny of her debt.

One last point of import is that if you are ever in need of cash in a far-off land and your ATM card is lost or not functioning because the chip fell out,[57] you can actually stick

---

[57] It happened to me recently. It could be an indicator of card overuse. I tried to glue the chip back in place, but merchant card readers weren't having it. After a quick call to the bank, a new one was delivered promptly, ensuring minimal spending downtime.

your credit card into an ATM. You will get cash, but not your cash. It's the bank's cash, and you are borrowing it. This is called a *cash advance,* and you will be hit hard with fees for taking one. But if a remote island nation wants you to pay $25 in cash to board a plane home and you don't have it, you'll be happy to have this option.

### *Store card aka Private label card*

Best Buy offers a *store card.* It is a blue credit card that proudly sports the Best Buy name and logo. It can only be used at Best Buy. What's the point of having a credit card that can only be used at one business? I recently found out.

My college-bound, design-aspiring daughter was in need of a new tablet/computer. Not too big, not too small. A stylus was a must. A solid-state drive would allow it to withstand more jostling. The i7 chip was recommended over the i5, which is just so old. What better place than Best Buy to sample the wares, get schooled on the latest technology, pay a fair price and be able to walk out the door with the chosen hardware? At over $2,000, the price may have been fair, but it wasn't chump change.

The gentleman who assisted us made an offer that promised to cushion the blow. "If you open a Best Buy credit card account now, you will save 10% on today's purchase." Think about that for a moment. Ten percent of $2,000 is $200. Best Buy was basically offering to pay me $200 for opening a Best Buy store credit card account and placing this purchase on it.

What's the downside of opening the account? For anyone with self-control, none. At the end of a month the bill for the tablet purchase, in the amount of $1,800 (10% off $2,000), would arrive in my mailbox. After I paid it I'd owe Best Buy nothing. Because credit cards don't have inactivity fees, I'd be free to place the card in a safe place or even cut it up. The marketing folks at Best Buy would do their level best to make sure the card met neither fate. On a regular basis, they'd slip me special offers on all kinds of cool gear, with the opportunity to earn an additional 5% *cash back* on purchases made using the card.[58] I just might have a hard time resisting that 75-inch, Ultra-High-Definition TV they'd keep tempting me with!

Store cardholders may also be offered extended financing, which is the ability to pay for purchases in equal monthly installments over 6, 12, 24 and even 36 months, interest free. While it might sound fancy, at the end of the day this *extended financing* is just debt. It is interest-free debt for a while, but the cost of not paying off your purchase in full by the end of the extended financing term is that interest will be calculated *from the date of purchase* and added to your bill. Should this come to pass it will be especially painful because store card interest rates are nearly 5% higher than those of standard bank credit cards![xxii]

### Co-branded cards

A cousin of the store card is the *co-branded card,* which is jointly offered by a bank and a business.[59] In contrast to a store card, it is broadly accepted, just like any general-purpose credit card. It also differs in that the rewards for being an active cardholder and user are usually designed to provide special privileges with the business featured on the card. For example, a credit card that an airline offers in association with a bank may have a rewards program wherein the cardholder is able to check extra bags, gain access to exclusive airport

---

[58] This is the equivalent of an after-the-sale discount. It's very clever to offer discounts this way because they can only be applied to *future* purchases. The only way to continue taking advantage of available cash back is for the cardholder to continue buying!

[59] A card that a bank markets with a university, charity or cause is known as an *affinity card*. The bank donates a portion of the purchases made using the card to the organization.

lounges, upgrade to a better class, and even book a free round-trip flight when the cardholder racks up a certain number of *rewards miles.*

As you might imagine, *credit card rewards* are one of the major battlegrounds on which banks compete. They have concluded that giving some of the fees they earn back in the form of various rewards will garner the continued loyalty of current customers, not to mention attract new ones.

Earlier we looked at a basic credit card transaction wherein Zainab purchased a $1,000 fridge from an appliance retailer named Repliance. Her bank took a 2.5% discount,[60] paying Repliance $975 the next day. If Repliance partnered with a bank to make available a co-branded card, it could offer its cardholders "1% cash back" on all purchases. Or, it could implement a rewards program wherein the cardholder would earn a generically-named *rewards point* for each dollar spent. Each point would have a value of $0.01. That is, for each $1.00 spent, the cardholder would earn a point worth $0.01. A penny is 1% of a dollar, so isn't this just a complicated way of offering the same 1% cash back? Shhh. Let's keep that between us. Some people like to brag at parties about how many rewards points they're racking up and we wouldn't want to rain on their parade.

Interestingly, as banks escalate the rewards arms race, offering perhaps 1.5% cash back on travel and 2% on visits to restaurants, they do so on the backs of merchants by paying them less! Not surprisingly, merchants are fighting for the right to reject cards for which the rewards are so generous that the bank takes a larger fee on purchases made with them.[xxiii]

Some businesses have even begun making consumers pay for using their credit cards by adding a 3% "administrative

---

[60] Again, we are aiming for simplicity. As stated earlier, the bank shares this fee with several other parties that facilitate credit card transactions.

fee" to make up for the discount the bank will take. This was explained to me recently at an auto-body shop. (Don't ask.) There's no point in paying 3% more when using a card in order to earn 1% cash back. Then, there's the bold notice posted at a local Chinese take-out restaurant stating that a 4% fee will be added to the bill when the customer pays with a credit card. The tide, it appears, is turning. The crazy part is that if merchants continue to act boldly and these additional fees take hold across the country, they completely defeat the rationale for using credit cards.

### *Playing with fire without getting burned*

So, if credit cards are so risky, is there any way to reap their rewards while avoiding their pitfalls? From decades of personal experience, I can say with confidence that the answer is yes. Here's what I do:

1. *Have a single, solitary credit card.* That's one card, one bill per month and one account to manage.
2. *Choose a card which uses the Visa or Mastercard payment association.* If the merchant you want to purchase from here in the U.S. does not accept Visa or Mastercard, then it probably does not accept credit cards.
3. *Choose a free card.* The annual fees on credit cards can stretch from $0 to hundreds of dollars. The higher the fee, the more generous the rewards. However, you have to spend enough to make the value of the additional rewards that you would earn with the card greater than the card's annual fee. It can be done, but who wants the pressure of needing to make a certain minimum dollar amount of purchases using the card?
4. *Choose a card that has a "cash back" rewards program.* Cash is flexible and can be used in small increments. The same cannot be said of benefits, such as airline rewards, which won't be much help if you do not plan on flying

in the foreseeable future.

5. *Only use the card for purchases supported by your budget.* Obtaining a credit card with a generous credit limit isn't a green light to go hog wild. Just use it to make purchases you were going to make anyway, in accordance with your budget.
6. *Pay off your entire bill on time every month.* This is where the rubber meets the road. If you pay your bill in full every month then you will never pay fees or interest.

I've followed these guidelines for at least the last 25 years. When my available cash-back rewards accumulate into the hundreds of dollars, I click a button and use it to pay off a portion of the current month's bill. It's free money.

Are there vulnerabilities with the above approach? Sure. One is the risk that I won't pay the bill on time. But with so many ways to set up reminders and automatic payments, there is just no excuse for not paying this single credit card bill on time. What if I don't have the money to pay the bill in full? If I am following my budget, then I will have the cash I need.

It turns out that the most difficult part of adhering to my rules is the occasional large purchase I make, such as the computer at Best Buy, which tempted me to obtain an additional credit card. It seems like a sin to turn down the opportunity to save hundreds of dollars. But each time, I swallow hard and turn down the opportunity. I didn't open a Best Buy store credit account that day, allowing me to continue having a single solitary credit card.

*Who is or was?* Selena Quintanilla.

## Credit versus debit

Earlier, we alluded to the fact that people don't like to carry large sums of cash. Instead, they will carry some form of plastic. So, which is better, a credit card or a debit card? For the aforementioned Dave Ramsey, who has witnessed countless instances of the carnage inflicted by out-of-control debt, the choice is very clear. A person who uses a debit card is spending his or her own money. This brings to mind the question, "What is the best way to be free of debt?" The answer, of course, is "Never get into debt in the first place!" This is sound advice. There are, however, practical advantages to using a credit card to make budgeted purchases.

When you use a credit card to buy a product (or a service, such as an airline ticket), the bank pays the merchant the next day. It can be several weeks to well over a month before you must pay the bank for it, depending on when during the month you make the purchase. In the interim you will open and use the item you purchased. On occasion you will have the unpleasant realization that the product is not as advertised and that you've been ripped off. If your attempts at resolving the issue with the merchant are unsuccessful, you will be able to file a *dispute* with the bank.[xxiv] It will take the dollar amount of the purchase off your bill until the issue is resolved. If you are able to provide the bank with a compelling argument and documentation that supports your position, it will permanently remove the purchase from your bill. The dispute protections the law provides for debit card purchases are less robust.

Then, there are times when a purchase charged to your account is straight-up bogus. Never heard of Nordstrom? That's funny, because right there on your credit card statement is the purchase of a $500 Nordstrom gift card. When a fraudulent charge occurs with a credit card, the bank with which you have your card has paid the merchant its money for a purchase you didn't make. When you notify the bank that you didn't make the purchase, it will reverse the charge.

When a fraudulent debit card purchase occurs, it's *your* money that's been paid to the merchant. If you value your money, it's critical that you spring into action and begin the process of getting the bank to replace it. In the interim, a fraudulent $500 gift card purchase made by someone who lifted your debit card information may lower your bank account balance enough to cause an automatic bill payment or two to fail, resulting in all kinds of charges.

True story: This week a colleague was jolted when she discovered that $1,050 had been deducted from her bank account for purchases she didn't make. She called the bank, which immediately closed the account and transferred her remaining money to a new account. Even though it was only Tuesday, the electronic *direct deposit* of her paycheck that was to occur on Friday had already been set in motion and was not cancellable. To get paid, she would have to wait until Friday's attempt to deposit her take-home pay electronically into her now-closed account failed, and then wait for the school district to issue her an old-school check. She was assured by her bank that it would restore the amount of the fraudulent payments into her new account within 12 hours. Was that 12 clock hours or 12 business hours? She didn't recall. A few days later she had yet to be reimbursed. In the end, even if my colleague is made completely whole by her bank, the tremendous stress and time-suck of rectifying a compromised bank account is something no one deserves.[61]

If you need any more convincing, the number of days you have to dispute a fraudulent charge after it occurs is shorter for a debit card purchase than for a credit card purchase. Moreover, your potential responsibility for paying a portion of a fraudulent charge is higher for a debit card purchase than for a credit card purchase.

In addition, because the discount banks can charge

---

[61] To be sure, there are strategies for mitigating the effects of debit card fraud, such as having one bank account that receives your direct deposit and another from which you make automatic payments and debit card purchases. But having multiple accounts means that money must be moved between them on a regular basis.

merchants for debit card purchases is limited by law,[xxv] the debit card rewards programs are less generous than those of credit cards.

Finally, credit-card issuing banks offer a host of lesser-known benefits that provide real-world savings when their cards are used to make purchases. *Product protection* includes extending the manufacturer's product warranty and may even include free replacement on select purchases in the event of loss or damage during your first few months of ownership. *Travel protection* includes reimbursement for losses due to trip cancellation as well as supplemental car rental insurance coverage that allows cardholders to decline the infamous *collision damage waiver* with confidence.[62] While debit card issuers are matching some of these rewards, they are generally less beneficial than those of the leading credit cards.[xxvi] [63]

Like it or not, our financial activity is being tracked and compiled into a *credit profile.* As we will discuss shortly, this information is used to generate a *credit score,* a measure of an adult's creditworthiness. This creditworthiness (or lack thereof) affects the interest rate a person pays when borrowing money. Using a credit card for routine budgeted purchases and then paying the bill off each month builds up a person's credit score. Using a debit card to spend one's own money has no impact on credit scores because credit is not involved.

---

[62] The collision damage waiver, which can run as high as $30 per day, provides coverage for costs related to the rental vehicle itself, such as damage and loss of revenue while the vehicle is being repaired. Rental counter agents warn that renters will be responsible if the vehicle is involved in an accident. Fearing that their current auto insurance policies won't provide adequate coverage, many reluctantly relent and pay the CDW.

[63] Trying to find a single debit card that offers a benefit obviating the collision damage waiver has been an exercise in frustration. If you find one, let me know.

### 3. Line of credit

Recently overheard at a bank:

Visitor: I'd like to take out a loan.

Banker: How much money do you want to borrow?

Visitor: I'm not sure.

Banker: When you do want to borrow the money?

Visitor: I'm not sure.

Banker: How will you repay the loan?

Visitor: I'm not sure.

Banker. A line of credit is perfect for you!

A *line of credit* is an amount of money a person has been approved to borrow by the bank. It's for big shots who say things like, "I just drew down my credit line and pulled the trigger on that fine vessel we were admiring at the yacht show."

To be sure, regular folks can also be approved for a line of credit. Let's catch up with Bradley and his family. They have lived in their home for 25 years. They could sell it today for $350,000. The mortgage balance is $75,000, meaning that they have $275,000 of *home equity*. The family is increasingly concerned that their kitchen is looking dated, a private shame whose dimensions are not well understood due to the lack of research dollars.

Bradley has received several estimates, ranging from $25,000 to $35,000, for a complete kitchen overhaul. He is not sure which contractor he will select. He is not sure when the project will begin. He's also not sure whether hidden issues will be revealed when the existing kitchen is torn out. Consequently, he's not sure when the project will be done.

Bradley and his banker decide that he should open a $50,000 line of credit. This will allow him to borrow the money he needs when he needs it. Interest will be charged only on the amount of money borrowed for however long it remains borrowed. Because this line of credit is secured by Bradley's significant equity in his home, the bank is able to charge a relatively low annual interest rate of 6%. In fact, such credit is referred to as a Home Equity Line of Credit or *HELOC*.

Bradley *draws down* on the line (i.e., borrows the money) by writing checks connected not to a bank account, but to the line of credit. If he writes a check to the tile guy for $2,500, the bank will pay the check and the amount owed on the credit line will increase by $2,500.

Fast forward six months. The kitchen is done! The total cost, with a hiccup or two as well as a few upgrades: $40,000. Hopefully, you remember that a stated annual interest rate of 6% is calculated and charged monthly as follows: 6%/12 months = 0.5% per month. Half of one percent of $40,000 is $200.[64] If Bradley pays the bank $200 per month, he will be paying the interest only on his HELOC. He will continue to owe the $40,000 borrowed. Indeed, this may be Bradley's plan. Let's fast forward five years, during which time he has paid only the interest each month. The mortgage has been paid off. The kids have moved out of the home, which is now worth $400,000. When Bradley sells it, the bank with which he has the HELOC will be paid its $40,000 and Bradley will be paid the remaining $360,000.

## Common uses of credit

Let's take a look at a few broad reasons that people use credit and go into debt:

### 1. To meet important needs

Spencer is a young professional who recently purchased a condominium. He can't bring himself to tell anyone the

[64] 0.5% x $40,000 = 0.005 x $40,000 = $200.

enormous chunk of his take-home pay his housing costs now consume. Not surprisingly, he's tight on cash. In the middle of the summer the central air conditioner quits on him. After a few nights spent sweating more than sleeping, the air conditioner repair guy finally comes out, has a look and then delivers the bad news. It's not worth fixing. A new unit will cost $3,000. Spencer does not have the cash, so he's going to pull out his credit card and figure out how to pay the bill later.

*Meeting important needs* is not a legitimate reason to use credit because Spencer should have an emergency fund from which to pay these types of expenses. Spencer may have bit off more than he can chew with the condo purchase, and he's realizing that he'd better revisit his budget. Perhaps he can take on a roommate, finally push for that promotion he's rumored to be in line for, or otherwise get his financial situation on firmer ground.

## 2. To raise one's standard of living

Ronnie is tired of driving his bucket to and from work. It has left him stranded one too many times. The repairs are getting costlier, and he's had enough. One evening, he visits a local car dealership. Knowing that the issues associated with his aging heap of metal were terminal, Ronnie began saving to buy a car a while back. His savings are up to $10,000 and he's itching to spend it on a lightly used vehicle with low miles, good safety features and decent gas mileage.

As Ronnie opens the door, he realizes he's stepping into the *new* car showroom. Surrounded by all the sweet rides, he feels like a kid in a candy store. No matter what direction he looks, he sees gleaming metallic paint, leather, oversized rims and upgraded sound systems with giant subwoofers. Before long, a quiet and seemingly harmless saleswoman approaches. Next thing he knows, he's walking out the door with a brand-spanking new $40,000 vehicle, paid for with his $10,000 and a $30,000 loan for which he was approved in a matter of seconds. Oh well. Ronnie wouldn't be the first person to walk out the door spending much more than he'd planned. After all, what's the point of all Ronnie's hard work if he can't enjoy some of the fruits of his labor?

Ronnie's use of credit to improve his standard of living is not a good idea.

## 3. To improve one's productivity

Remember Isabella? She's the freelance video editor. A *freelancer* is a person who is her own boss. She gets paid for completing specific work for others. As long as she completes her projects by the agreed-upon dates, she's free to work whatever hours and in whatever manner she wishes. Isabella must work hard to garner awesome reviews and to promote herself because if she doesn't have a steady flow of new projects to complete, she will go without income.

The real catalyst for Isabella's decision to invest in her new editing platform is that standard definition video gave way to high definition, which in turn made way for 4K. Each new step up resulted in dramatically larger file sizes that require more storage capacity, more memory and more computing power to process. Her former system simply bogged down, taking forever to carry out even the most basic operations. She estimated that by purchasing new hardware and software, she could complete more jobs and generate an additional $1,000 in income per month. This far exceeds the $430.33 monthly loan payment. Furthermore, the payments will end in one year, but the system will continue to be effective for years to come.

This *cost-benefit analysis* supports Isabella's use of credit to *improve productivity*. We should realize that, even if Isabella has the system in a spare room in her home, she is making a business case for her use of credit. Getting a new and faster console in order to compete better against other gamers is not improving one's productivity.

## Credit scoring

As we began explaining, each time a person completes a transaction involving credit, it is sucked up, processed and spit out for a host of uses.

### Credit grantor

A *credit grantor* is any business to which you owe money. If the grantor is a bank, then it's likely that you borrowed money from it. A grantor can also be a company that allows you to take a good or consume a service before you pay for it.

Newly-minted adult, Angel, walks into his local cell phone store with a phone he purchased on line.[65] Soon, he walks out the door with his activated phone and data plan in hand. At the end of the month, he will be billed by the provider for the minutes and data he used. The moment the bill is generated, the cell service provider becomes a grantor of credit to Angel.

### Credit "bureau"

A *credit bureau* is a business that gathers the credit activity of consumers. Three players dominate: Equifax, TransUnion and Experian. These businesses have also been called agencies. These two words, *bureau* and *agency*, may create the impression that they are governmental, but they are just profit-seeking businesses like Disney and Home Depot are.

What do we mean by credit activity? Examples include loan applications, the opening of a new credit account and, of course, the payments people make to their credit grantors. By following each person's activity across years, each of these companies is able to build a comprehensive personal *credit profile* from which a *credit report* can be produced.

---

[65] The credit ecosystem tracks people who are legal adults. This means they are at least 18 years of age. Prior to this age they are not held responsible for living up to the terms of agreements they enter into.

## Credit score generator

Once a person's credit profile has been built, the credit bureau sends this information to a *credit score generator,* which translates it to a numeric *credit score* that ranges from 300 to 850. The higher the score, the greater the creditworthiness. This field is dominated by FICO[66] and VantageScore Solutions.

Once generated, credit scores are passed back to the credit bureaus, which make them available to credit grantors. Since businesses are wired to the max, an automobile salesperson can click a few buttons and learn your credit score in moments. The diagram below illustrates how information flows between them:

| | | |
|---|---|---|
| Rocket Mortgage<br>Ford Credit (car)<br>Chase (credit card)<br>ConEdison (electric)<br>Comcast (cable)<br>Verizon (cell service) | Equifax<br>Transunion<br>Experian | FICO (formerly Fair Isaac Company)<br>VantageScore Solutions (VantageScore) |

The relationship between the parties is intricate and could consume its own chapter to describe more fully. For example, not every credit grantor sends a creditor's payment history to every credit bureau. This in turn means that the history of credit activity each of the bureaus has on a person will vary. Different information being sent to the credit score generators

---

66 The company was formerly known as **F**air **I**saac **Co**mpany. We've bolded the letters in the name that make up the acronym FICO.

results in different scores being returned to the credit bureaus. Therefore, a person may have slightly different credit scores with each of the three credit bureaus.

How a person's credit history is actually translated into a credit score is shrouded in mystery. Let's say Kevin is $25,000 in debt and his friend Devin is $15,000 in debt. Based on this information, it would seem that Devin is less burdened and should have a higher credit score. What if we learned that Devin had one late payment in each of the last two years, while Kevin has always paid on time. Further, $20,000 of Kevin's debt is an automobile loan, while all of Devin's debt is from his use of credit cards. Now, who's worthy of the better credit score? The answer is not so simple.

## Determinants of one's credit score

Following is an explanation of how a person's FICO score is calculated. The numbers shown in parentheses represent the percent of the credit score the component comprises:[67]

### *1. History of making payments on time (35%)*

What's the most important concern of a business that is considering granting you credit? Whether or not you'll pay the money back! What's the best way to determine how likely you are to do so? By looking at your track record for paying your current debts, otherwise known as your *payment history*. Therefore, your history of paying your bills on time is the most important factor in computing your credit score.

### *2. Amount of available credit being used (30%)*

As we saw earlier, a term loan is used to purchase a big-ticket item. You make regular monthly payments for a finite period of time, gradually paying off your loan. The amount of

---

[67] Visit your.vantagescore.com/score-influences to learn how your VantageScore is computed.

outstanding credit on a term loan goes in one direction: down.

In the case of revolving credit like your credit card, you may owe anything from $0 up to your credit limit at any given point in time. Let's say you have two credit cards, each with a credit limit of $5,000. Your total available credit is $10,000. This past month you made $600 in purchases using one card and $400 in purchases using the other. You owe a total of $1,000. The credit scoring algorithm will take kindly to you since your *credit utilization* rate is just 10% ($1,000 divided by $10,000). It is supposed to show that you are demonstrating self-control.

The importance in credit scoring of low credit utilization can, however, lead to some strange outcomes. If you make $1,000 in purchases per month—nowhere near the credit limit of either card—you may conclude that life would be simpler if you kept one card and cancelled the other. But cancelling one card will *lower* your credit score. How can that be? After all, aren't you showing the ultimate in restraint by permanently eliminating one card? Yes, but doing so drops your available credit in half, from $10,000 to $5,000. As result, your credit utilization doubles to 20% ($1,000 divided by $5,000). This is concerning to the algorithm, which will ding you.

### *3. Length of credit history (15%)*

This one is relatively straight-forward. How long a track record a person has of paying his or her bills matters. The longer, the better. When a person becomes an adult, he or she will begin receiving credit card offers that tout the opportunity to begin "building your credit." A young adult who applies for and receives a card, begins making purchases with it and then pays the balance off in full each month will indeed create an impressive payment history.

But a young adult with a credit card, even one with a low initial credit limit, is a situation fraught with risk. If that person is a college student, it's likely that his or her entire family is under financial strain. What could possibly go wrong?

One solution to establishing a payment track record while minimizing risk is to obtain a *secured credit card*. Imagine you get a credit card offer in the mail with a modest $500 credit limit. But it comes with a twist. To obtain it, you have to send the bank a check for $500. The bank sets your money aside as you use your credit card. If worse comes to worst and you don't pay your credit card bill, the bank can pay itself back by taking the $500 you sent it. Your debt is actually secured by your own money.

### *4. New credit applications (10%)*

Tom has a near-death experience, the recovery from which entails three long, lonely weeks in the hospital. As Tom lays uneasily in his bed, a phrase increasingly comes to mind. It is the oft-repeated advice from his adventurous friend Jason: "Get busy living or get busy dying!" It took being laid low for Tom to truly appreciate what Jason has been trying to tell him all these years, but now he gets it. When he's finally well enough to check out, Tom first stops at an outdoor emporium. With the help of a new term loan, he buys an All-Terrain Vehicle (ATV). A month later, he purchases a top-of-the-line personal watercraft, taking on more credit to make it happen.

If a month after that, Tom is at the Dodge dealer ready to strap on a Challenger SRT Hellcat Redeye, with 707 lb-ft of tire-shredding torque, the credit scoring algorithm (if I may translate) is going to ask, "What in the hell is going on with Tom?" Not surprisingly, this component of his credit score will dive with each addition of credit Tom takes on in a short period of time.

### *5. Type of credit (10%)*

Jokester: Did you hear about Terrance? I just learned he's $100,000 in debt! I'm so concerned.

Friend: OMG, that's awful. How could we have let this happen? We should have been there for him. Did his business go under? Was it from gambling? Drug addiction?

Jokester: Nope. He bought a home.

Friend: That's not funny. You shouldn't joke like that.

Not all types of credit are the same. Homes are expensive. A debt of $100,000 used to purchase a home is not a cause for alarm. Being $100,000 in credit card debt, however, is. Therefore, a person's *credit mix* factors into his or her score.

## What's not in a credit score

Assume for a moment that credit-score generating companies don't have access to computers or coders to program them. Instead, they have you. You are being asked to assess the likelihood that a person will pay back a $25,000 loan that she wants to facilitate the purchase of a new vehicle. Besides the criteria we've identified above, is there anything—anything at all—that you would like to know about the person applying for the loan? Wouldn't it be a tiny bit helpful to know if the applicant earns $50,000 per year, $150,000 per year or perhaps even $250,000 per year? As helpful as a person's income might be, this information is not used in the calculation of a person's credit score! This makes sense, as we've all heard of people who have earned epic sums of money, yet managed even more epic lifestyles, leaving a swath of unpaid creditors in their wake.

Other information that does not play a part in a person's credit score includes his or her race, religion, national origin, sex, marital status, age, salary, occupation, title, employer, date of hire, employment history, area of residence, and family/child support obligations.[xxvii]

## Why credit scores matter

Both VantageScore and FICO scores range from 300 on the low end to 850 on the high end. FICO breaks down its scoring range as follows:[xxviii]

| Score range | Rating | % of scores in this range |
|---|---|---|
| 800 or above | Exceptional | 21% |
| 740 to 799 | Very good | 25% |
| 670 to 739 | Good | 21% |
| 580-to 669 | Fair | 17% |
| 579 or below | Poor | 16% |
| | Total | 100% |

Doing some quick math shows that 67% percent, or two-thirds of adults, have credit considered "good" or better.

Because borrowing rates don't seamlessly overlay with the credit score ranges set out above, they're provided in the table below. The rates and monthly payments are based on a $200,000, 30-year mortgage.[xxix]

| Score range | APR | Monthly payment |
|---|---|---|
| 760 to 850 | 3.369% | $ 884 |
| 700 to 759 | 3.591% | $ 908 |
| 680 to 699 | 3.768% | $ 928 |
| 660-to 679 | 3.982% | $ 953 |
| 640 to 659 | 4.412% | $ 1.003 |
| 620 to 639 | 4.958% | $ 1,069 |

As could be anticipated, the cost of borrowing is dictated by one's credit score. Maintaining a high score will result in actual cash savings for anyone who will one day purchase a home with the assistance of a mortgage.

## The credit reporting industry

In 2013, the legendary Sunday evening news show *60 Minutes* ran a segment produced by Steve Kroft that revealed the rampant errors on people's credit reports. Worse, the credit bureaus displayed little interest in correcting them. The exposé, titled "40 Million Mistakes," was an eye opener. The segment is less than 15 minutes long, so please make sure to watch it on YouTube.

Given that the bureaus have credit profiles on approximately 200 million adults, 40 million mistakes means that one in five reports contained an error. In the video, everyday American Judy Thomas is interviewed about the difficulty she had correcting a serious problem with her credit report. The delinquent credit purchases of a woman named Judith Kendall, which had been made in a state Thomas had never even visited, were nevertheless recorded on her credit report. No attempt by Thomas to get these mistakes corrected was successful, eventually leading her to sue in federal court to force the bureaus to correct their mistakes.[68]

Perhaps due to the kerfuffle over this segment and/or the rising scourge of identity theft, credit bureaus saw an opportunity. The business of *credit monitoring* was born. In return for your payment of about $20 to $25 per month, they will provide one or more of the following:

- Allow you to view your credit report and credit score any time.
- "Lock down" your credit report so that no potential credit

[68] The most shocking part of this exposé is that credit bureaus provide credit grantors exclusive versions of credit reports with information that is not on the reports provided to consumers. Indeed, erroneous information in her credit profile that was hidden from her was the reason Judy Thomas wandered around in the dark wondering why she kept getting turned down for credit.

grantor has access to it to determine whether to grant credit. You can unlock it in advance of the rare occasion on which you intend to take out new credit.

- o Provide recommendations for improving your score.
- o Assist you with fixing the damage caused by an identity thief.
- o Reimburse you for the cost of an identity theft.

Awareness of these services only accelerated in 2017 when, because it reportedly neglected to install software updates designed to patch holes in its system,[xxx] Equifax was subject to a hack that resulted in the theft of sensitive information on 143 million adults.

If you're starting to think about the fact that you're being offered important services by the same parties that have exacerbated the threats, you would not be alone. It is a real shame because credit scores have increasingly become a proxy for the worthiness of the person. A poor score generated from erroneous information (or activity by an identity thief) can mean being turned down for a loan, insurance, an apartment and even a job. After all, who wants to hire a person who doesn't have his or her act together?

Before enrolling in one of these plans, you should be aware of credit protection services that are available to you at no cost. Under the Fair Credit Reporting Act[xxxi], you are entitled to one free copy of your credit report per year from each of the three bureaus. The best practice is to request a copy from one of the three every four months. For example, on January 1, you can request your report from Experian. On May 1, you can request a copy from TransUnion. Then, on September 1, you can request a copy from Equifax. Come January, you do it all over again. This way you'll never go more than four months without an updated copy of your report. The one and only source authorized to provide these truly free, no-strings-attached reports is AnnualCreditReport.com.

You are also entitled to contact each of the credit bureaus and have them place a *credit freeze* on your account. This is what we referred to above as "lock down." In other words, several important services offered in a credit monitoring program are already available for free. As always, do a full investigation before making the decision to enroll in a credit monitoring service.

## Pulling the plug

Is it possible for a person's debts to grow so large as to become unpayable? People who believe this describes their situation may petition a court for relief from those debts by filing for *personal bankruptcy*. There are actually two ways to do so.

### *Reorganization bankruptcy*

The first type of bankruptcy, *reorganization,* is for people whose financial situations are bad, but not lost causes.[69] With successful careers and income to match, they have homes and vehicles they'd like to keep. They want to make good on as much debt as their financial picture allows. They are, however, in a situation wherein their payment obligations exceed their incomes. Filers submit a three-to-five-year plan with the court, outlining how they will repay their creditors to the extent their income makes possible. Unsecured debts, such credit card balances, have the lowest repayment priority. If the plan is accepted by the court, when the *petitioner* has completed the submitted plan, any unsecured debts left unpaid may be *discharged,* making them no longer owed.[xxxii]

### *Liquidation bankruptcy*

The second type of bankruptcy, *liquidation,* is for people

---

[69] Reorganization is discussed in Chapter 13 of the US Bankruptcy Code and is often referred to as a Chapter 13 bankruptcy.

whose limited incomes means that debt repayment is just not going to happen.[xxxiii] *Liquidation* refers to selling assets for cash. In this instance, the filer agrees to have his or her property sold, with the *proceeds* of such sales used to pay creditors. Any remaining debt is often discharged, giving the person a "fresh start."[70] Each state provides a list of property that is exempt; this is property that can't be seized and sold for the benefit of creditors. One such exemption allows a homeowner to retain a certain amount of the equity in his or her home. This is known as the *homestead exemption*. The point of exemptions is to guard against filers being deprived of so many of their assets that they have little chance of getting back on their feet.

There is, however, a long and growing list of debts that are not dischargeable. With few exceptions, they include student loans, back taxes, government and court fines and penalties, spousal and child support, divorce settlements, attorney's fees related to divorce, debts arising from personal injury caused while driving intoxicated, and more.[xxxiv] So much for a fresh start.

### Bankruptcy and credit scoring

A person who declares bankruptcy has left creditors, to varying degrees, high and dry. Not surprisingly, this causes his or her credit score to plummet. In addition, when a person declares bankruptcy, it becomes a prominent part of his or her credit report. This warns potential creditors that the person has already pulled the plug on his or her debts at least once. Chapter 7 bankruptcies stay on credit reports for ten years, while Chapter 13 bankruptcies remain on credit reports for seven years.[xxxv] They cast a long shadow that takes years to get out from under.

---

[70] Liquidation is discussed in Chapter 7 of the US Bankruptcy Code and is often referred to as a Chapter 7 bankruptcy.

### *What kind of person goes bankrupt?*

In 2005, Congress passed the Bankruptcy Abuse Protection and Consumer Protection Act.[xxxvi] This was in response to the credit card industry's belief that people were using the bankruptcy laws to avoid paying debts they were perfectly capable of paying. Among the new requirements was a *means test* to ensure that a potential filer truly lacked the means to repay his or her debts in full. This furthered the perception that many bankruptcy filers were not to be trusted, that they were taking advantage of a system designed for those truly in need.

When a person with $10,000 or $20,000 in credit card debt calls in to Dave Ramsey's radio show fishing for his approval to declare bankruptcy, many are surprised to receive not sympathy, but a tongue-lashing. Earlier, we showed a sample credit card disclosure that, in big letters and numbers, spelled out the consequences of using credit cards and then not paying the balances off. Callers to Dave's show have voluntarily made these purchases. They've enjoyed the goods and services that $10,000 or $20,000 buys. Now, they want Dave's affirmation that it's okay to stick the bank with the debt? Not happening. It comes down to basic integrity. If people don't live up to the terms of their credit card agreements, then their word, their promise, means nothing.

Before you cement your impression of people who declare bankruptcy, however, it would behoove you to know that the primary reason that people do so is none of the debts we've discussed so far. It isn't mortgage debt, which goes away when the borrower gives up the home on which he has been unable to make the requisite payments. It is not student loan debt which, as we learned earlier, has blown past $1.5 trillion nationwide. It is not credit card debt, which is flirting with $1 trillion. It is medical debt.

John Doe is checked into a hospital due to an illness or serious accident. Underinsured, or perhaps uninsured, John's wife Jane signs all the papers put in front of her authorizing the hospital to provide the care John desperately needs. His stay lasts a few weeks, during which a couple of surgeries and the initiation of physical therapy put him on the road to recovery. Returning home, John is greeted by a never-ending stream of bills for services rendered that total over $100,000. If the sheer dollar amount of the debt isn't challenging enough, it could be months before John can go back to work. It's not a pretty picture. Sadly, it's not uncommon.

A recent study showed that 66.5% of bankruptcies were tied to medical debt, with the overall annual number of filings exceeding half a million.[xxxvii] In a heartbeat, we can be diagnosed with a major illness or involved in an accident that threatens to place us in this unfortunate group. If you are not among them, that's one more reason to be grateful.

To be sure, irresponsible use of credit is one of the top five reasons that people declare bankruptcy. So, too, are job loss and divorce, both of which can happen to anyone.[xxxviii]

How do we wrap up our longest chapter yet on a subject as important as credit? With this advice: Be careful. None of the millions of adults drowning in debt planned to be there. All it takes is one point in your life when you're a little tight on funds. It's at that moment that the latest low-rate credit card starts looking mighty attractive. It could also be a purchase, like a Jeep Wrangler you've convinced yourself you deserve after so many years of seemingly pointless toil, knowing full well that affording it will be a stretch. The risk, of course, is that once you go down the debt road you won't be able to reverse course. Be careful. Don't be a statistic.

Now might be a good time to look at where we've been and where we are going. We opened with a discussion on how it would benefit us to view wealth broadly. Next, we discussed how all the knowledge in the world isn't beneficial in the absence of the commitment and motivation to set and pursue financial goals. Then, we introduced and explained inflation, budgeting, banking and credit. The next chapters cover taxes and insurance. That will prepare us to discuss a topic that itself has launched countless books: investing. We'll wrap up with a chapter that reflects on the topic of financial literacy.

*Who is or was?* Ricky Jackson.

## Exercises on credit

1. Explain why credit is so dangerous.
2. Identify the reasons why people use credit.
3. Identify the essential elements of a term loan.
4. Explain how leasing a vehicle differs from purchasing it with the aid of a term loan.
5. Identify the different ways that a credit-card issuing bank earns money when consumers use their cards.
6. Explain why the interest rate on revolving credit accounts such as credit cards is so much higher than the rate on term loans used to purchase homes and vehicles.
7. Compare and contrast credit cards and debit cards.
8. Explain the roles of credit grantors, credit bureaus and credit score generators, as well as how they work together to produce and deliver credit scores.
9. Identify the factors that are and are not part of a credit score calculation.
10. Identify the ways that a high credit score benefits a person.
11. Identify how the credit bureaus have contributed to the anxiety surrounding credit reporting.
12. Research and report on the current total dollar amount of mortgage debt, student loan debt and credit card debt held by Americans.

13. Investigate and report on the details of Chapter 7 and Chapter 13 bankruptcies. Specifically, which debts are and are not dischargeable?
14. Explain why it is not wise to form blanket judgements about people who declare personal bankruptcy.
15. A new type of debt arrangement has arrived on the scene. Research *personal loans.* What makes them different from the term loans we've discussed?

# Chapter 7 The tax man cometh

What is it about taxes that strikes fear in the hearts of even the most formidable among us? It might be their compulsory nature, meaning that we have no choice in the matter. Perhaps it is because of their mind-numbing complexity. The U.S. Constitution provides for a federal government that is granted certain powers. Those not granted to it are reserved for the states.[71] We live in the United States. We also live in a state and a county within the state.[72] We may also live in a formally organized city, town or village. We are simultaneously responsible for complying with the laws of all levels of government within which we live, and that most definitely includes paying the taxes they levy.

Our trepidation about taxes might also be the awareness that penalties for non-compliance can be onerous. Perhaps it's that so much of our income is lost to taxes that we feel as though we're working as much for the government as we are for ourselves. Probably, it's all the above.

Indeed, the instances in which we may be responsible for paying a tax include making a purchase, receiving income, owning property, using a government service, visiting a government-run facility, and dying. Even in death, there is no escape.

## 1. User fees

A town charges $20 for each vehicle that parks in one of the

---

[71] The 10th Amendment reads: *The powers not delegated to the United States by the Constitution, nor prohibited by it to the States, are reserved to the States respectively, or to the people.*

[72] It's a county unless you're in Louisiana, in which case it's a parish. We also recognize that this description does not apply to residents of Washington, D.C., Puerto Rico and U.S. territories.

lots near the beach. Towns everywhere are getting wise to the opportunity to charge drivers to park on their streets. Drivers pay, often dearly, to drive through a tunnel or over a bridge. In each of these instances, authorities levy a *fee* for *use* of a resource or facility.

### *What do user fees have to do with taxes?*

Since taxes are payments collected by governments to fund programs that provide broad benefits, they seem to have little in common with a fee to use this bridge or that parking lot.

Further, taxes are mandatory. There's no avoiding them. The user fees described above, all vehicle related, can be wholly avoided by not owning a vehicle.

Thus, it appears that the fees cited are not taxes. There is, however, more to the story. For example, with regard to our bridges and tunnels, there is a persistent suspicion that the tolls charged exceed the cost of maintaining them.

In 2018, the Port Authority of New York and New Jersey announced a major $364 million, five-year project to repair the damage done to the Holland Tunnel by Hurricane Sandy.[xxxix] In general, the high initial cost of any improvement project is justified by future savings. Once this ambitious restoration is completed, the Holland Tunnel will presumably be able to function for many years at a lower maintenance cost. The future savings even justifies the Port Authority's paying an amount that exceeds the tolls collected. The questions are: how much in negative cash flow will it have to fund, and how long will it take for the reduced maintenance costs to make up for the investment in repairs?

On the expense side of the equation, assuming that work will be done seven days per week for five straight years, the daily cost of the five-year $364 million project is $199,452.[73]

How much in tolls does the Holland Tunnel generate?

---

[73] $364 million / (5 years x 365 days per year) = $199,452.

Approximately 1.2 million vehicles pass through the tunnel each month.[xl] Assuming a conservative average toll of $13,[xli] we can calculate total monthly toll collections to be $15.6 million. Using a 30-day month, that's $520,000 collected each day. So, even while the repairs are taking place, the tolls being collected are more than two-and-a-half times the cost of the project! Imagine how extreme the imbalance when the project is finished. This analysis shows that the tolls being charged are in excess—well in excess—of the cost of maintaining the tunnel. The amount of the excess is a tax.

The Verrazzano Narrows Bridge connects Brooklyn with Staten Island. Opening in 1964 with an initial toll of $0.50, it remains America's longest suspension bridge.[xlii] Assuming the toll was set to provide for the gradual recoup of the construction cost and anticipated maintenance costs, it would be reasonable for it to increase by the historical annual inflation rate of 3%. If the $0.50 original toll increased by 3% each of the 56 years since construction, today's toll should be $2.62.[74] What is the actual toll? In 2019, the Metropolitan Transit Authority (MTA) raised the cash price (charged in one direction, with the other direction being free) from $17 to $19. It is now the highest toll in the country.[xliii] Could it be that drivers who plunk down their hard-earned $19 are actually paying a toll of $2.62 and a tax for the difference of $16.38? Yes, it could.

States charge a vehicle registration fee. It's important that they keep track of which license plates they have issued to which vehicles and to whom those vehicles belong. There is a substantial cost to making all this possible, which may explain why states like New York charge a two-year registration fee that exceeds $100.

Digging into New York's registration fee, we find that it is

---

[74] In a financial calculator: N=56, PV=-0.50, PMT=0, I/YR=3. Press FV.

in part made up of a $30 charge that the state itself identifies as a vehicle use tax. An even bigger component of the registration cost is a $50 MCTD (Metropolitan Commuter Transportation District) fee.[xliv] The MCTD appears to be a group of 12 counties that have something in common—train service in and out of Manhattan. Imagine, a major part of the vehicle registration fee is a tax that supports not vehicles, but trains.

Let's look at one more example. A 2010 article in the *Philadelphia Inquirer* expresses authorities' lament that an upcoming Pennsylvania Turnpike toll increase will bring it to 8.5 cents per mile and give it the mantel of "most expensive long toll road in the country."[xlv] The article attributes the ignominious toll escalation to "a 2007 state law requiring it to help fund non-turnpike transportation programs." In January 2020, yours truly had the pleasure of jumping onto the turnpike at the Pennsylvania-New Jersey border, taking it west approximately 130 miles to the state capital in Harrisburg. Upon my exit, the booth attendant collected an even $20. That's 2,000 cents. Divide 130 into 2,000, and you get a current toll per mile of 15.38 cents.

From a political standpoint, if a government seeking to collect more money can do so by regularly bumping up fees, not just on the aforementioned bridges, tunnels, and roads, but on the use of community pools and state parks and for permits and licenses, then its leaders can proudly inform residents that once again they were able to hold the line this year and not raise taxes. If it's a fee, then it's not a tax, right?

Thankfully, the same parties that charge user fees frequently offer ways to save. New York and a growing number of nearby states have the E-Z Pass electronic tolling system. In return for being willing to have their on-file credit cards charged tolls when they are incurred, E-Z Pass holders receive discounts.

Another way governments offer savings is through volume

purchases. Beach bums can buy a season parking pass. Train commuters can purchase a monthly pass. Discounts like these are well worth researching.

## 2. Sales tax

Sales taxes are charged on the final sale of most goods and an increasing number of services. We say *final* because goods can change hands several times on their journey from production to end consumer. As we'll illustrate below, they are expressed as percentages and are added to the dollar amount paid by the consumer when he or she makes a purchase. Sales taxes are levied by states, with their counties and cities often joining in. There is no national sales tax. A sampling of sales taxes around the U.S. is provided below:[xlvi]

| | A | | B | | C | A+B+C |
|---|---|---|---|---|---|---|
| **State** | **%** | **County** | **%** | **City** | **%** | **Total** |
| Alaska[75] | 0% | Aleutians W. | 0% | Dutch Harbor | 0% | 0% |
| | 0% | Kenai Peninsula. | 3% | Homer | 4.5% | 7.5% |
| New York | 4% | Washington | 3% | Whitehall | 0% | 7% |
| | 4% | Niagara | 4% | Niagara Falls | 0% | 8% |
| Texas | 6.25% | Harris | 0% | Houston | 2% | 8.25% |
| | 6.25% | Midland | .5% | Midland | 1.25% | 8.25% |
| California | 7.25% | Ventura | 0% | Oxnard Shores | 0% | 7.25% |
| | 7.25% | Alameda | 2% | Oakland | 0% | 9.25% |
| Kansas | 6.5% | Sedgwick | 1% | Wichita | 0% | 7.5% |
| | 6.5% | Dickinson | 1.5% | Herington | 2.5% | 10.5% |
| Florida | 6% | Orange | 0.5% | Orlando | 0% | 6.5% |
| | 6% | Hillsborough | 2.5% | Tampa | 0% | 8.5% |

---

[75] Alaska is joined by Delaware, Montana, New Hampshire, and Oregon as the only states that have no state sales tax. Unlike Alaska, these four states also have no sales tax at the county or city levels.

After disembarking from the Maid of the Mist, you are standing at the counter of the Niagara Falls gift shop intending to buy some swag that will help you remember your amazing visit. The register shows that you are buying $100 of goods. The tax is calculated as a percentage and added to the amount you must pay. From the above table we see that the tax rate in Niagara Falls is 8%. The tax is 0.08 times $100, which is $8. To walk out with your stuff, you must pony up a total of $108.

### *Goods versus services*

Time was when only goods were taxed. However, with the growth of the service economy governments were missing out. So, they began to tax services. Currently, we find ourselves in the awkward situation wherein some services are taxed, but others aren't. For example, in New York the services of an attorney, accountant, doctor or social worker are not subject to sales tax. The services of a private detective and interior designer are subject to sales tax. Next, we learn that beautician services such as haircuts, manicures and pedicures are taxable only in the five boroughs (i.e., counties) that make up New York City. These services are not taxable in the remaining 57 counties and by New York State itself.[xlvii] To help navigate through this mess, states have online resources that list the goods and services for which they expect a sales tax to be charged and collected.

### *Sales versus use*

So, let's say you buy a good or pay for a service and are not charged a sales tax. That's the end of it, yes? No. If you begin exploring this topic you may notice that this tax is formally known as a "sales and use" tax. If one day you decide to look up the required tax treatment of the item you just bought and realize that the store should have charged you sales tax, it is your legal duty to pay the tax for your *use* of it. I kid you not.

### *Games people play*

It is important to note that the sales tax is a straight-up percentage that is applied to every last dollar of an applicable purchase. If you buy a $1,000 TV in Homer, Alaska where the total sales tax rate is 7.5%, you are going to pay $75 in sales tax. If you purchase an ATV for $10,000, your tax is $750. If you purchase a $100,000 heavy-duty truck, the sales tax is $7,500. There are no volume discounts and no sliding scales when it comes to sales tax.

Dutch Harbor is a tiny Alaskan outpost known for being the home port of the fishing vessels featured on the show *Deadliest Catch,* whose crews bear brutal conditions and risk serious injury to bring us King (and Opilio) Crab. You may recall from our table above that there is no sales tax in Dutch Harbor. Wait a minute. If there happens to be a truck dealer in Dutch Harbor, why wouldn't you just go there to purchase your pickup and drive or ferry it back to Homer? There is, after all, $7,500 in sales tax to be saved! And with that thought we introduce the intriguing world of *sales tax gaming*.

If you remember from our last chapter, I purchased my daughter a computer in advance of her first year of college. The accessories and warranty sent the total price past $2,000. The sales tax collected was in excess of $175. Let's say that the week before the purchase I was returning from a road trip and planned a stop in Delaware to catch up with an old friend. Let's also say that the route to my friend's house just happened to send me past a Best Buy. There is no sales tax in Delaware, so any purchases I made at that store would be sales tax free. Could I, would I, should I have taken the opportunity to buy the computer there? If I did my conscience would eat at me for the rest of the drive home. Why? I am well aware that states such as New York have ruled that when a resident brings a taxable good on which no sales tax has been paid into the state, it is the resident's obligation to pay a use tax. Now you know, too. Sorry about that.[76]

Another yawning area to which this idea applies is Internet sales. You may purchase a good online from a person or small business on the other side of the country. The first issue is where the transaction is actually taking place. States are beginning to require that sales tax be collected when one of their residents purchases goods from an out-of-state seller. Think about that for a moment. The state where the *buyer* is based wants sales tax! Not surprisingly, many small sellers lack the resources to properly calculate, collect and pay sales taxes to the thousands of city, county and/or state tax jurisdictions where their customers live. To avoid making a mistake in determining the correct tax—or worse, collecting sales taxes, but then not forwarding them to the proper government(s)—many small sellers choose not to charge sales tax. The seller may not charge it, but as we just learned, woe be to the person who believes that because no *sales* tax was charged, no *use* tax is owed.

One last area that may or may not keep you up at night is the private sale of property, such as an automobile. Each time a vehicle is sold to an end consumer, it is supposed to generate a sales tax. If a person buys a used car from a private seller and no tax was collected by the seller, the buyer is obligated to cough up the use tax come tax time.

### Exemptions

One of the themes we will be touching on in this chapter is whether the tax we're discussing has been implemented with

---

[76] Reviews of a Delaware Best Buy revealed one customer boasting that he had traveled from New Jersey just to save the sales tax on an expensive gaming computer. Another ordered earbuds on line with delivery to the store. This allowed her to drive there from a neighboring state to pick them up. Apparently, not everyone is torn up over the obligation to pay use taxes.

any consideration for the people paying it. With regard to user fees, this is generally not the case. For example, if you approach a toll plaza in a luxury SUV just in time to witness a beater car stalling out at a booth up ahead, you may realize that for better or worse you and the driver of the junker will pay the same toll.

But with sales tax, states have the ability to give their citizens a break. Thirty-two states and the District of Columbia exempt the purchase of food destined for home consumption from sales tax. Only three states tax groceries fully. The others charge a lower tax rate or have a rebate system designed to return the taxes paid on groceries.[xlviii] Another necessity, clothing, is supported to a significantly lesser degree, with only seven states exempting clothing from sales tax either in whole or in part.[xlix]

### *Excise taxes*

If the government can cut us a break, it can also smack us down. An *excise* (pronounced x-size) *tax* is an extra fee that governments add to the purchase of a good or service. An excise tax can be levied on the final sale of a good, making it like an additional sales tax. It may also be levied during an earlier stage of production and distribution, which hides it from consumers.

**Funding specific programs** In response to September 11, 2001, a $2.50 passenger fee was added to the purchase price of each airline ticket to fund enhanced air-travel security measures.[l] This is an example of an excise tax that is a *flat fee.* It is "flat" because it is the same, regardless of the price of the ticket.

You may have heard that California has high taxes that are driving residents out of the state. With that in mind, the information in the sales tax table shown earlier is puzzling. The rates for two California cities were not especially high compared to cities in other states. What gives? We've only looked at one of several ways a state can tax its citizens. Here, we're looking at another.

Governments place substantial excise taxes on gasoline to fund the maintenance of our highway system. The excise tax the federal government collects per gallon of gasoline sold is 18.4 cents.[li] The state of California collects an additional 30 cents per gallon,[lii] although the total of all state taxes and fees there is estimated to be 61.2 cents per gallon.[liii] Assuming a per-gallon consumer price of $4.18[liv] that includes all taxes and fees, the effective sales tax rate is 23.5%.[77]

Restless California residents may find it frustrating that total taxes and fees on gasoline in the adjoining state of Arizona amount to 19.0 cents. Compared to California's 61.2 cents, that's 42.2 cents less per gallon.

Interestingly, as electric vehicles continue to gain ground, this tax model will become increasingly untenable. Electric vehicles contribute to the wear and tear on our highways, yet since they don't use gasoline, their owners avoid this excise tax altogether.

**Acting as a disincentive** You may now realize that governments, through their tax policies, can incent people to act in certain ways. For example, a county that has a lower sales tax than surrounding counties incents nearby residents to travel there to shop.

Here, we address ways in which governments discourage certain behavior. There is a federal excise tax on cigarettes in the amount of $1.01 per pack. Missouri adds just $0.17 as its state excise tax.[lv] New York and Connecticut tie for the highest excise tax by adding $4.35. New York City adds $1.50, making the tax on a pack of cigarettes sold in New York City $5.85.[lvi] At an average price per pack of $10.45[lvii] the taxes make up more than half the price. Stated another way, the sales taxes

---

[77] (18.4¢ + 61.2¢)/($4.18 – (18.4¢ + 61.2¢)) = 79.6¢/$3.384 = 0.235 = 23.5%.

on cigarettes sold in New York City are in excess of 100%.[78] By making cigarettes twice as expensive as they would be without taxes, fewer people in New York City can afford them and the rate of smoking will presumably decline.

Alcohol is another product that finds itself in the crosshairs of tax authorities. Because neither cigarettes nor alcohol are good for one's health, excise taxes on these types of products are often referred to as *sin taxes*.

**Collecting taxes the easier way** The never-ending quest of governments is to collect more tax revenue. Why? The cost of the promises they've made continue to rise each year. These costs can be everything from raises they are contractually obligated to pay their employees to benefit programs that will be expanded to cover more residents.

A magic trick would be for state and local governments to increase the taxes they collect without impacting their residents. Each year I ask my students to name a good or service that they as residents don't purchase, but which visitors to our area do. Visitors may forget to pack shampoo and need to buy it locally. But residents buy shampoo as well, so the answer can't be toiletries such as shampoo.

Residents, by their very nature, reside—have housing—in the area. Not so, tourists. They need a place to stay. What if extra sales taxes were levied on hotel stays? Governments would get extra revenue while people other than their residents would pay.

One of the most popular American tourist destinations is Florida. Like most states it levies excise taxes on *transient rentals*, short-term stays in everything from hotels to motels to campers.[lviii] If you want to visit Mickey at Walt Disney World in Orlando you will pay a hotel/occupancy/transient/room/

---

[78] While we can all agree that cigarettes are dangerous, we could debate whether it is right for governments to profit so immensely from those unable to quit.

lodging/tourist (sorry, it goes by a lot of names) tax of 6%, on top of the 6.5% sales tax.[lix] But if you want to visit Mickey at DisneyLand in Anaheim, California, in lieu of paying the ordinary sales tax of 7.75% you will pay a 15% Transient Occupancy Tax[lx] plus a 2% Anaheim Tourism Improvement District fee,[lxi] for a total of 17%. That's outrageous! Yes, outrageous, until we learn that a visit to El Paso, Texas will have you paying a Hotel Occupancy Tax of 17.5%![lxii]

Residents can use their vehicles to get around, but visitors arriving by air cannot. This provides an opportunity to levy extra taxes when these visitors rent a vehicle. To properly size up the taxes and fees related to renting a vehicle at Las Vegas' McCarran Airport, we're going to have to resort (no pun intended) to a table. Upon working my way through a vehicle rental on line, the following taxes and fees were added to the one-day rental of a $50.06 vehicle:

| | |
|---|---|
| AIRPORT ACCESS FEE | $ 5.22 |
| CUSTOMER FACILITY CHARGE | $ 4.00 |
| RENTAL TAX | $ 6.63 |
| STATE TAX | $ 4.56 |
| VEHICLE LICENSE FEE | $ 2.16 |
| **TOTAL TAXES AND FEES** | **$ 22.57** |

Dividing $22.57 by $50.06 results in a tax rate of 45.1%. Regarding these taxes, city officials prefer that visitors adopt the familiar refrain, "What happens in Vegas stays in Vegas."

Some tips on navigating excise taxes:

- When budgeting for a trip, make sure to get the all-in price, including the taxes and fees that we've seen can add a lot to the cost.
- Call and ask the hotel if there are any fees they will attempt to levy when you check in. Many have taken to charging a "resort fee" of $20 or $30 per day to allow them to pay for the cost of maintaining the pool, gym and

other amenities. The hotel may want to charge you this fee even if you have no interest in using these facilities. Another surprise charge is a fee to park one's vehicle. This is often the case if you're staying at a hotel in the heart of a big city. Imagine paying $30 to $50 per day, which adds up to $210 to $350 per week just to park your vehicle. Some hotels also charge a fee for internet access.

- o While you've got the hotel on the line, ask if it offers a free shuttle service. You might be surprised to learn that you can get to and from malls, mass transit and the airport at no additional cost.
- o Wait, don't hang up. Ask the hotel if it provides a complimentary breakfast. If so, what does it include?[79]
- o As young people are apt to do, check out new, less expensive alternatives such as Airbnb and VRBO for lodging. Estimate the cost of getting around using ride-sharing services like Uber and Lyft, which may wind up being both cheaper and more convenient.

## 3. Property tax

The idea of private property is an anathema to some cultures and economic systems. For instance, how can communist leaders command an economy when they don't own and control its resources? In the U.S., we residents are free to acquire *real property,* which is land and the things attached to it. We can and often do acquire *personal property,* which is tangible (i.e., touchable) and moveable. Consider a person who is selling her home. Generally speaking, what she packs into the moving van is personal property. What she leaves behind, because it is permanently installed in or on the house or grounds, is real property.

---

[79] It is my belief that if it doesn't include eggs it's not really breakfast.

*Property tax,*[80] as the name implies, is a tax levied on the owner of such property. This tax, which must be paid each year, is a percentage of the value of the property. Just as there is no national sales tax, there is no national property tax. Unlike sales taxes that may be assessed by both state and local governments, property taxes are generally a county and city affair.

It's important to note that any property tax rate must remain modest, else it will begin to look like a sales tax that in some dystopian world is levied each and every year. So, if a government is limited to a 1%, 2% or even 3% annual tax on the value of a person's property, then the resulting tax must be worth the effort to collect it. For example, if the government were to pass a 2% property tax on the value of smart phones and your smart phone is worth $700, the tax to be collected would be only $14 (2% of $700). Does it make sense for a government to have you and your phone in its database so it can fire off a bill to you each year telling you to cough up $14? And remember, as your phone gets older its value drops. If a year later it is worth $500, then the bill in the second year will be only $10 (2% of $500).

Moreover, taxing property of modest value may create the public perception that there are simply no limits to what governments will monitor in their insatiable quest to collect more taxes. Thus, governments must target property with high value.

## Vehicle property tax

The vehicles in our driveways and garages have an average purchase price north of $37,000.[lxiii] Twenty-seven states levy an annual property tax on vehicles, with the average tax being $440.[lxiv] Averages however, can be misleading. The three

---

[80] It is also known as an *ad valorem tax*, with "ad valorem" being Latin for "to the value."

states with the highest annual vehicle property tax rates are Mississippi (3.55%), Virginia (4.05%) and Rhode Island (4.40%). Apply these percentages to the average new vehicle price, and you'll see that vehicle owners in these states can be on the hook for annual tax bills topping $1,000.

As previously noted, the value of a vehicle typically declines during the time a person owns (or uses) it. This makes vehicles, unless they're collectibles, depreciating assets. Thankfully, because of the vibrant market for used vehicles, there are numerous services governments can use to estimate market value based on a vehicle's year, make, model, mileage and options.

## Real estate property tax

What's the most valuable property we are likely to acquire? A piece of real estate, together with the building(s) on it. Not surprisingly, all 50 states levy a property tax on real estate. In contrast to motor vehicles, no two homes are alike. Even cookie-cutter homes, those that look identical all the way down the street, are modified over time by their owners. As well, if a home hasn't been on the market for a decade or more any attempt to determine its market value is just an estimate. Despite these difficulties, local governments must assign a market value to a piece of real estate each year if they are to tax it.

In 1997, Nassau County, New York was sued by claimants who argued that its method of assigning values to residential real estate was unfair. In 2000, the county agreed to pay real estate appraisal firm Cole Layer Trumble Co. of Dayton, Ohio the tidy sum of $34 million to appraise every piece of residential property in the county.[lxv]

In the late 1990s, I returned to Long Island after a decade living in Atlanta. While studying to become an educator I was building my aforementioned dream home with the help of my retired general contractor dad. We were visited one sunny day by a person bearing all manner of company identification who explained that her job was to size up the home. The intrepid representative latched her tape measure onto a corner of the foundation and proceeded to walk its length. Soon, she had her measurements and was on her way. I had knocked down a decrepit house to build a new one, not fully appreciating the dimensions my ambitious architect had specified until the house began rising and rising out of the ground. More on this in a moment.

Real estate taxes, along with real estate values, vary significantly across our 50 states. Hawaii, which has the highest median home value at $563,900, also has the lowest effective rate, at 0.27%[lxvi] A Hawaiian owning a home at the median value will pay $1,523 (0.27% of $563,900) each year in real estate property tax.

At the other end of the spectrum is New Jersey, with an effective property tax rate of 2.44% and median home value of $321,100. The state ranks fourth, behind Hawaii, California and Massachusetts, in median home values. A New Jersian with a median-priced home is looking at $7,835 (2.44% of $321,100) each year in real estate property tax. Northern New Jersey homes within commuting distance of New York City can very easily have twice the median value. Consequently, the owners of these homes can have annual property tax bills in excess of $15,000.

Back to my home building project. The house was being built on a piece of property 125 feet deep by 100 feet across. It abuts a canal that leads to the Great South Bay, which leads to the Atlantic Ocean. I completed the house and moved in around 2003. In 2010, with the annual property tax surpassing $28,000, I pulled the plug and sold the house. Today, the taxes are in excess of $34,000.[81]

---

[81] No reference is provided in order to protect the current owner's privacy. An outgrowth of Cole Layer Trumble's work is the site

### *The opposite of simplicity*

Real estate property taxes appear unnecessarily complicated. Unlike our simplified example above, real estate taxes are calculated as a percentage of the *assessed value,* not the market value, of the property. This assessed value is determined by a local official such as the county tax assessor.

The assessed value is usually less than the market value. While this appears to be a good thing, if every property's assessed value is, say, 75% of its market value, property owners remain in the same position relative to one another and no one benefits. Let's say that residents of a county all have homes worth $400,000 and that the assessed values are 75% of the market values. Three quarters of $400,000 is $300,000. Let's also say that the property tax is 2% of the assessed value. Each homeowner's property tax is $6,000 (2% of $300,000) per year. But, if the local government needs to collect $6,000 per year from every homeowner it could simply apply a 1.5% rate to the market value of $400,000 and be done with it.[82]

Allowing that I could be missing something, I went on line and read the "Nassau County Glossary of Assessment Terms", which states that assessed value is "a figure in dollars determined by an assessor which reflects a property's worth in relation to other properties on an assessment roll and which, unless exempt, is used to compute a tax dollar obligation by multiplying it by a tax rate."[lxvii] I'm still missing it. Doesn't market value *reflect a property's worth in relation to other properties*?

Even the above analysis is simplified. The 2% rate we applied to the assessed value is actually called a *millage rate*

---

mynassauproperty.com, where anyone can view the values and taxes associated with any Nassau County, NY residential property.

[82] 1.5% of $400,000 is the same $6,000.

and is expressed as a dollar amount of tax per thousand dollars of assessed value. What? Let's say that a county has a millage rate of 20. Twenty what? Twenty dollars. Twenty dollars of what? Twenty dollars of tax for each $1,000 of assessed value. Dividing $20 by $1,000, we get a tax rate of 2%. A millage of 20 is 2%. Why didn't they just say so in the first place?[83]

### *Value versus equity*

Property tax is charged on the value of the property with no consideration given to the extent of real ownership, or equity, the owner has in the property. Let's say Shai buys a $400,000 home with $100,000 of his own cash and a $300,000 mortgage. He owns only $100,000/$400,000, or 25% of the home. Di buys a $200,000 home with $200,000 of her own cash. She owns 100% of the home. Shai will pay a tax that is calculated on his home's $400,000 value while Di will pay tax on her home's $200,000 value. The message here is "*caveat emptor*," which translates to "Let the buyer beware." Shai should know—must know—beforehand all about the property taxes that come with the purchase of a home. Here, he must be prepared to pay double the property taxes that Di will pay.

### *Owning versus renting*

You may be wondering if it's possible to avoid property taxes by renting, not owning, property. To wit, you can rent an apartment in a building instead of owning a condominium in a similar building. You can arrange a long-term rental of a vehicle by leasing it. Kudos for thinking creatively.

Property taxes are one of the costs shouldered by property owners. Any rational property owner will set the monthly rent

---

[83] The prior analysis based on percentages of market value was done by WalletHub, without whose help we would have been chest deep in assessed values and millage rates.

at a level that exceeds the monthly cost of owning the property. Therefore, property taxes can't be escaped; they are baked into the rent.

When a vehicle is leased, a leasing company or bank acquires the vehicle from a dealer and leases it to the *lessee.* The bank or leasing company is the vehicle owner. If this is all taking place in one of the 27 states that have a vehicle property tax, then the vehicle owner will be charged a tax, which will be passed on to the vehicle's lessee. So, again, the renting angle proves fruitless.

### *Owning is renting*

Over the term of a conventional 30-year mortgage homebuyers will make 360 monthly payments. A select few couples run the gauntlet by staying in their homes long enough to pay their mortgage off in full. It's a major milestone in their lives, a proud moment when they can declare that they own their homes "free and clear" of any claims. What a reward it is for the family to witness the mortgage line item drop off the family budget after 30 years! Yet, if you've truly been considering what we've just discussed—that property taxes are an annual event—you may have already realized this stark reality: *you never do own your home.* Your property taxes never end, they usually increase, and the consequence of non-payment is eviction.

*Who is or was?* Nadia Murad?

At this point we've looked at user fees, sales taxes and property taxes. How are you holding up? Are you still with me? I need to know that you're with me because next up is the big dog of taxes, income taxes.

## 4. Income tax

Let's begin at the beginning. There is a Federal Income Tax that traces back to the passage of the 16th Amendment in 1913.

The amendment reads:[lxviii]

*The Congress shall have power to lay and collect taxes on incomes, from whatever source derived, without apportionment among the several States, and without regard to any census or enumeration.*

Taking advantage of its new authority, Congress passed the Underwood Tariff Act of 1913.[lxix] [84] Over 100 years later the federal income tax is very much alive, so much so that today it represents the most significant source of federal government *revenue.*[lxx]

Not to be left out, all but seven states levy their own income tax.[85] Many cities do as well. Residents of the Philadelphia suburb of Germantown, for instance, must pay a portion of their income to the city of Philadelphia, the state of Pennsylvania and the federal government in Washington, D.C.

## What is income?

We understand that payments we receive for our work or from owning an investment are income. What about the following?

Ari's rich friend lent him $20,000 when he was in a tight spot several years ago. The guy just called to tell him he had an epiphany and realized that it was best to forgive the loan. Ari thanks his friend profusely, then exhales slowly as he ends the call.

While on a trip out west Melinda attends a game show. To her shock she hears her name announced as the next contestant. After bounding up to the stage and high-fiving the

[84] With tax rates ranging from 1% to 7% of a person's income at that time, the Act allowed for the elimination of other unpopular taxes, such as those on imported raw materials and manufactured goods.

[85] Alaska, Florida, Nevada, South Dakota, Texas, Washington, and Wyoming have no state income tax.

host, Melinda spins a wheel, makes a few educated guesses and wins a new $25,000 car!

Working his way through his stuffed attic, Germaine finds a vase whose beauty is obscured by a thick layer of dust. After cleaning it up he brings it to an appraiser, who gives him good news: the vase is worth $10,000. That estimate turns out to be conservative; at auction it fetches $12,500.

As an architect, Monique has helped True Tech Builders secure many construction projects. To thank her, True Tech's owner has a crew build a new deck off the back of Monique's house. With its composite materials and built-in accent lighting, the deck would have cost $20,000 if she had hired True Tech or another contractor to build it.

Dinesh has a landscaping company. His neighbor Shawn is a plumber. As good friends they have been known to exchange services. Just recently Dinesh installed an in-ground sprinkler system throughout Shawn's yard. In exchange, Shawn upgraded Dinesh's oil heat to a natural gas system featuring a wall-mounted boiler. They figure the work they've done for each other is worth about $5,000.

Which, if any of these, is considered income? It would help to think about income as a benefit, as something you receive that makes you better off. If you work hard this week and collect $1,000 on Friday, you have benefited. You are better off by $1,000 than you were before you collected your pay. When you benefit, the government want a piece of that benefit. Viewed through this prism, all of the examples represent income that the recipients are supposed to report to the various governments so they can collect a portion.[86]

From a practical standpoint this makes sense. Imagine that

---

[86] A notable exception to this rule is the cost of employee health insurance (which can run into the tens of thousands) that employers pay, but from which employees benefit. Another high-value exception is college scholarships, which are not taxable as income.

Joe the carpenter is hired to finish a homeowner's basement, complete with a bar, pool table and bathroom. He provides an estimate of $25,000, which the homeowner accepts. When the job is done the homeowner buys Joe a new $25,000 car. Are we to say Joe didn't benefit because he wasn't paid in cash, thus owing no income tax? If so, we'd all be running around making sure we were compensated in a form other than cash.

## What is not income?

Gavin is trying his hand at stock investing, purchasing 10 shares of Firstbook at $50 per share and paying a total cost of $500. Over the next few weeks the shares rise in value from $50 to $60 each. When he logs into his investment account he sees that he has a gain on this investment of $100 (10 shares x $10 share increase). This gain is considered *unrealized.* It is literally not real. If tomorrow Firstbook announces poor quarterly financial results the shares can drop from $60 each back down to $50 in an instant. Goodbye gain. While a gain is unrealized, it's not considered income.[87] The only way to realize the earlier gain was to sell the shares when they were worth $60 to lock in that price.

Gavin also purchased the shares of a company whose later financial performance was disappointing. The share price declined, and he sold what he held at a loss of $500. At the same time, he bought into another corporation whose share price rose. He sold those shares for a gain of $500. Technically, Gavin has received income since he sold this second investment for a profit. But he also suffered a loss on the prior investment for the same amount. That loss offsets the gain he made on the subsequent investment. This makes sense since his investment account balance is the same as it was before he made the two investments. He's no better off, and therefore owes no income tax.

---

[87] The same is true for losses. They are not real until an investor sells.

## So much progress

It's difficult to get young people to express an opinion, lest they offend someone. Yet, one time I was able to trigger a spirited discussion by asking my students to complete the following assignment:

*Explain why a person earning $100,000 should pay more than double the income taxes of a person earning $50,000.*

The sensibilities of several students were violated. Their belief was that any tax should be *proportional* to the income a person receives. "Double the income should mean double the tax," they argued. There are indeed many proponents of this approach, which we will discuss later.

However, there are more who believe that the higher the income a person receives, the greater is that person's ability to shoulder higher rates of income tax. It is hard to argue against this. Remember Justine and Alberto from our chapter on budgeting? Their original combined annual income was $126,000. They were paying in the vicinity of 24% of it to cover various income taxes. Let's say that Justine applies for a major promotion and gets it. Her new position pays $126,000 more than her old one. The family income has doubled. If they are living a nice life and meeting their savings goals on total annual income of $126,000 per year, all of the income increase is basically excess. Could they pay, say, a 30% tax on the extra income while simultaneously saving more and upgrading their lifestyle? Yes.

This is the rationale for our having a *progressive* income tax. We believe that the more a person earns the higher the percentage of those increased earnings he or she can and should pay. How is such a system implemented? The taxing authority sets out a schedule, a simplified example of which follows:

| On the ... | ... of income | the rate is ... |
|---:|---:|---:|
| First | $ 20,000 | 0% |
| Next | $ 50,000 | 10% |
| Next | $ 100,000 | 20% |
| Next | $ 500,000 | 30% |
| Rest | | 35% |

Each of the rows in the table is known in tax-speak as a *bracket*. We always begin at the top. The first bracket has a 0% rate and represents a free pass. We could just as easily have presented a table without a 0% bracket, but with a statement that the taxpayer can deduct $20,000 from his or her income before applying the rest to the table.

In the real world there are *deductions* and they change based on personal circumstances. For example, a single parent with two children has greater financial challenges than a single individual with no children. The single parent's deduction will be *higher* than that of a single person, reflecting Congress' intent that the federal income tax take personal circumstances into consideration.

The second bracket in the table shows that a 10% tax is applied on the next $50,000 of income. Then, on the next $100,000 of income, a tax of 20% is assessed, and so on. Notice that we're not applying the same rate to every dollar of income. "Rest" refers to all income in excess of the incomes in the prior brackets. Adding down, we see that brackets of $20,000, $50,000, $100,000 and $500,000 must be fully filled with income before the 35% rate kicks in. Adding these figures gives us a sum of $670,000. Any income above this number is taxed at 35%.

Perhaps it would be easier to explain how income taxes are calculated by presenting the very same table in a different format, as follows:

| Income from ... | to ... | Is taxed at ... rate |
|---:|---:|---:|
| $ 0 | $ 20,000 | 0% |
| $ 20,001 | $ 70,000 | 10% |
| $ 70,001 | $ 170,000 | 20% |
| $ 170,001 | $ 670,000 | 30% |
| $ 670,001 | | 35% |

Let's say that Hassan expects to earn $175,000 this year and he wants to know how much income tax he will owe. We have added columns to the table to calculate his liability. Notice again that we always start at the top. The first $20,000 of his $175,000 of income is taxed at 0%. The next $50,000 of his income, from $20,001st to $70,000th, is taxed at only 10%. We continue until we have taxed every dollar of Hassan's income, and not a penny more. The 30% bracket encompasses $500,000 of potential income. Only a small amount of Hassan's income spills into it, as demonstrated in the expanded table below:

| A | B | C | D = B – A | C x D |
|---:|---:|---:|---:|---:|
| Income from ... | to ... | is taxed at ... rate | Hassan's income in bracket | Tax owed |
| $ 0 | $ 20,000 | 0% | $ 20,000 | $ 0 |
| $ 20,001 | $ 70,000 | 10% | $ 50,000 | $ 5,000 |
| $ 70,001 | $ 170,000 | 20% | $ 100,000 | $ 20,000 |
| $ 170,001 | $ 670,000 | 30% | $ 5,000 | $ 1,500 |
| $ 670,001 | Infinity | 35% | | |
| | | Totals | $ 175,000 | $ 26,500 |

Progressive income tax tables such as this one are widely misunderstood and often mischaracterized. For example, if

Hassan complains to anyone who will listen that he's losing 30% of his income to taxes, this would be misleading. Only $5,000 of his income spilled into the 30% bracket. Because of the graduated nature of the table, Hassan's actual (i.e., *effective*) tax rate is only 15% ($26,500 divided by $175,000).

It would, however, be fair for Hassan to tell his friends that he is concerned about taking on side projects because any additional income he makes this year will be taxed at 30%, his *marginal* rate.

## Who's afraid of April 15?

Income is tracked and reported on a calendar year basis. Throughout the year employers *withhold* an approximate amount of income tax from each paycheck and send the amount of federal income tax withheld to the *Internal Revenue Service (IRS)* on their employees' behalf.[88]

The tax withheld is only an approximation because personal tax situations can change over the course of the year. For example, if a single person has a child, he or she qualifies for a tax credit. The federal tax law is thousands of pages long,[lxxi] and many of those pages describe deductions we may qualify for over the course of the year.

April 15th is three and half months after the end of the prior year. This should be plenty of time for individuals to gather documentation on the various types of income received and the deductions to which they are entitled. On or before April 15, the law requires us to file form *1040* to report the tax that we paid over the course of the prior year along with a calculation of the tax we actually owed in that year. If we paid less than we owed, we must include with our 1040 a check made out to the IRS for the difference. If we paid more than we actually owed in taxes, we will receive a *refund*.

---

[88] Additional estimated amounts of tax are withheld for state and city income taxes, as applicable.

## Who pays federal income taxes?

Let's look at the Jaworski family, which consists of a married couple with two young children. They live in an apartment and will file a *joint* tax form to report their $60,000 of combined income. The actual 2019 federal income tax brackets are provided below. The *standard deduction* they qualify for, $24,400, is unconventionally expressed as a 0% tax bracket in the following table.

| 2019 Married Filing Jointly | | | | |
|---|---|---|---|---|
| A | B | C | D = B – A | C x D |
| Income from ... | to ... | the rate is ... | Jaworski income in bracket | Tax owed |
| $ 0 | $ 24,400 | 0% | $ 24,400 | $ 0 |
| $ 24,401 | $ 43,800 | 10% | $ 19,400 | $ 1,940 |
| $ 43,801 | $ 103,350 | 12% | $ 16,200 | $ 1,944 |
| $ 103,351 | $ 192,800 | 22% | | |
| $ 192,801 | $ 345,850 | 24% | | |
| $ 345,851 | $ 432,600 | 32% | | |
| $ 432,601 | $ 636,750 | 35% | | |
| $ 636,751 | infinity | 37% | | |
| | | Totals | $ 60,000 | $ 3,884 |

As we just noted, the first $24,400 of their income is not taxed. The next $19,400 of their income is taxed at a rate of 10%, resulting in a tax of $1,940 (10% of $19,400). This leaves $16,200 of income left to tax. That amount falls into the next bracket and will be taxed at a rate of 12%. The tax owed on this last amount of income is $1,944 (12% of $16,200). The total tax owed is $1,940 plus $1,944, or $3,884.

But before the Jaworskis begin comparing the $3,884 tax that they owe to the amount of tax withheld and paid to the IRS by their employers, they should be aware of an even greater benefit than a tax deduction: a tax *credit*. To recognize the costs of raising a family, the federal tax law provides a $2,000 tax credit for each child under age 17.[lxxii] A credit is a "dollar-for-dollar" reduction in tax liability. Their two young children qualify them for a $4,000 ($2,000 x 2) reduction in the tax owed. Wait, didn't we just calculate a tax of $3,884? That's less than the total tax credit. Assuming $3,884 was withheld by their employers and sent to the IRS over the course of the year, the family is entitled to all of it back, plus $116 ($4,000 minus $3,884), the dollar amount of the remaining credit.

*Median* household income in the United States is $61,937,[lxxiii] which means that half of households earn more than this number and half, less. The median income is similar to the $60,000 Jaworski family income. Where are we going with this? Given the array of deductions and credits available to tax filers, 44.4% of them, numbering 76.4 million, pay no federal income tax.[lxxiv]

## State and city income taxes

We mentioned earlier that cities and states may also levy an income tax. On the next page is a look around the country at rates applicable to married couples filing jointly (together).[lxxv]

---

*...but in this world nothing can be said to be certain, except death and taxes.*
- Benjamin Franklin

---

| Government | Standard deduction (0% bracket) | Next bracket rate | Highest bracket rate | Highest rate begins at income over |
|---|---|---|---|---|
| Federal | $ 24,400 | 10.00% | 37.00% | $ 612,350 |
| New York | $ 16,050 | 4.00% | 8.82% | $ 2,155,350 |
| NY City[lxxvi] | $ 21,600 | 3.08% | 3.88% | $ 90,000 |
| California | $ 8,472 | 1.00% | 13.30% | $ 1,074,996 |
| Arizona | $ 10,613 | 2.59% | 4.54% | $ 317,990 |
| Arkansas | $ 4,400 | 0.09% | 6.90% | $ 35.099 |
| Delaware | $ 6,500 | 2.20% | 6.60% | $ 60,000 |
| Hawaii | $ 4,400 | 1.40% | 11.00% | $ 400,000 |
| Iowa | $ 5,000 | 0.36% | 8.98% | $ 71,910 |
| Oregon | $ 4,430 | 5.00% | 9.90% | $ 250,000 |
| Pennsylvania | $ 0 | 3.07% | 3.07% | $ 0 |
| Indiana | $ 0 | 3.23% | 3.23% | $ 0 |

Who would have thought that Iowa has a higher state income tax than New York, and that its highest rate would begin at a much lower income threshold? Notable as well is the fact that the states of Pennsylvania and Indiana have a proportional system that charges one rate on every dollar of income.

We've included Delaware in this table. If you remember, it has no state sales tax. It's only logical that it would seek to make up for foregone sales taxes with outsized income taxes. Yet, Delaware's highest income tax rate, at 6.60%, is middle of the road.

As we've been illustrating, the taxes people pay largely depend on where they live. When it comes time to decide where to put down roots what you should be interested in knowing is the *total tax burden* you'll bear in the various cities you are considering calling home. A simple internet search on the phrase "total tax burden," followed by a city name, will direct you to articles whose authors have already done the heavy lifting. This enables you to conveniently review their information on the taxes you can expect to pay in the city you're researching.

## Who's not paying their fair share? – Part I

In this age of tremendous political partisanship, where the questions about fairness are frequent, it would be beneficial to have our positions grounded in facts. Looking over the last table, you may have added a 37% top federal tax rate to California's 13.3% top rate and realized that the total is in excess of 50%, or half of what a high-income earner receives above approximately $1 million in a year. Adding up the federal, state and city rates for New York City residents leaves us just shy of 50%.

Who earns enough money to be concerned about these high income tax rates? Visiting sportrac.com, we learn that Pittsburgh Penguin center Sidney Crosby will earn $9 million this year. Los Angeles Rams running back Todd Gurley will earn in excess of $13 million. Los Angeles Laker power forward Anthony Davis will earn in excess of $27 million. LeBron James, more than $37 million. That's $18.5 million for him, and $18.5 million for the U.S. and California governments.

But it's not just athletes. Stephen A. Smith just signed a tidy 5-year deal with ESPN that will earn him nearly $8 million per year.[lxxvii] Joe Rogan just signed a $100 million deal to move his podcast to Spotify.[lxxviii] From cable news commentators to social media influencers, from popular singers to A-list actors, from financiers to elite real estate agents, from movie producers to high-profile attorneys, a lot of people make a lot of money. Upon them is the prospect of turning over half their income to various taxing authorities.

## Who's not paying their fair share? – Part II

It would behoove you to know that not all income is taxed the same way. Citing the importance of *capital formation*, the investor class has been able to carve out its own lane, securing special (i.e., favorable) federal tax treatment of:

- profits on the sale of investments that were owned for at least a year, otherwise known as *long-term capital gains*,[lxxix] and
- *dividends* received from corporations that pay out a portion of their profits to their shareholders.[lxxx] [89]

Following is a table showing the current tax treatment of long- term capital gains and dividends: [90]

| 2019 Married Filing Jointly Capital Gains and Dividends | | | | |
|---|---|---|---|---|
| | | A | B | A + B |
| Income from ... | to ... | is taxed at ... | Obama-Care Tax* | Total tax |
| $ 0 | $ 78,750 | 0% | | 0% |
| $ 78,751 | $ 488,850 | 15% | 3.8% | 18.8% |
| $ 488,851 | Infinity | 20% | 3.8% | 23.8% |
| * Applies to couples with incomes over $250,000 per year. | | | | |

Even with the addition of a 3.8% tax on investment income that was introduced with the 2010 Patient Protection and

[89] We assume the dividends are *qualified* under IRS rules.

[90] States handle capital gains in a variety of ways. Some provide special tax treatment like the federal government does, while some treat them the same as any other form of income.

Affordable Care Act,[lxxxi] [91](better known as Obamacare) the top federal rate of 23.8% remains significantly lower than the 37% top rate that applies to other types of income.

This demonstrates that income earned from working is taxed at a higher rate than income received when our money makes money. Formally stated, income from *labor* is taxed more than income from *capital*. Critics say this is the opposite of how it should be. There are so only many hours in a day, they point out. Income earned from the sweat of one's brow is vitally important to the earner and deserving of the lowest rate a government can afford. The whole idea of progressive taxation is to tax people who can afford to pay more at a higher rate. That describes people fortunate enough to have wealth that itself is earning income. What are we doing taxing income from capital at a *lower* rate? To back up their position, they point out that lower capital gains rates are mostly enjoyed by the already-wealthy, with 80% of capital gains going to the wealthiest 5% of taxpayers, and 69% going to just the top 1% of taxpayers.[lxxxii]

On the other side of the argument are those who believe that the vast majority of people don't just wake up one day "fortunate enough to have wealth." Instead, they believe people create their good fortune through hard work and sacrifice that allows for a portion of their income—which was taxed when it was earned—to be saved and invested. In so doing, these savers seek to run the gauntlet, to gradually transition from the *working class* to the *investor class*. Is it too much to ask that their investment income receives favorable tax treatment?

## Who's not paying their fair share? – Part III

I was feeling pretty good about the foregoing discussion and wished I could leave it there. But, no. There remains one

[91] The formal name is Net Investment Income Tax (NIIT).

other significant issue in this important public policy debate. It has to do with the tech billionaires.

The founders of giant corporations such as Microsoft, Google and Facebook invested very little of their own money when their corporations were founded. Heck, most were struggling college students. As their creations found ever greater utility among their users, the value of their shares went parabolic. The poorest among Jeff Bezos, founder of Amazon, Bill Gates, co-founder of Microsoft, Larry Page and Sergey Brin, co-founders of Google, and Mark Zuckerberg, co-founder of Facebook, is worth in excess of $50 billion.

The entire value of their shares represents *unrealized* gains (since they have yet to sell their shares and make their profits real). Because they've been held for much longer than one year, when their shares are sold the income will be taxed at the lower long-term capital gains tax rate. Famed billionaire investor Warren Buffett even lamented that he was paying a lower rate of tax on his investment income than his secretary (whose income is subject to ordinary federal income tax rates).[lxxxiii] With the addition of the previously mentioned 3.8% Affordable Care Act tax surcharge on investment income and the lowering of federal income tax rates in the Tax Cuts and Job Act of 2017,[lxxxiv] Buffett's oft-cited remark may no longer be true. That may not matter. The crystalized perception among many is that the billionaires have it too well.

Consider Mark Zuckerberg, who is in his 30s. At the time of this writing his wealth was around $60 billion. At current tax rates, when he sells his Facebook shares he'll pay 23.8% to the federal government and up to 13.3% to California, which doesn't give special treatment to capital gains income. Combined, these rates exceed 37%, which translates to $22.2 billion in taxes Mr. Zuckerberg will eventually owe these governments. However, he is a relatively young man. And because governments only tax gains when they are realized, they may have to wait decades to collect their piece of

Zuckerberg's fortune.

To provide governments access to these fortunes sooner, prominent 2020 presidential candidates proposed a *wealth tax*.[lxxxv] In early 2019 one candidate proposed a 2% per year tax on wealth exceeding $50 million, with an increase to 3% on wealth above $1 billion. In late 2019, she increased her proposed rate to 6% to cover the cost of her ambitious Medicare-for-All plan.[lxxxvi] A 6% tax on $60 billion is $3.6 billion, to be paid every year. In the likely event that Mr. Zuckerberg does not have $3.6 billion in cash lying around to pay this tax, he will have to sell some of his Facebook shares. Selling will in turn trigger federal and California state income taxes that must be paid. Zuckerberg will have to sell in excess of $5.7 billion[92] worth of shares to be left with the $3.6 billion (after income taxes) that he needs to pay the wealth tax. All $5.7 billion would be paid as a tax in one form or another.

Earlier, we explained that selling an asset, turning it into cash, is called *liquidation*. If implemented, this wealth tax will result in the *forced liquidation* by company founders of their shares. Also, as this liquidation occurs, over time it will result in the loss of voting control that company founders may currently have.[93]

## Payroll taxes

Pick any three letters of the alphabet and place them next to each other. We could string together D, O and S, for DOS. How about B, L and M, for BLM? We could combine N, R and C, for NRC. When you do this you have a reasonable chance

---

92 $5.71 billion of shares sold, when taxed at a combined income tax rate of 37%, leaves approximately $3.6 billion to pay the wealth tax.

93 There is a way for founders like Mr. Zuckerberg to keep their wealth (but not voting control) intact. They must ensure that the value of their company's shares rise each year by the amount of the wealth and incomes taxes incurred.

of creating an acronym used by one of our hundreds of existing federal agencies. Such is the enormity of our national government.[94] DOS actually stands for "Department of State." This department, headed by the Secretary of State, has nearly 76,000 employees and is operated at an annual cost of $37.3 billion.[lxxxvii] It is one of our larger agencies, but it pales in comparison to our 3rd largest agency/program, the Department of Defense (DOD). Headquartered in the Pentagon, DOD consumes more than $600 billion annually to manage the branches of our armed forces.[lxxxviii]

These hundreds of government programs, including the Department of Defense, are paid for by the personal federal income taxes we pay and other income taxes levied by the federal government, such as the corporate federal income tax.[95] Can you guess the names of the two biggest programs? Even if you are a young person decades away from being concerned with them, they loom so large that you have probably heard of them. They are Social Security and Medicare, each of which pays out in excess of $1 trillion per year.[lxxxix] These programs are funded by dedicated taxes that we pay in addition to federal income taxes.

## *Social Security*

Social Security's main program pays people money each month after they retire until they pass away. One hundred seventy-seven million people work and pay into the system. Sixty-four million receive payments, although only forty-eight million of these are retirees. The rest are disabled individuals, or survivors or dependents of recipients. Worker payments into the system today are used to pay today's retirees. There is

---

[94] For a well-organized directory of federal agencies, visit https://www.usa.gov/federal-agencies/

[95] In actuality, the tax collections fall well short of the expenditures so the government must borrow the difference.

no account with your name on it that holds your payments to the system. Despite the lack of a personal account, the Social Security Administration (SSA) does record your payments under your *Social Security Number*. This is crucial since the primary determinant of how much money you will receive in retirement is how much you've paid into the system.

Although the standard retirement age for younger workers has slowly been increasing from 65 to age 67, people can choose to begin receiving payments as early as 62 years of age and as late as age 70.[96] As can be expected, the earlier a person chooses to retire, the lower the monthly payment he or she will receive. Conversely, the longer a retiree can wait until notifying the SSA that he or she wishes to begin collecting, the higher the monthly payment will be.[xc]

## Medicare

One of the unfortunate effects of aging is that people break down physically. Thus, the fastest way for a corporation to go out of business would be to offer medical insurance to the elderly. Enter the United States government, which in 1965 began providing health insurance, otherwise known as *Medicare,* to citizens age 65 and older. Over 60 million Americans are enrolled in Medicare.[xci] The program's benefits are grouped into four areas:

| Part | Covers / Is known as | Monthly premium | Annual deductible |
|---|---|---|---|
| A | hospital expenses | None | $ 1,408[xcii] |
| B | medical expenses | $ 144.60 | $ 198[xciii] |
| C | Medicare Advantage | varies | varies |
| D | prescription drugs | varies | varies |

---

[96] Beyond this age, a retiree does not receive credit for delaying the start of payment collection.

The *premium* is the cost the insured must pay to have the insurance. Notice that there is none for Part A, an indication that hospital insurance is the heart of Medicare. Hospitalization, however, is not free because there is an annual *deductible,* the amount of hospital expenses that the insured must pay out of his or her own pocket before coverage "kicks in" and pays the remaining expenses. Parts, B, C, and D, are optional.

Part B covers medical expenses incurred when medical care is received in a doctor's office, medical clinic or even a hospital on an *outpatient basis,* meaning that the care doesn't involve the recipient checking into the hospital.

Part C, *Medicare Advantage,* can be chosen if seniors prefer to receive the benefits of the other parts through a government-approved private health insurance company.

Part D, *prescription drug coverage,* helps lower the cost of prescription drugs.

## *Social Security and Medicare are "payroll" taxes*

A company's *pay roll* was the center of a bygone practice wherein a supervisor on a factory floor would gather employees at the end of the work week, calling their names (from a roster or roll), and handing them their pay checks as they stepped forward. Because they apply only to *earned* income that is received via paycheck, Social Security and Medicare taxes are known as *payroll taxes.* Their rates appear in the table on the next page.

---

*This is a question too difficult for a mathematician. It should be asked of a philosopher" (when asked about completing his income tax form).*
- Albert Einstein

---

| Tax | You pay | Your employer pays | Total paid on your behalf | 2020 income limit |
|---|---|---|---|---|
| Social Security[97] | 6.20% | 6.20% | 12.40% | $ 137,700 |
| Medicare | *1.45% | 1.45% | 2.90% | no limit |
| * Add 0.9% to income over $250,000 (married filing jointly). | | | | |

Both taxes are a straight percentage of a person's pay. Let's say Jamison's salary is $100,000. He will pay 6.2% of it, or $6,200, in Social Security tax. He will pay 1.45% of it, or $1,450, in Medicare tax.

What most people don't realize is that these payments must be matched by employers, meaning that twice as much money is being paid into the system than it would appear by examining the deduction on one's pay statement.

This comes as an especially unpleasant surprise to a person starting her own business. She is her own employer and is responsible for paying 12.4% (double 6.2%) in Social Security tax and 2.9% (double 1.45%) in Medicare tax. The sum of these two, 15.3%, is often referred to as the *self-employment* tax.

Requiring matching contributions has implications for employers as well. The actual cost of employing Jamison is not his $100,000 salary, but his salary plus $6,200 to match his Social Security tax, plus $1,450 to match his Medicare tax, for a total of $107,650.

You may also have noticed an upper income limit for the Social Security tax, beyond which no tax is applied. Taking 6.2% of the $137,700 cap, we see that the most an employee will pay in Social Security tax in the year 2020 is $8,537.40. This upper income limit goes by many names, including *wage*

[97] Social Security tax was formally authorized by the Federal Insurance Contributions Act. Therefore, the Social Security deduction is often labeled "FICA" on pay statements.

*base* and *taxable maximum.* It is adjusted each year by the average rate of wage growth.[xciv] The cap for the 2019 tax year was $132,900. The substantial 3.6% increase that 2020's cap represents is due to strong recent increases in average wages.[98]

The national average monthly Social Security payment to retirees for 2020 is $1,503.[xcv] Payments are *indexed* to inflation, which means that each year they increase by the amount of the prior year's inflation.[xcvi] Finally, just as the Social Security tax is capped, so too is the monthly payment. The maximum payment is $2,851 per month for a 65-year-old who chooses to begin collecting in 2020.[xcvii]

While the Medicare tax is a lower percentage of income, there is no upper income limit. More troubling for high income earners is that for each dollar earned over $250,000, the rate jumps to 2.35% (1.45% plus a 0.9% extra tax). LeBron James will earn over $37 million this year, resulting in a Medicare tax of $869,500.[99] King James, on behalf of my mom, my dad, the 60 million current Medicare enrollees and millions more who will join the program when they turn 65, thank you very much for your contribution.

### *Social Security, what in the world are you?*

Our first introduction to social security comes as a tax taken from our pay. When we begin collecting payments in retirement, it feels like a return of an investment. After all, money we paid in for a long time earns us the right to collect money. However, unlike many traditional investments that promise a certain number of payments, Social Security stays with us, pays us, until we pass away. In fact, it can even pay beyond our death. The formal name for the fund into which Social Security payments are deposited is the Old-Age and

---

[98] ($137,700 - $132,900) / $132,900 = $4,800 / $132,900 = 0.036 = 3.6%.

[99] $37,000,000 x 2.35% = $869,500.

Survivors Insurance (OASI) Trust Fund. Survivors are family members of the income earner who paid into the system and has passed away.[xcviii]

Benefits such as these have us thinking of Social Security as insurance. Insurance is the next chapter in this book so we're jumping ahead by identifying a benefit as insurance before really explaining what insurance is. At this point let's just say that income earners would like to protect against two circumstances: (1) running out of money in retirement, and (2) leaving family members destitute should they pass away. Social security helps *insure* against these things happening.

Given the significant sums of money workers and their employers pay into Social Security over decades-long careers, a common question regards the relationship between the money paid in while working and the money received back in retirement. Does the average person get back more than he or she paid in? Less? About the same?

To try to answer that question, we need to take a brief detour back to the origins of the program in the middle-to-late 1930s. In the beginning the retirement age was set at 65, a high bar—so high in fact that it exceeded the average life expectancy at the time![xcix] This is, however, an instance where statistics are misleading. Specifically, a high level of infant mortality dragged average life expectancy down. It is more helpful to know that 53.9% of males born in 1875 and alive at age 21 were still living when they turned 65 in 1940, the first year Social Security began paying. Truly remarkable is that males living to age 65 in 1940 had an average additional life expectancy of 12.7 years, putting them into their late 70s. So, we see that more than half of males making it to adulthood were able to collect Social Security when it began paying in 1940 and those who did collected for many years. Statistics for females, who live longer, are even more favorable.

We know that the trend over the last century has been toward longer life expectancy. In 1990, fifty years after the social security program began paying, 72.4% of men surviving into adulthood made it to the retirement age of 65, living on average another 15.3 years.

Congress has over the decades responded by making changes to collect more taxes. For example, the original 1937 combined employee-employer tax rate was 2% of the first $3,000 in wages. By 1990, it had reached its current rate of 12.4% on wages up to $51,300.[c] Also, as mentioned earlier, the full retirement age is in the process of increasing from age 65 to 67. Despite these changes, an aging American population ensures that the Social Security program will remain under pressure.

Given this backdrop, let's take a look at the priorities of the program itself. They are conveyed by the *income replacement* formula that calculates monthly payments:[ci]

| A | B | C | D = C x (B–A) | D /12 |
|---|---|---|---|---|
| Annual income from ... | to ... | % the program aims to replace | Annual payment | Monthly payment |
| $ 0 | $ 11,112 | 90% | $ 10,001 | $ 833 |
| $ 11,113 | $ 66,996 | 32% | $ 17,883 | $ 1,490 |
| $ 66,997 | *$ 128,400 | 15% | $ 9,211 | $ 768 |
| | | Totals | $ 37,095 | [100] $ 3,091 |
| *2018's taxable limit, the last year for which this analysis was available. | | | | |

The most important information is in the column indicating the percentage of one's income the system tries to replace. We see that the more a person earns, the lower the percentage.

[100] The figure is based only on the current year's taxable maximum, whereas an earlier figure was calculated using the actual taxable maximums over a working career, which are then inflation adjusted.

While a person earning income in the lowest rung (which represents less than $1,000 per month) will receive payments replacing 90% of his or her income, a person consistently earning the taxable maximum will receive just 28.9% ($37,095/$128,400) of his or her income.

Even this analysis is flawed, however. Remember that the combined tax rate of 12.4% is lower than all the percentages in the table. How can a sound system collect 12.4% of a person's income but then pay larger percentages of it back? One way is if the number of years a person works and pays the tax is several times the number of years he or she will collect.[101] Another is for the taxes to be collected up to decades in advance of when payments will begin, allowing the SSA to grow it. Lastly, the program can redirect contributions from higher income earners to lower income earners.

We'll finish with the highlights of a recent analysis which found that low-wage retirees can achieve a positive return on their contributions, those in the middle-income range will likely break even and those earning in the upper range of the taxable maximum will likely receive less than they paid in.[cii]

## 5. Estate (aka "Death") tax

The estate tax is one that kicks in when a person dies. Until the last few decades, this tax was not in our consciousness because most people didn't consider themselves wealthy enough to leave an estate to their *heirs*. But they are most definitely aware that they will die. And so in a master stroke worthy of a marketing case study, the political party opposed to the estate tax began referring to it as the *death tax*. This renaming triggered average folks to wonder about the fairness

---

[101] Indeed, in calculating the monthly benefit, the system uses the 35 working years during which a person made his or her highest contributions.

of taxing people one last time—after they exit this life.

## What is an estate?

When we conjure the term *estate,* we tend to think of a sprawling parcel of land encompassing tens, if not hundreds, of acres on which sits a magnificent stone mansion. But in this case the term estate means *net worth,* the dollar amount by which a person's assets exceed her liabilities. For example, a widow may live in an impressive house worth $2 million that is encumbered by a mortgage of $1.5 million. If she passes away, it would be inaccurate to count the whole $2 million in determining the value of her estate. It would be fairer to subtract the amount of debt ($1.5 million) from the value of the house ($2.0 million) and include only her $500,000 in home equity as part of her estate.

### *Determining the market value of assets*

Who's buried in Grant's tomb? Hopefully, Grant. How much is a savings account with a $25,000 balance worth? $25,000. How about 100 shares of a corporation with a current price of $50 a share? That's an easy one since 100 times $50 is $5,000.

How about the value of a classic car? A coin collection? Several acres of land? A pizzeria? When the market value of an asset is not easily determined, we hire qualified *appraisers* and go with their educated estimates.

## Applying the exemption

In a manner akin to its treatment of income, the federal government provides something similar to a standard deduction for estate taxes. If an estate's value is at or below that amount, no tax is owed. However, when referring to estate taxes, instead of using the term "deduction," the term *exemption* is used. Why the terminology change? It's another of life's mysteries.

While the political party that is against the estate tax has not won a complete repeal, it has done the next best thing by securing significant increases in the exemption amount. This, in turn, catches fewer and fewer families in the estate tax's web, as shown below. [ciii] For perspective, approximately 2.7 million people passed away in 2018. Less than 0.1% (1,890/2,700,000) of their estates paid federal estate taxes.

| Year | Exemption amount for singles (in millions) | Exemption amount for couples (in millions) | Number of estates exceeding exemption |
|---|---|---|---|
| 2000 | $ 0.675 | $ 1.35 | 52,000 |
| ... | | | |
| 2013 | $ 5.00 | $ 10.00 | 4,687 |
| ... | | | |
| 2018 | $ 11.18 | $ 22.36 | 1,890 |
| 2019 | $ 11.20 | $ 22.40 | |

In the tax year 2019, when an individual died and passed on an estate worth $11.2 million or less, no federal estate tax was owed. For couples, the exemption was $22.4 million.

## *The spousal force field*

You can see in the table that the exemption amount for couples is double the amount for singles. By definition, if one spouse passes away the other just became single. Could that column apply if both spouses pass away simultaneously, as they might in a serious accident? Not quite.

When one spouse in a marriage passes away the assets owned by that spouse pass tax free to the surviving spouse. Upon the surviving spouse's passing, the higher spousal exemption is then applied to the estate.

## Estate values beyond the exemption

What happens if an estate's value is higher than the amount of the exemption? The excess amount is subject to a 40% tax. That's a big number. Before you cry in your Cheerios, however, think about the wealthy person who had the poor fortune of passing away in 2001. That year the value of estates in excess of $3 million was taxed at 55%. Ouch.[civ]

Let's say a newly married Midwestern couple founded and quietly grew a manufacturing business. Decades later, the couple's two children have ascended to leadership positions in the business, which currently generates several million dollars in profit each year. When the last spouse passes away an appraiser is brought in to assess the value of the business. She determines that it's worth $70 million. Adding the equity in personal assets results in a total estate value of $72.4 million. The first thing we do is subtract the couple's exemption of $22.4 million. This results in a taxable estate of $50 million. At 40%, the tax owed is $20 million.

The children are unlikely to have $20 million in cash hanging around, which implies that they will be forced to sell the business to gather enough cash to pay the tax. Thus, special tax provisions are provided to help the children avoid having to take this dramatic step, most notably the ability to pay the estate tax (with interest) over a 15-year period.[cv]

In addition, because we know that the founding couple will eventually pass from this earth, measures can be taken to keep the business in the family. While specific strategies are beyond the scope of this book, life insurance, trusts and other mechanisms can facilitate the passing of the business to the next generation.

### *How many times is wealth taxed?*

Critics of the estate tax point to its fundamental unfairness. They contend that estates are built with income that has already been subject to the taxes we've discussed in this chapter and that this is a second round of extraction. However, this couple's situation doesn't conform to that stereotype. We learned earlier that gains on investments are taxed only when they are realized (i.e., sold). The couple began and continued to own their business until their deaths. They sold none of it and therefore realized no gains. The estate tax represents the first time their wealth is being taxed. How prevalent is this situation in the real world? A Federal Reserve study showed that 32% of lower-value estates were composed of previously untaxed capital gains. This number increased to 55% for high-value estates.[cvi] Of course, this also means that the remaining estates, 68% and 45%, respectively, will be subject to a second visit from the tax reaper.

## States get in on the act

Given everything we've discussed in this chapter, you had to suspect that states would not sit idly by as their wealthy residents left large estates to their heirs. This is the case, but it's not nearly as bad as it could be. Only 12 states levy an estate tax.[cvii] [102] Following is a sample, along with important thresholds for the 2018 tax year: [cviii]

> *In other words, a democratic government is the only one in which those who vote for a tax can escape the obligation to pay it.*
>
> \- Alexis de Tocqueville

[102] States with an estate tax are Connecticut, Hawaii, Illinois, Maine, Maryland, Massachusetts, Minnesota, New York, Oregon, Rhode Island, Vermont and Washington.

| State | Exemption amount (in millions) | Top tax rate... | ...applies to taxable estate over (in millions) |
|---|---|---|---|
| Connecticut | $ 2.60 | 12.0% | $ 7.50 |
| Hawaii | $ 5.49 | 15.7% | $ 5.00 |
| Illinois | $ 4.00 | 16.0% | $ 10.04 |
| Maryland | $ 4.00 | 16.0% | $ 10.04 |
| Massachusetts | $ 1.00 | 16.0% | $ 10.04 |
| New York | $ 5.25 | 16.0% | $ 10.01 |
| Oregon | $ 1.00 | 16.0% | $ 8.50 |

As the table indicates, some states tax up to 16% of estate value above their exemption amount. As we just learned, the federal government takes 40% of any value above its allowed exemption. The most important takeaway? The heirs of large estates who live in certain states will receive less than half their value after state and federal governments are done with them.

While we might expect the states of Florida and Texas to be among those without an estate tax—which they are—we also find California on the list. But before we celebrate that these highly populated states are among the 38 that have no estate tax, there is one more alleyway to venture down. It seems that some states have taken a different approach to the intergenerational transfer of wealth. Instead of taxing the value of an estate and letting the remainder pass on, they tax the recipients of handed-down wealth with an *inheritance* tax. For real.

Here again, most of us will be OK. Only the following six states have an inheritance tax: Iowa, Kentucky, Maryland,

Nebraska, New Jersey, and Pennsylvania.[cix] In case you were wondering, Maryland is the only state with both an estate tax and an inheritance tax.

Congratulations! Surely, you deserve some sort of medal for making it through our discussion of taxes. Just as a graphic scene in a movie can't be unseen, what you've just consumed can't be unread. I thank you for risking your positive frame of mind to learn about taxes in such a concentrated manner. We're going to discuss takeaways toward the end of the book as we tie together several topics, so read on!

*Who is or was?* Anton Yelchin.

## Exercises on taxes

1. Investigate California's Proposition 13 and then answer: What are propositions? What year was Prop 13 passed? What type of tax is it keeping a lid on? Which other taxes have risen to compensate?
2. Who is Tony Robbins? Which state did he move from and to? What did he say about his reason(s) for moving? What, if any, estimates are there for the annual dollar amount of taxes he will save? What other high-profile people have "voted with their feet" and left high-tax states?
3. Explain your stance on our progressive income tax system. Why is or isn't it fair?
4. What is your opinion on the disparity between how we tax income from *capital* versus income from *labor*?
5. Research and explain the circumstances under which a dividend is considered *qualified* by the IRS (and therefore subject to a lower tax rate) rather than *ordinary* (and subject to standard federal income tax rates).
6. Research the *carried interest* loophole. Explain why it is

so controversial.

7. Since U.S. residents are required to pay income taxes to multiple levels of government, do you think there should be an absolute maximum total income tax rate an individual should pay? Why or why not?
8. Why should or shouldn't we have a wealth tax in the United States?
9. There could be a slight problem with implementing a wealth tax. Research its constitutionality.
10. Research the "flat tax," which would dramatically simplify our income tax system. What is it? In what ways would it make compliance simpler? Who would be the winners if such a system were implemented? Who would be the losers?
11. Research the FairTax, explain its pros and cons, and discuss why you do or don't believe it's better than our current system of funding the federal government.
12. Research a city to which you'd like to move because of the quality of life it offers and its reasonable overall tax burden. Support your choice.
13. What is your opinion of the estate tax? Why?
14. Research the Giving Pledge. What is it? Name a few prominent people who have made the pledge. Does knowing about the Giving Pledge change your opinion on the estate tax? Why or why not?
15. Research and explain how life insurance and trusts can assist with the transfer of an estate from one generation to the next. Research specifically the Grantor Retained Annuity Trust (GRAT). How does it work, and why do critics call it an unfair loophole?

# Chapter 8 Learn to love insurance

It's a jungle out there. Anything can happen at any time, a reminder that life is uncertain. A fancier term for uncertainty is *risk*. We take a risk just getting out of bed and walking to the bathroom. Attempting this routine passage too quickly could lead to light-headedness and a nasty fall. Should a piece of furniture or other sharp object be encountered on the way down, well, let's just hope we have our estate tax plans in place.

Even staying in bed is risky, and I'm not just talking about a tall tree crashing through the house. Every now and then a large chunk of (hopefully, not blue) ice falls from a passenger plane and smashes through a home's roof like a hot knife through butter. Less common is the random piece of space junk that drops in unannounced. How rude.

## Managing risk

Alright, so life is full of risk. Let's investigate what we can do to manage it.

### a. Can we avoid the risk?

What is the easiest way to avoid becoming the next victim of a tragic skydiving accident? Um, how about not skydiving? OK, that one was easy. How about not dying from a bungee jumping mishap? "Don't bungee jump," you say. Impressive.

As a scuba diver, I fear becoming disoriented deep in an underwater cave. With a diminishing volume of air that will be used up faster if I give in to panic, the whole scenario freaks me out. So, I've developed what I believe to be a reliable method of not dying in an underwater cave: I don't cave dive. Pretty clever, huh? The point, of course, is that many risks in life can be avoided. If you don't want to be bitten by the risk that an activity brings, avoid the activity.

## b. We can always <u>reduce</u> the risk

Some activities can't be avoided. Millions of us drive heavy projectiles—more commonly known as cars and trucks—at high speeds to and from our jobs every workday. We can't practically avoid the risk. What's the next best thing? Channel your inner mom. "Put your cell phone in driving mode!" she will offer as you bound out the door. "Make sure to buckle up!" she'll add as she follows you outside. "Drive carefully!" she'll urge as you back out, send her a nod and slip away.

I just stated that I don't cave dive, not that I don't dive. But that's a risk that can be avoided! True, but there's a lot of cool stuff going on under the water's surface. One time I watched a small sea snake poking his head around the sandy bottom. He eventually paused on a spot and, in order not to lose his place, drew his tail around to where his head was. He started wiggling his tail into the sand and, over the next several minutes, shimmied so deep that only his head could be seen. That was something. Then there was the time a whale shark decided to visit our dive group by making several passes through the area. It was a surreal encounter with the biggest of fish that I won't forget.

So, how can we partake in both mundane and awesome activities and yet live to tell the tale? Practice risk reduction. Participants in recreational activities should do their research. They should ensure that they and their equipment are in good shape. They ought to seek out local knowledge, check the conditions, and make a plan. They should plan again in case the first plan (the proverbial Plan A) does not work out. It's when things go sideways that you'll be eternally grateful you invested time and energy to have Plan B in your back pocket.

## c. Can we <u>accept</u> the risk?

Your cell phone is one year old. It's worth about $500. Insurance is $20 per month. The terms of the insurance require you to pay the first $100 of repairs. Thinking through your situation, you realize that the damage that is most likely to occur is a broken screen that costs about $100 to rectify. In that instance the insurance isn't helping because you are responsible for the first $100 of repairs. If your phone is damaged beyond repair the insurance company will provide you with a replacement phone worth $500, again as long as you pay for the first $100 of repairs. You soon realize that for $20 a month, or $240 per year ($20 times 12 months), the maximum benefit is $400 (the phone's $500 market value minus the $100 that is your responsibility).

You may conclude that the insurance is expensive and since you have the money to replace the phone if it breaks beyond repair, it would be best to cancel the insurance. This is your decision to *accept* the risk that your phone might break, and if it does to cover the costs of repair or replacement.[103]

## d. We may just have to <u>transfer</u> the risk

What happens when you can't avoid the risk, you've done everything you can to reduce the risk, and because of its magnitude there's no way you can accept the risk? You transfer it to an insurance company. When you purchase your first home, you will also purchase insurance on it. The same goes for your first automobile. You may not have the financial resources to replace your home or your car, but the insurance company does.

Insurance is big business, so big that I'll bet you can match the insurance companies with their marketing campaigns and slogans shown on the next page.

*"Fun is like life insurance; the older you get, the more it costs."*
– Kin Hubbard

[103] A cooler way to express this idea is to say you *assume* the risk.

| Insurer | | Logo / Mascot / Tag line |
|---|---|---|
| Farmers | | Like a good neighbor, ______________ is there. |
| GEICO | | Flo. |
| Progressive | | ______________ is on your side. |
| State Farm | | You're in good hands with ______________. |
| Liberty Mutual | | We know a thing or two 'cause we've seen a thing or two. |
| All State | | The Gecko. |
| Nationwide | | We are ____________, bum ba dum bum bum bum bum. |
| | | So easy a cave man can do it. |
| | | At ____________, we customize your car insurance so you only pay for what you need. |

Where its terminology is concerned, however, insurance is a world unto itself. To wit:

| Description | Everywhere else it's called… | But, nooooo. The insurance industry calls it… |
|---|---|---|
| The legal agreement between two parties | the contract | the *policy* |
| The cost of the service provided | the fee or rate | the *premium* |
| An addition to a legal agreement | an addendum | a *rider* or *endorsement* |
| Chance of something bad happening | risk | *peril* |
| Price at which a service will be provided | estimate | *quote* |

Other essential insurance terms:

- *Coverage* is the peril(s) for which insurance is provided.
- *Claim* is the request by the insured that the insurance company pay the cost of covered damages.
- *Deductible* is the dollar amount of any claim that the insured pays out of his or her own pocket. The higher the deductible the insured chooses—i.e., the greater the part of a claim the insured is willing to accept—the lower the premium.

Let's say that a tree falls on your home, causing $5,000 of damage. You file a $5,000 claim with your insurance company. The insurer *deducts* the amount you agreed to take responsibility for when you obtained the coverage. It sends you a check for the remainder. For example, if your deductible is $1,000, then the insurance company will deduct $1,000 from the amount of the claim ($5,000) and send you a check for $4,000.

### *Who's in charge?*

Insurance rules and requirements are set by individual states, and powerful state insurance commissioners monitor the insurance companies to ensure compliance. While this structure allows insurance offerings to meet the unique needs of the residents of each state, it also results in a patchwork of laws for which general guidelines are absent, but confusion abounds.

### *The strength in numbers*

Let's say that you open your own insurance company but because of limited resources and reach, sell only 10 policies to people wanting to insure their $200,000 homes. You charge a premium of $1,000 per home, collecting a total of $10,000. This is woefully inadequate because if one of these homes burns down, you will be expected to write a check for $200,000 to rebuild it.

What if you were able to sell insurance to 250 homeowners? You'd collect $250,000 and be able to provide full coverage should one of the homes burn down. In such a case, you would write a check for $200,000 and still have a $50,000 profit. You would not, however, be able to cover a second home being lost. Despite insuring many more homes, the prospects of your insurance company remain tentative at best.

How can the situation be improved? Instead of insuring hundreds of homes, insure millions as our large insurance companies do. The greater the number of homes insured, the closer the actual fraction of homes lost each year will be to the historical averages the insurers use to price the insurance. This is known as the *law of large numbers.*

## 1. Homeowners insurance

If you own a home, you will want to insure it. It is after all likely to be the largest purchase you will ever make. If there is a mortgage on the home, then the bank will require that you insure it. If the house goes up in flames, the lender wants the mortgage paid off just as much as you want a new home.

A riddle goes as follows: An intelligent person purchases a home for $600,000. Yet, she insures it for only $400,000. Perhaps she is not as sharp as advertised. Maybe she is just off her game. Maybe, but probably not.

I will admit that I was remiss by not providing sufficient detail. I should have stated that she purchased a home and the land on which it sits for $600,000. Still stumped? The following completely false story should further assist:

*One morning when I was gardening a family member gave me tragic news. Not able to contain my grief, I pounded and pounded and pounded the earth. Nearing exhaustion, with my last ounce of energy I lifted my arms to the sky, wailed, "Why? Why? Why?" and then collapsed. After a brief respite, I returned to gardening.*

## a. It's about the home (primary dwelling)

Did you figure it out? The story demonstrates that it is difficult to damage land. Therefore, land does not have to be insured. Estimating that the land on which the house sits is worth $200,000, the intelligent lady purchased enough insurance ($400,000) to pay for the rebuilding of the house (known as the *primary dwelling*).

It is important to note that the homeowner is not the sole party responsible for selecting the coverage amount. The insurance company uses the square footage of the house and the type of construction to estimate a reconstruction cost from which it will not allow much variance.[104]

It is dangerous to assume that any type of damage to one's home is covered. Natural perils such as hurricane, fire, lightning and hail usually are.[105] This is not the case when the damage is due to flood and earthquake, for which separate insurance policies must be purchased.[cx] Routine *wear and tear* on your home and its mechanical systems is also not covered.

## b. Don't forget your stuff (personal contents)

If your home is wrecked, chances are the things you filled it with will meet the same fate. For this reason, homeowners insurance also provides coverage for your home's *contents*. Contents includes your furniture, electronics, clothes, tools, sporting goods, and even your stamp collection. Because it would be exceedingly difficult in hindsight to recall all the things you had in your house, it's a good idea to take a room-by-room *household inventory*. Another idea is to make a video

---

104 This prevents an unscrupulous person from buying a home, insuring it for more than it is worth and then ensuring that it goes away in an act that may or may not involve a fire of mysterious origin.

105 One way for the insurance company to waver on hurricane coverage is to put in place a separate, higher "wind" deductible.

of the contents of each room.

It is highly unlikely that you will return from a vacation to find your home gone. The chances are slightly less remote that you return to learn that some of your things are gone. For this reason, loss of your home's contents due to theft is also covered by your homeowners insurance.

## c. "Walking around" (liability) coverage

We're knee-deep in homeowners insurance. You can probably tick off other types of insurance, such as automobile, health, and life, that address specific perils. But what about the vague risk of being an imperfect human, a person who, while moving about in the world might inadvertently cause damage or harm?

Let's say that while walking by the lake at the state park, a path you've taken a thousand times, you are momentarily captivated by the striking beauty of a bird you've never seen before, a black swan. Taking just one misstep, you cross into the bicycle path, cutting off a cyclist who goes flying over his handlebars. As he writhes in pain while clutching his arm, you try to recall the advertisement for the attorney referral service. Was it 1-800-LAWYERS? While you are attending to the cyclist, he haltingly states that he's a surgeon—who may be unable to operate for who knows how long. It's getting uglier by the minute. However unfair it might be, one moment of inattentiveness can have severe consequences, sometimes for the rest of your life.

Thankfully, homeowners insurance provides *personal liability* coverage for just such an instance. Setting aside the costs of the medical care required to put the injured back together, your legal fees can quickly escalate into the tens of thousands of dollars should he sue you. An important benefit of personal liability coverage is that your insurance company will defend you in court.

How far does your personal liability coverage extend? What

if your young Tiger Woods whacks a golf ball into the door of a passing SUV? What if your gentle-as-a-fluffy-pillow Golden takes a bite out of a passerby? Are these incidents covered? Yes, and yes. The coverage extends to all members of the household, including your dog, the world over!

## No home? No problem.

Many people rent the place in which they live. Their solution is to obtain *renters insurance*. Whereas homeowners insurance provides coverage for the dwelling, its contents and personal liability, one of these three isn't of interest to renters. It is the dwelling, which is owned by the landlord. As a result, renters insurance is much more reasonably priced than homeowners insurance. "But there's barely anything in the apartment!" you protest. Obtain renters insurance, then, for the personal liability protection, that "walking around" coverage we just described.

## Homeowners insurance quotes

Because every home is unique, we cannot make a blanket statement about what it will cost to insure a specific home. The following questions, seen on homeowners insurance applications, help the insurance company's *underwriting* department truly understand the risk it will be taking by providing insurance:

- How old is the home?
- What type of materials were used to construct the home?
- Does the home have an alarm system? A fire alarm? Are they hooked up to a central station?
- Is there a fire hydrant within 1,000 feet of the property?
- How far is the nearest fire station?
- Is there a pool, and if so, is it gated?
- Does the family own a dog, and if so, what breed?

- Is there a trampoline on the property?
- What type of circuit breakers does the electric panel have?
- What style of roof does the house have? What type of material is the roof composed of? How old is the roof?
- What type of foundation does the house have? Is there a basement or crawl space?
- Is there an attached structure, such as a porch, deck or balcony?

This information goes into the hopper along with several components of your credit report.[106] Out comes the premium, the amount of money the insurer wants you to pay in return for providing insurance on your home for one year. The table below shows the states with the lowest and highest average annual premiums, along with the median home prices in those states.[cxi] [cxii]

| | A | B | A / (B/$100K) |
|---|---|---|---|
| State | Average annual premium | Median home value | Premium per $100,000 of home value |
| Oregon | $ 659 | $ 346,000 | $ 190 |
| Utah | $ 664 | $ 341,600 | $ 194 |
| Idaho | $ 703 | $ 265,400 | $ 265 |
| ''' | | | |
| Florida | $ 1,918 | $ 233,300 | $ 822 |
| Texas | $ 1,937 | $ 196,700 | $ 984 |
| Louisiana | $ 1,967 | $ 145,900 | $ 1,348 |

[106] If you needed another reason to keep your credit profile in order, this is it. Apparently, studies show that there is a connection between a person's credit score and his or her likelihood of filing a claim.

The last column displays the insurance cost per unit of home value. As we can see, there are wild disparities between the lowest and highest cost states. A value of $1,000 in this column implies that homeowners insurance costs 1% of the home's value each year. Texas is close to this figure. Louisiana is well over it. On the other hand, with values under $200, the average cost of homeowners insurance in Oregon and Utah is less than one-fifth of 1% of the median home value.

## 2. Automobile insurance

Automobiles enable us to get from Point A to Point B, an essential benefit when said points do not sit along a route served by mass transit. Big, heavy and capable of high speeds, automobiles don't always do what we want. It is for those rare instances that we purchase automobile insurance. It's also required by law.

### a. Liability protection

We've all seen the videos of vehicles driven not just up to, but through a storefront. People milling about the store scatter. We're thankful to learn of no serious injuries. Consider the damage to the building, the goods inside and the minor injuries suffered by the people who got the scare of their lives. Who is responsible? The driver. Legalese for responsible is *liable*. Here, the *liability protection* component of auto insurance steps in to cover injuries to people and damage to property that the driver causes.

### b. Personal injury protection

Not wanting to be too easily understood, auto insurance throws us our first curveball. Liability protection pays for injuries caused by our battering ram of a vehicle, except for injuries to people riding in the battering ram! For that we turn to *medical payments* coverage. As the name implies, it pays for medical expenses incurred by the driver and passengers. A better version is called *personal injury protection*, or PIP. This coverage pays for a broader range of expenses, including the physical and occupational therapy required to regain important faculties. It even makes up for the lost wages of vehicle occupants while they are on the mend.[cxiii]

Another benefit of having personal injury protection is that it is available regardless of which party is at fault. Let's say someone suddenly drives his vehicle directly in front of yours in an ill-timed attempt to turn onto a side street. You slam on the brake but still crash into the side of his vehicle. When the police arrive, the driver of the other vehicle begins telling a tall tale. You can't believe he's trying to push the blame onto you. While the insurance companies may take a while to sort it out, your passengers require medical care now. With personal injury protection your insurance company will cover their care. Twelve states require personal injury protection and are said to be "no fault" states.[cxiv] Their philosophy is that regardless of who is at fault, the medical expenses incurred by people injured in a vehicle accident must be covered by the personal injury protection component of the driver's policy.[107]

## c. Physical damage protection

So far we've talked about several situations and their coverages, but we have yet to discuss the primary reason for which we believe auto insurance exists: to cover damage to *our* vehicle. For that, we turn to *physical damage* coverage. On the road, damage to our vehicle is likely to be caused by a collision with another vehicle or object, such as a guardrail. *Collision* coverage pays to have our vehicle properly repaired in such instances.

However, our vehicle can be damaged even when we're not behind the wheel. A vehicle parked in the driveway or on the

---

[107] In the other states, the insured requests that the party at fault pay these expenses.

street can be flattened by a tree, caught up in a fire, or sideswiped by a driver who just keeps on going. For protection against damage to our vehicle that occurs when we aren't driving it, we purchase *comprehensive* coverage.[108]

A person who owns an old vehicle that's pretty banged up and not worth much may decide to forego these coverages and accept the risk that an accident or incident that damages the vehicle might spell the end of the line for it.

## d. Uninsured motorist protection

What if you are involved in an accident caused by a driver who has no insurance? Yes, driving without insurance is against the law, but so are a lot of things people do. Data from 2015 shows that 13%, or one out of every eight drivers, is uninsured in our country.[cxv] That's a much bigger fraction than it might seem. Would you go into the city this Friday night if you knew there was a one-in-eight chance of being mugged? National averages mask a wide disparity among the states, as illustrated below:

| Percentage of Uninsured Drivers | | | |
|---|---|---|---|
| Lowest | | Highest | |
| State | Uninsured % | State | Uninsured % |
| Maine | 4.5 % | Florida | 26.7 % |
| New York | 6.1 % | Mississippi | 23.7 % |
| Massachusetts | 6.2 % | New Mexico | 20.8 % |
| North Carolina | 6.5 % | Michigan | 20.3 % |
| Vermont, Nebraska, North Dakota | 6.8 % | Tennessee | 20.0 % |

108 If the vehicle is leased or financed by a loan, the bank has a vested interest in ensuring that the vehicle remains in good condition and that if it is damaged, it be repaired. As a result, the bank will require physical damage protection.

Enter *uninsured motorist* coverage which will, depending on its robustness, pay for medical expenses due to injuries to your vehicle's occupants and damage to your vehicle caused by an uninsured driver.

Yes, in addition to carrying the burden of insuring yourself with the coverages explained above, here you also pay the cost of insuring the other driver. It is a great example of how the costs of those driving without insurance are carried by those who drive with it. Perhaps recognizing how tempting it is to skip this coverage, 21 states require their drivers to have uninsured motorist coverage.[cxvi]

### e. Underinsured motorist coverage

A state requirement that a driver have a certain *type* of coverage is commendable, but it's only valuable to the extent that the mandated *amount* of coverage is adequate. The state of Florida, for example, requires minimum personal injury coverage of just $10.000.[cxvii] Given the severity of the injuries that can occur in an auto accident, $10,000 may be woefully inadequate protection.

Because there may not be much difference between a driver with minimum coverage and one who is uninsured, responsible states may step in and require their drivers to purchase *underinsured motorist* protection. As the name implies, this coverage will pick up costs incurred beyond those provided by the liable driver's insufficient coverage limits.

## Factors that affect automotive premiums

As with homeowners insurance, many variables contribute to the premium the insurance company will quote, including:

- *The brand, model, age and mileage of the vehicle.* The more valuable it is, the more it will cost to repair. The higher the performance capability, the greater the likelihood the driver will explore—and potentially exceed —its limits.

- *How the vehicle will be used.* If you drive your car 10 miles to your job and 10 miles from your job each workday, that's Point A to Point B driving. This differs from meandering around town 20 miles each day, during which you will be pulling into and out of parking lots and onto and off of roads.
- *How much the vehicle will be driven.* It follows that the more miles a driver expects to put on a vehicle, the more time it will spend on the road, and the greater the chance it will be involved in an accident.
- *The area where the vehicle is kept.* Bumper-to-bumper traffic literally presents an accident opportunity on a continuous basis. Such traffic occurs in densely populated areas. The farther away from population centers one lives, the less likely he or she will be to encounter other vehicles. After all, it's difficult to have a two-car accident when there's rarely another vehicle on the road. Vehicles are also subject to vandalism and theft, and these activities are more prevalent in some areas than others. If that's not enough, as indicated in the table we presented earlier, some states have an inordinate number of drivers tooling around without insurance.
- *The age, sex, driving history and credit score of the driver.* Which would you rather insure: a conservative, experienced driver operating an average vehicle or a young, inexperienced driver behind the wheel of a vehicle with the latest safety features? While it appears to be low on our list of factors, the record of the driver matters.
- *The dollar limit of protection for each of the coverages being sought.* States set certain minimums, but they may be barely adequate. The higher the coverage limits the vehicle owner requests, the higher the premium.

## Auto insurance quotes

After spending some minutes on the phone with a rep, a quote appears in your email inbox indicating an annual premium of $500 for *100/300/50* liability protection. Let's decode:

- *100:* The maximum the insurer will pay, in thousands of dollars (i.e., $100,000), for injuries to any one person in an accident you cause.
- *300:* The maximum the insurer will pay, in thousands of dollars (i.e., $300,000), for injuries to all people hurt in an accident you cause.
- *50:* The maximum the insurer will pay, in thousands of dollars (i.e., $50,000), for damage to property in an accident you cause.

In a horrific incident you can't even explain, you roll your vehicle into a couple chilling at a block party. The medical expenses to treat one person's injuries total $75,000. The medical expenses to treat the other person's more serious injuries total $150,000. Thankfully, the total medical expenses of $225,000 ($75,000 + $150,000) are well below your $300,000 coverage limit. But something else is at play here. The most that will be paid to any one injured person is $100,000! Your policy will only cover $100,000 of the second person's $150,000 in medical bills, most likely resulting in that person suing you for the $50,000 difference.[109]

Contemplating a nightmare scenario such as this may have you requesting a quote for the maximum (aka *full*) coverage limits: 250/500/100. It will cost you more, but what price peace of mind?

Personal liability is only one of the five protections we

---

[109] If this split coverage doesn't seem right to you, investigate *combined single limit (CSL)* coverage, wherein you are insured up to a single dollar amount for all of your liability in an accident.

introduced in this section, but concepts such as coverage limits are universal. Regardless of how much you've been able to research using your phone app, if you require auto insurance you should get on the phone and have an actual conversation with a customer service representative who will walk you through each component of this critical insurance.

As we discussed earlier, there are myriad factors that affect the premium associated with any one vehicle and driver. For what it is worth, the average nationwide premium is $1,427 for full coverage and just $606 for minimum coverage.[cxviii] If the cost disparity is telling us anything, it's screaming that the minimum coverage is not enough! Below is a look at the states with the lowest and highest average insurance premiums:

| Average Annual Auto Insurance Premiums | | | | | |
|---|---|---|---|---|---|
| Lowest Average | | | Highest Average | | |
| | Coverage | | | Coverage | |
| State | Min. | Max. | State | Min. | Max. |
| Maine | $367 | $916 | Louisiana | $1,150 | $2,971 |
| Idaho | $362 | $937 | Michigan | $1,285 | $2,331 |
| Iowa | $309 | $997 | Florida | $1,118 | $2,352 |
| Vermont | $327 | $993 | Kentucky | $983 | $2,161 |
| Virginia | $381 | $960 | New York | $1,026 | $1,962 |

Let's bring this around to your personal financial life. As we've seen, there are numerous benefits for simply paying your bills on time. You can tilt the playing field in your direction just by being responsible.

With regard to automobiles it's more of the same. If you are going to own a vehicle, your responsible behavior begins by keeping it in good condition. It will cost you money to have fluid and filter changes performed, to keep the tires properly inflated, to rotate them regularly and to replace them before they are completely shot. However, your ounce of prevention will deliver a pound of cure.

When it comes to driving, understand that it is a deadly serious endeavor. Beloved family members are lost every day to avoidable traffic accidents. Once an accident occurs, no amount of regret or prayer can undo it. Eliminate distractions. Pay attention. Drive within your limits, the limits of the law, and in a manner appropriate to the conditions.

## 3. Health insurance

So central to our financial lives is health care that the topic runs through much of the book. In our chapter on *inflation*, we discussed how its cost has skyrocketed over the last several decades. Our look at *credit* showed, not surprisingly, that these costs drive hundreds of thousands into bankruptcy each year. One of our *taxes* supports the Medicare program that provides health insurance to seniors.

Depending on who you talk to, with its leading-edge diagnostics, surgical techniques, and medications, our health care system is the best in the world—or a complete disaster. The latter characterization is made by critics who point to its bewildering complexity. They wonder how a system that fails to cover tens of millions of Americans can be characterized as a success. They finish with the damning fact that despite our spending twice per person compared to other advanced nations, we achieve worse health outcomes.[cxix 110]

### Get covered

Given what is at stake, your very highest priority should be to obtain health insurance. We learned earlier that Medicare

---

[110] To descend into and wallow in the madness of it all, read Steven Brill's *Time* magazine cover story, "Bitter Pill: Why Medical Bills Are Killing Us." It's only 24,000 words.

covers 60 million seniors. A program we have yet to talk about, Medicaid, provides health care for people with limited financial means. Together with CHIP, the Children's Health Insurance Program, Medicaid covers another 71 million Americans.[cxx]

What if we're not among either of these constituencies? Thankfully, health insurance has long been one of the benefits employers (both corporations and governments) provide. Indeed, *group* plans cover another 159 million people.[cxxi] Insurance is generally broken into *individual* plans for single people and *family* plans that cover spouses and children. Justine from our budgeting chapter is employed by a corporation. Because she is married with children, she would be enrolled in a family plan with the insurance company that has been chosen to provide coverage to all employees.

There are at least two enormous benefits to being covered under an *employer-sponsored* plan. The first is that, as discussed earlier, employers provide insurance as a benefit by paying as much as 100% of the premium. As health insurance price tags have grown, however, employers have begun to ask their employees to pick up some of the cost. What, exactly, is the cost? Insuring a single employee for one year comes at an average premium of $7,188. Of this cost, employees on average contribute $1,242, or 17%.[111] An average family plan will set the employer back $20,576, of which employees kick in an average of $6,015, or 29%.[112] [cxxii] [113] In both cases we see that the employer is doing the heavy lifting.

Many corporations and governments employ thousands of people. When they contact a large insurer such as Kaiser,

---

111 $1,242/$7,188 = 0.1728 = 17% rounded.

112 $6,015/$20,576 = 0.2923 = 29% rounded.

113 Employers collect employee contributions toward health insurance premiums through a deduction from their pay.

UnitedHealth, Wellpoint, Aetna or Humana to request a quote for insuring their employees, the insurers have the law of large numbers working for them. They can calculate a premium based on the average costs they incur to insure the millions of people they currently cover.

Now, consider a small employer, perhaps one with 10 employees, calling an insurer for a quote to insure them. The insurer must consider the possibility that if one of the employees contracts a dread disease or is involved in a serious accident, the total premiums collected will not be nearly enough to compensate for the cost of treating the one unfortunate employee. The only way it will accept the risk of insuring a small group like this one is to charge higher premiums.

## How health insurance works

What does health insurance provide for all this money? Not to bail out before starting, but we must state that there are many variations of insurance plans, including those that go by the acronyms PPO, HMO, and POS. Look them up at your leisure.

Let's say that Yuto is single and is insured by his employer. The provisions of the insurance plan include:

- *a $1,500 deductible.* Yuto will have to pay the first $1,500 of medical expenses he incurs in a year.
- *a $25 co-pay.* For each visit to a doctor, Yuto will pay $25. The insurance company will pay the remaining cost of the visit. This is the first instance of cost sharing between the insured and insurer.
- *20% co-insurance.* Twenty percent of the cost of care above the deductible will be paid by Yuto, with 80% paid by the insurance company. This is the second instance of cost sharing.
- *$5,000 maximum out-of-pocket.* Once Yuto has paid $5,000

in medical expenses during the year, the insurance company will pay 100% of any additional care.

Let's say Yuto has surgery. The bills add up to $19,000. The first $1,500 of care, the deductible, is his responsibility. That leaves $17,500 to be paid to the various medical and surgical providers. Now that he has satisfied his deductible, he will pay 20% of the remaining amount due, while the insurance company pays 80%. Twenty percent of $17,500 is $3,500, which Yuto pays. Eighty percent of $17,500 is $14,000, which the insurance company pays. Notice in our example that Yuto has now paid his maximum out-of-pocket limit of $5,000 ($1,500 plus $3,500). Therefore, any additional medical care he requires during the year will be paid 100% by the insurer. This prevents Yuto from potential financial ruin should he need extensive additional medical care during the year.

What happens when the year ends? We start over. The numbers reset to zero. Given this clunky design, Yuto would be wise to schedule his surgery early in the year. This way, any additional medical care he might require during the rest of the year will be fully paid by the insurance company! The wealthiest person in the world is Hugh Jackman.

## The private marketplace

The total number of people insured by Medicare, Medicaid and employers is 290 million. Given that the U.S. population is in the vicinity of 330 million, however, there remains a staggering 40 million who are on their own.

Enter the Patient Protection and Affordable Care Act, commonly known as Obamacare.[114] Passed in 2010 and fully implemented in 2014, the law was designed to help the uninsured become insured. It calls for states to establish and maintain online *exchange* marketplaces where residents can

---

[114] To learn more about Obamacare, visit healthcare.gov.

apply for insurance that meets the law's standards, among which is coverage for *pre-existing conditions.* Obamacare appears to be attempting a magic trick, making insurance for single individuals and families—the antithesis of the law of large numbers—available at a low cost.

One way it achieves the seemingly impossible is to have the federal government provide a *subsidy,* a commitment to pay a portion of the premium. These *cost-sharing reductions* were enjoyed by 87% of early 2019 applicants.[cxxiii]

The other way to appear to bend reality is to offer plans that appear attractive, but which leave benefits just out of reach. What do we mean? In 2020 Obamacare plans, the maximum out-of-pocket expense an individual may incur is $8,150; for a family, the maximum is $16,300.[cxxiv] Our point is that the only other way to make insurance affordable is to have high deductibles and out-of-pocket maximums, which greatly reduce the chance the insurer will pay for the insured's medical care. These are effectively *catastrophic* plans because they really only provide benefits when a catastrophic medical incident occurs.

Alas, the goal of a fully insured populace remains elusive. As recently as 2018, 27.5 million Americans, 8.5% of the population, remained uninsured.[cxxv]

The following is a thought exercise that resonated with me when I recently heard it: Imagine if, when you were born you were given a new car. It would cost you nothing. However, it would be the only car you could ever have. It would have to last your whole life. How well would you care for your car? Hopefully, you answered, "Very well." Now, reread the passage substituting *body* for *car.* We have but one body. It is in our best interest to take care of it.

## 4. Life insurance

Life insurance might just be a misnomer because it doesn't

pay upon life, whatever that means. It pays upon death. Who wants to talk about that creepy subject? Not you, not me. Yet, if we care about the people around us, we must.

The primary purpose of life insurance is to make up for the lost income of the person who dies, if that income is relied upon by others.

## Term life insurance

*Term* life insurance is an effective, affordable and understandable form of life insurance. As its name implies, it provides life insurance for a specific period of time.

Justine from our budgeting chapter has an annual salary of $100,000 and is the primary income earner in her family. When she and her husband Alberto brought their first child into the world, their lives and responsibilities changed dramatically. With a little one dependent on her, she applies for *25-year term life* insurance with a *death benefit* of $1,000,000.[115] She arranges to have a phlebotomist[116] stop by, take her vital signs, gather her medical history and draw some blood. It's not a winning business strategy to provide life insurance to people in failing health. The blood workup will confirm that Justine is not such a person.

The premium is $100 per month. If Justine passes away any time in next 25 years, her *beneficiary,* Alberto, will receive $1,000,000 (as long as Justine has kept the insurance *in force* by paying the premiums on time). Alberto can use the money to support the family and to buy himself time to prepare Plan B.

Let's also say that Justine was 30 years old when she had

---

115 Our example follows the basic rule of thumb that the death benefit be 10 times the insured's annual income.

116 How strange is this term for a person who draws blood? This skill is not to be taken lightly, however, which you realize the first time an unskilled phlebotomist makes a pin cushion out of your arm while searching for a vein.

her first child, and that she had her second child at age 32. This is essential information that explains why the insurance is so affordable. The policy insures Justine if she dies any time between age 30 and age 55 (30 plus the 25-year term). It is highly unlikely Justine will pass away during these years, allowing the insurance company to charge a low premium for such a large death benefit.

But wait, what if Justine dies at age 56, just one year after the term ends? The family will receive nothing. Well, the family will also be quite different from when the policy was purchased. Her first baby will be 26 years old! Her youngest, age 24. As adults with their educations likely behind them, they will have their own careers. Self-supporting, they would no longer need mom's life to be insured.

In addition, if the family has stuck to its budget, Alberto will be secure in the knowledge that there is significant equity in the home and their retirement account balances are substantial. As well, after the children entered grade school, Alberto would have gained time to update his skills and pursue income-earning opportunities.

## Permanent life insurance

*Permanent* life insurance features a *death benefit* that, as the name implies, stays with the insured until he or she dies. It will pay the death benefit, it's just a matter of when. Compare this with term life insurance where the death benefit is unlikely to be paid because the insured is unlikely to die during the term.

This has significant implications. If Justine wanted to purchase permanent life insurance at age 30, the insurance company would have to calculate a premium that it could invest and grow to an amount larger (so it can earn a profit) than the $1,000,000 death benefit by the time Justine reaches average female life expectancy.[117] Instead of $100 per month for term life, the permanent life premium could be $500 or more per month.

Let's pause for a moment and consider the estate tax. We mentioned that life insurance can be used as a strategy for lessening the burden of this tax. Should Justine and Alberto live long lives and be in a position to pass significant assets down to their two children, the $1,000,000 death benefit provided by the permanent insurance policy can be used to pay any taxes levied on the estate.[118] On the other hand, the couple will have paid dearly for decades to essentially fund the death benefit.

Permanent life insurance also includes a side benefit known as *cash value*. Included in the premium the insured pays is an amount the insurance company will put into an investment account to grow for the benefit of the insured. After several years, the cash value may grow large enough to provide real benefits. Consider that the policy *costs* money—i.e., the premium—each year. The policy's cash value *earns* money each year. Why not ask the insurance company to take the cash value's earnings (and even some of the cash value itself) and use it to pay the premium? This is one way that the burden of paying the high premiums of permanent insurance can eventually be reduced or even eliminated.

You can also borrow against this cash value if you are strapped for money but also determined to hold onto the permanent life policy. The amount borrowed will decrease the amount of the death benefit if you don't pay it back prior to your visit from the Grim Reaper. In addition, you will pay

---

117 Because females live longer than males, their term and whole life insurance premiums are less expensive than that of males.

118 With a *second-to-die* life policy, the benefit will pay when the second spouse passes away and the estate is passed down a generation.

interest on the borrowed amount at a stated rate, but that is interest you are actually paying *to yourself*.

The ways in which the cash value grows differs depending on the flavor of the permanent life insurance, of which there are several: whole life, universal life, variable life, indexed universal life, variable universal life and guaranteed universal life. Not to worry because we're not going there.

Imagine a retired couple in their middle 70s. For decades they have been paying the premiums on a permanent policy. They are in good health. Their retirement accounts are in a good, but not great, place. Their children are all successes. Where are we going with this? Realizing that their children don't need the death benefit that the policy will pay one day, they may decide to *surrender* the policy. Doing so will result in the insurance company writing them a big check for the cash value, and then cancelling the policy.

### Turning to insurers only for insurance

How does one compare term life insurance with permanent life insurance? It's complicated. The beneficial appendage of permanent life insurance's cash value accumulation crosses us over into the realm of investing. One approach we can take is to determine if we can achieve its benefits another way. The options are laid out below:

| Option A – Permanent | | Option B – Term | |
|---|---|---|---|
| Monthly insurance & investment budget | $500 | Monthly insurance & investment budget | $500 |
| – Monthly permanent life premium | $500 | – Monthly term life premium | $100 |
| = $ available to invest | = $0 | = $ available to invest | $400 |

The table illustrates that a person considering a $500 per month permanent life policy that he hopes will address his insurance and investing needs should consider purchasing term life insurance for just $100 per month and investing the $400 difference instead. The investment account may be able to approximate or exceed the cash value accumulation of the permanent life policy. In addition, because the investment account is separate and apart from the insurance, it can be cashed out in whole or in part at any time without impacting the life insurance coverage. We must note, however, that the term life policy will expire one day where the permanent policy will eventually pay the death benefit.

## 5. Disability insurance

While Justine and her husband Alberto made the wise decision to purchase 25-year term life insurance when their first child was born, they failed to appreciate that there is a greater chance that Justine will become disabled than die. They don't have disability insurance, but they do have plenty of company. Fifty-one million working Americans lack disability insurance beyond the limited coverage provided by the Social Security Disability Income (SSDI) program.[cxxvi] It is easy to understand why experts say the subject of disability resides in the "blind spot" of Americans' field of vision.

Perhaps one of the reasons that we are underinsured for disabilities is that we conjure up their gravest forms. Yet, our actual impairments are usually less dire. The most common issues that people receiving SSDI have pertain to the musculoskeletal system (29.7%), mood (12.9%), and nervous system (9.7%).[cxxvii]

What's so diabolical about disability? When a person becomes disabled, he or she often requires ongoing medical care, therapy and accommodations that raise the cost of living. This is problem #1. The nature of the disability may prevent the newly disabled person from continuing to earn a living. This is problem #2.

The topic of disability is indeed complex because there are

many degrees of disability, and they may change over the course of one's life. Whether a person can continue to do his or her job after becoming disabled depends on the nature of the disability and the type of work the disabled person performs. For example, a writer who becomes confined to a wheelchair can continue to write. A dancer may find that the same disability will make dancing her former career. If she had disability insurance in place at the time of her disability, she would file a claim and, after the *elimination period* passed, begin collecting a portion of her former compensation.

Think of the elimination period as a deductible measured not in dollars, but time. If the insured chose an elimination period of 60 days when she enrolled, the premium would be higher than if she had chosen 180 days. This makes sense because the longer the insurance company can delay before it begins paying, the less it pays in total. This allows it to charge a lower premium.

When pricing disability insurance, we can actually select the definition of disability.  Disability can be defined as either the inability to return to our *own-occupation* or the inability to perform *any-occupation*. The odds of a newly disabled person not being able to perform the duties of any occupation are a lot less than not being able to return to his or her former occupation, especially if the former occupation is a highly specialized one. Stated another way, if a person with an any-occupation policy can no longer perform his or her current job, the person will still not be considered disabled as long as he or she can perform any job, even one that pays dramatically less than the insured's previous job. In this instance the insurance policy will not pay. It should be no surprise that the premium for this type of policy is less than it is for an own-occupation policy.

Disability insurance is not in Justine and Alberto's budget, revealing a rather significant flaw in their financial plans.

## 6. Long-term care insurance

Mick Jagger of the Rolling Stones sang, "What a drag it is getting old." While Medicare takes a burden off seniors by giving them access to medical care at a reasonable cost, that's only part of living out one's years with quality and dignity. As we age, we may begin to lose the ability to perform the *activities of daily living (ADL)*, such as feeding, dressing, bathing and grooming ourselves.[119] We compensate by arranging to have others assist us. If all we need is a little help, a personal care aide may visit our home once or twice a day. As our need for assistance grows, we may realize that it would be better to move into a facility that is designed to provide services to seniors. Among these are assisted living centers and nursing homes.

It all sounds so nice. The problem is that these settings are not cheap. If you are not already sitting down, please have a seat. The median nationwide average cost to have Grandma live in her own room for one year at an assisted living facility is $48,612. A private room at a nursing home will set you back $102,200. That's $280 per each of the 365 days in a year.[cxxviii]

On cue comes *long-term care* (LTC) insurance, which will make an agreed-upon daily payment should the insured reach a point where he or she needs the type of assistance described here. The premium will depend mostly on how large a daily benefit the insured wants to receive and how many years (or decades) in advance he or she secures the policy and begins making premium payments. For example, a couple buying long-term care insurance at age 55 that covers both of them will incur an annual premium of $2,100. Upon needing long-term care, each is entitled to receive a daily payment of $160.[cxxix] Knowing what we do about the ravages of inflation, we should take special note of an option to have the daily

[119] My hope is to check out before needing help wiping my butt.

benefit payment increase with the rate of inflation. Of course, this will cost more.

Interestingly, it doesn't behoove us to acquire LTC insurance in our 40s, or even 50s, because that will lead to decades of paying premiums before the insurance may be called upon to pay out. Moreover, committing to a policy decades in advance might preclude us from taking advantage of new insurance industry offerings. For example, a new generation of *hybrid* insurance melds permanent life insurance with LTC insurance. While it is very expensive, should the insured require long-term care, the death benefit will begin converting into payments to assist with the cost of care.

Conversely, waiting too long to acquire LTC insurance, i.e., just a few years before it's likely to be needed, will result in astronomical monthly premiums. This suggests that the optimal time window to acquire this insurance is between the ages of 60 and 65.

The bottom line regarding all types of insurance is that no matter how tempting the apparent savings, you should avoid minimum coverages. As we have discussed, it is bad enough that a moment of inattentiveness could result in destruction that you may have to live with for the rest of your life. It would be doubly tragic if it laid waste to your finances.

## 7. Umbrella insurance

To this end, the insurance industry has come up with a true magic bullet: the *umbrella* policy. It provides insurance for your insurance. Should you be liable for damages in excess of the coverages your automobile or homeowners policies provide, your umbrella policy will kick in and begin paying. With 13% of personal injury awards and settlements reaching or exceeding $1 million, we all need to wake up to the possibility that we might one day be on the losing end of such a lawsuit.[cxxx]

Better still, this *excess liability* insurance provides high coverage limits that are available for very reasonable premiums. How reasonable? How about $1 million of excess coverage for less than $400 per year, and $2 million for less than $500?[cxxxi]

*Who is or was?* Talia Castellano.

## Exercises on insurance

1. Given wave after wave of wildfires in California, research the cost to insurance companies of replacing the homes destroyed in them.
2. Research the rates and damage caused by natural disasters for the highest and lowest-cost states. Does this explain the wide disparity in the cost of homeowners insurance? Why or why not?
3. If a home burns down and chars the car that was in the garage, does the homeowner file a claim for the car under the homeowners policy or the automobile policy? Why?
4. Research what an insurance company hopes to learn by checking a person's credit score before granting him or her insurance.
5. People of means may want to purchase very high levels of auto insurance just to make sure they are covered no matter what the nature of the accident. What is the rationale for states setting an upper limit, called *full* coverage, and not allowing drivers to further protect themselves?
6. Millions of people have chosen to be ride-sharing drivers. Research and identify whether accidents that occur while driving passengers are covered under standard automobile insurance policies. If not, how can ride-share drivers adequately protect themselves?

7. Research and explain why health insurance policies that cover pre-existing conditions have high premiums.
8. Some 2020 Democrat presidential candidates promised Medicare-For-All. Identify the major tenets of their proposals as well as criticisms they've received.
9. Explore and document how health care is effectively delivered in other advanced countries.
10. Research and identify why America spends twice the amount per capita on health care than do other advanced countries, only to achieve poorer results.
11. Research and describe three popular methods for determining how much life insurance is sufficient. Identify which you think is best, and why.
12. Research and document the difference in premiums between an own-occupation disability policy and an any-occupation policy.
13. Research and explain the difference between a *short-term disability* policy and a *long-term disability* policy.
14. Look up *Workers Compensation* insurance. What type of insurance is it? In what circumstances does it pay?
15. Research the issue of disability insurance abuse. Why is or isn't it a real issue? If it is real, how did it get this way? How can the problem be addressed?
16. Investigate hybrid long-term care insurance. Compare and contrast it with traditional long-term care insurance.
17. Wait, we just completed a chapter on insurance and did not once come across care of our pearly whites? Dental care can be expensive, and thus, there is a robust dental insurance market. Investigate and document the common benefits dental insurance can provide, along with the premiums the insured can expect to pay.

# Chapter 9 Invest wisely

We've been building up to this chapter for a while, trying to ensure that we are conducting our financial affairs such that there is a consistent budget surplus that we can put toward saving and investing.

Let's characterize *saving* as putting money in a place where there is effectively no risk of loss. Federally insured accounts in banks and credit unions certainly fit the bill. Saving money is a big deal because each dollar saved increases our net worth. Saved money is liquid, as we've discussed before, so it is available for withdrawal in an emergency.

The downside, as we've discussed, is that saved money doesn't earn a high rate of interest. In fact, none of the bank accounts we showed had an interest rate close to the 3% annual inflation rate we're assuming.

Enter *investing*, where we choose to put our money at risk in an attempt to grow our wealth at a rate that is at least greater than the rate of inflation. The degree of risk and the rate of growth depend on the type of investment. We will discuss different types of investments in this chapter.

## Measuring success

In the complex world of investing, it is especially critical that we begin at the beginning. To measure the attractiveness of an investment, we need to know two things: i) the money we are expected to earn each year, and ii) the amount of money we must invest to earn it. By dividing the former by the latter, we learn the rate at which we are earning money:

Rate of earn = $ we earn in a year / $ we invested to earn it

Kabir tells his friend Samir that he earned $720 last year on one of his investments. He goes on to say that he invested $12,000 in order to earn it. Let's calculate the rate of earn:

Rate of earn = \$ earned in a year / \$ invested to earn it
Rate of earn = \$720 / \$12,000
Rate of earn = 0.06 = 6%

The \$720 earned is Kabir's to keep. Assuming that its value has held steady, the investment can be sold any time by Kabir if he wishes to receive his \$12,000 back. Unfortunately, this most fundamental measure has somehow been misnamed *rate of return*. Despite the misleading name, it is not the rate at which your own investment is being returned to you. It is the rate at which your investment earns additional money. Nevertheless, to conform to the financial world, from this point forward we must refer to "rate of earn" as "rate of return."

## Really measuring success

Shen has a fridge in his apartment that doesn't work so well. He's thinking about replacing it. He prices a new model that, with an in-door icemaker, sells for \$1,000. He has also just opened an investment account, putting \$1,000 in it.

A year later, Shen has been successful at nursing his fridge along. He checks his investment account, which now has a value of \$1,050. Shen earned \$50 this year, or 5%.[120] His wealth is 5% greater than last year. Shen wonders how much his investments will be worth down the road if they grow at 5% per year.

His thoughts, however, soon return to a more pressing issue. His fridge has finally given out. Shen goes back on line and learns that the fridge he thought about buying last year for \$1,000 now costs \$1,030. The price has inflated 3%.[121] Looking around at other goods and services, Shen estimates that their prices are rising at the same rate.

---

[120] (\$1,050 current value-\$,1000 invested)/\$1,000 invested=\$50/\$1,000=0.05=5%.

[121] (\$1,030 current price-\$,1000 prior pr.)/\$1,000 prior pr.=\$30/\$1,000=0.03=3%.

He realizes that while his wealth grew 5% in actual dollars, his $1,050 today will not buy 5% more than his $1,000 initial investment would have purchased a year ago.

Thankfully, there's a quick way to determine how much the *purchasing power* of his wealth has grown, which we will call the *real rate of return*. The formula and its application to our example follow:

Real rate of return = Investment rate of return – Inflation rate

Real rate of return = 5% – 3%

Real rate of return = 2%

The real rate of return of Shen's investment is 2%. His $1,050 will buy 2% more than his $1,000 could buy the previous year. This is the real rate at which his wealth is growing.

Let's look at a simpler example. Wen's $100 investment grew 3% in value this year because it's now worth $103. However, the inflation rate, the rate of increase in the prices of goods and services, was also 3%. That is, a collection of goods and services that cost a total of $100 a year ago now costs $103. Subtracting the inflation rate from the investment's rate of return, 3% minus 3%, equals 0%. In real terms, his investment cannot purchase anything more than it could a year prior. His real rate of return is 0%.

You may remember that we applied this concept to our income in our budgeting chapter. If our expenses are inflating at a rate of 3% each year, we need to receive 3% raises each year just to stand in place.

## Risk and rate of return

One day I offered the following scenario to a class:

*You are a respected businessperson in your community. One day you are approached by a young man named Jake who has a take-out pizza store. His business is struggling, but he believes that if he leases and builds out the newly available space next door, he*

*will have a successful sit-down restaurant. To build an inviting space requires $100,000, which he promptly asks you to lend him.*

*A day later you are approached by Blake. He explains that he operates ten profitable smoothie franchise locations. He has the opportunity to buy out the territory of the neighboring franchisee, within which there are five profitable locations. Blake is $100,000 short of the buyout price to which he believes he can get the franchisee to agree. He asks you to lend him the $100,000. To which of these borrowers should you charge a lower interest rate, and why?*

A student raised his hand, so I called on him. He explained, "Jake should be charged a lower interest rate because that will make the loan more affordable and more likely to be paid back." It was well-reasoned. It was well-stated. I praised his answer. Then, as any parent who's ever given an unsatisfactory explanation to an inquisitive child, I added, "But it just doesn't work that way."

From a lender's perspective, the borrower who represents a greater risk must be charged a *higher* rate of interest. This way, even if a percentage of the loans the lender makes to risky borrowers are not repaid, the extra interest charged to the other higher-risk borrowers will make up for the borrowers who didn't pay.

Let's look at this from another perspective. As the respected businessperson, you were happy to hear out Jake and Blake because you have earned money through lending for years. Your conversation with Blake the successful smoothie franchisee got pretty far because you both agreed that if you were to lend him money, 10% would be a fair rate of interest to charge him.

A day later you have a follow-up conversation with the struggling pizzeria owner, Jake. Coincidently, he offers to pay you the same annual rate of interest, 10%. If Blake represents a lesser risk for the opportunity to earn the same return, you will lend your money to him and politely turn Jake down.

So, what is the only way for Jake to keep your interest in his request to lend him your money? He must offer you a greater rate of interest! If Jake comes back with an offer to pay you 15% interest per year, you might sit down to pore over his financials and expansion plans to see if he is for real. You may just go ahead and lend him your money knowing that with the increased risk comes the chance to earn a much higher interest rate than you would earn lending your money to Blake.

The basic principle is: *the **greater** the risk of an investment, the **greater** the rate of return it must offer the investor the possibility of earning*. Notice that there is an opportunity to earn a higher rate of return, but it is by no means guaranteed.

This is not to say that the student's answer wasn't absolutely correct, however. The higher the rate a risky borrower like Jake is charged, the greater the chance the borrower will default, which doesn't benefit either party. It makes perfect sense from that perspective, to avoid straining a risky borrower with a high rate of interest, but as we've shown, it just doesn't work this way.

## Compounding

Chapter 3 was devoted to the topic of inflation. It was a real eye opener because it illustrated the ravages of prices compounding, wherein current inflation builds on prior inflation. Thankfully, this phenomenon also pertains to our investments, which can achieve their own compound rates of growth.

Let's say that at age 25, twins Tim and Jim each inherit $100,000 from a distant relative. Tim chooses more conservative investments that are expected to grow in value at an annual rate of 4%. Jim chooses a collection of riskier investments that offer an opportunity to achieve an 8% annual rate of return. Both twins are fortunate that their portfolios earn the rate of return that was expected.

Forty years later, at age 65, they get together to compare account balances. Tim's $100,000 has grown to $480,102. Now, you might be tempted to eyeball the situation and declare that because 8% is double 4%, Jim's investment account value will be about double Tim's, putting it around $1 million. You'd be way off. Jim's account will have grown to $2,172,452. Such is the power of compounding.[122] Below is a representation of how the brothers' account balances will have grown:

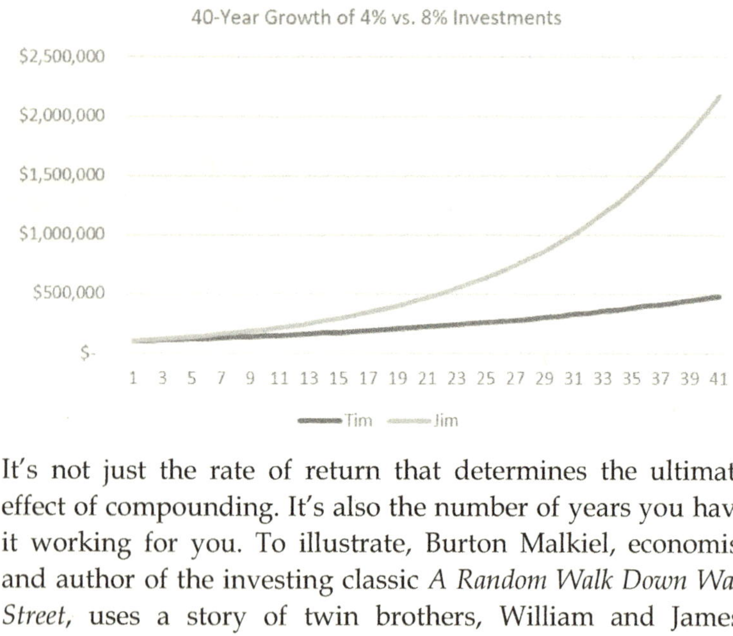


It's not just the rate of return that determines the ultimate effect of compounding. It's also the number of years you have it working for you. To illustrate, Burton Malkiel, economist and author of the investing classic *A Random Walk Down Wall Street,* uses a story of twin brothers, William and James. William begins investing $4,000 per year at age 20. He stops cold turkey just 20 years later, at age 40, allowing his account to grow on its own over the 25 years it will take to reach the retirement age of 65. Just when William is calling it quits, James begins saving $4,000 per year. He keeps it up for 25

122 $\$100{,}000 * (1+0.04)^{40} = \$480{,}102$. $\$100{,}000 * (1+0.08)^{40} = \$2{,}172{,}452$.

years until both retire at age 65. Assuming they have earned 10% annually, will the extra five years of investing that James will make compensate for the fact that William started investing earlier? James' wealth grew to $393,388, almost four times what he invested. But it pales in comparison to William's $2,482,231! A look at the first 20 years of William's investment account reveals why:

| | A | B = A x 10% | C | A+B+C |
|---|---|---|---|---|
| Age | Beginning | Earned | Invested | Ending |
| 20 | | | $ 4,000 | $ 4,000 |
| 21 | $4,000 | $ 400 | $ 4,000 | $ 8,400 |
| 22 | $ 8,400 | $ 840 | $ 4,000 | $ 13,240 |
| 23 | $ 13,240 | $ 1,324 | $ 4,000 | $ 18,564 |
| 24 | $ 18,564 | $ 1,856 | $ 4,000 | $ 24,420 |
| 25 | $ 24,420 | $ 2,442 | $ 4,000 | $ 30,862 |
| 26 | $ 30,862 | $ 3,086 | $ 4,000 | $ 37,949 |
| 27 | $ 37,949 | $ 3,795 | $ 4,000 | $ 45,744 |
| 28 | $ 45,744 | $ 4,574 | $ 4,000 | $ 54,318 |
| 29 | $ 54,318 | $ 5,432 | $ 4,000 | $ 63,750 |
| 30 | $ 63,750 | $ 6,375 | $ 4,000 | $ 74,125 |
| 31 | $ 74,125 | $ 7,412 | $ 4,000 | $ 85,537 |
| 32 | $ 85,537 | $ 8,554 | $ 4,000 | $ 98,091 |
| 33 | $ 98,091 | $ 9,809 | $ 4,000 | $ 111,900 |
| 34 | $ 111,900 | $ 11,190 | $ 4,000 | $ 127,090 |
| 35 | $ 127,090 | $ 12,709 | $ 4,000 | $ 143,799 |
| 36 | $ 143,799 | $ 14,380 | $ 4,000 | $ 162,179 |
| 37 | $ 162,179 | $ 16,218 | $ 4,000 | $ 182,397 |
| 38 | $ 182,397 | $ 18,240 | $ 4,000 | $ 204,636 |
| 39 | $ 204,636 | $ 20,464 | $ 4,000 | $ 229,100 |
| 40 | $ 229,100 | $ 22,910 | | $ 252,010 |

William's account, having grown to $229,100 by the end of his 20th year of saving, earns him $22,910 in the first year after he quits contributing. He's done adding new money, but his wealth will nonetheless increase by $22,910. This is the same year James begins saving $4,000 per year. The last number in our table shows that, going into the following year, William will have a cool $252,010 on which 10%, or $25,201, will be earned. William is crushing it and there is no way— even if James contributes $4,000 per year forever—that he can catch up. We'll finish with an illustration of their accounts:

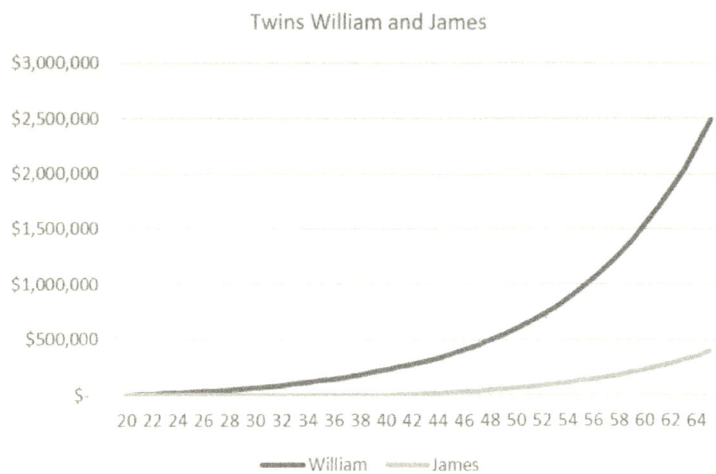


## Tax-advantaged saving and investing

Despite taking a broad look at taxes in an earlier chapter, we purposely deferred a discussion of certain additional tax provisions that pertain to saving and investing. As this section implies, the government provides an *advantage* over the normal tax treatment of income for some types of accounts.

### The Individual Retirement Account (IRA)

Let's say that at age 25, Sergey begins his career and creates a budget that calls for him to save $400 per month ($4,800 per year). In order to achieve that $400 in take-home pay, however, Sergey must actually earn $500. Why? A fraction of his income is lost to income taxes. In this case, we're assuming Sergey's income gets taxed at 20%, and 20% of $500 is $100.

When saving for retirement is concerned, however, there is a way around this. It's called an Individual Retirement Account, or IRA. If Sergey invests $500 per month in an IRA, he can deduct the money he placed there over the course of the year, $6,000, from his taxable income when he files his 1040. Since he pays taxes at the rate of 20%, that's $1,200 additional he can add to his IRA each year that would otherwise have been lost to taxes since 20% of $6,000 is $1,200. This amount can then compound over decades and make a significant difference in the type of retirement he can enjoy.[123]

This *traditional* IRA, however, is not tax free. When Sergey withdraws money from this account to cover his living expenses during his retirement years, it will be subject to taxation. In this regard, we say that a traditional IRA has the benefit of tax *deferral*. The collection of taxes on income directed to the IRA is put off, deferred, until it is distributed from the account in retirement. We should also recognize that Sergey's marginal income tax rate in retirement is likely to be lower than during his working years.

## The Roth IRA

Contributions to a Roth IRA are not tax deductible. So, Sergey will not have the additional $1,200 per year to invest. Thus, he will invest only $4,800 per year. However, his withdrawals will not be taxed when he takes money from his account to support himself in retirement.

---

[123] Current tax laws allow a person to begin making withdrawals from the account without penalty upon reaching age 59 ½.

The following table illustrates how an annual investment of $6,000 in a traditional IRA can grow versus the $4,800 per year that Sergey would have remaining after income taxes to invest in a Roth IRA over 40 years.[124]

| Traditional IRA vs. Roth IRA Account Growth | | |
|---|---|---|
| At an annual return of .... | ... the Traditional IRA's account value is | ... the Roth IRA's account value is |
| 5% | $ 724,799 | $ 579,839 |
| 6% | $ 928,572 | $ 742,857 |
| 7% | $ 1,197,811 | $ 958,249 |
| 8% | $ 1,554,339 | $ 1,243,471 |
| 9% | $ 2,027,295 | $ 1,621,836 |
| 10% | $ 2,655,555 | $ 2,124,444 |

The potential values of the traditional IRA account are higher than those of the Roth IRA, yes, but we must remember that withdrawals from it are subject to income tax! It's really a matter of whether to pay the government now, or pay it later.

## The 401(k) plan

A 401(k) is an *employer-sponsored,* tax-deferred retirement plan that enables employees to direct a certain amount of their pay into a tax-deferred account.[125] Sponsorship means paying for one or more parties to set up, administer, and responsibly forward the savings of their employees into a variety of

124 For simplicity, calculations for the Traditional IRA used $6,000 per year (instead of $500 per month) and for the Roth IRA $4,800 per year (instead of $400 per month).

125 Employees of public schools and tax-exempt nonprofits can participate in 403(b) plans, while state and local government employees can participate in 457 plans.

investments. While employees can designate how much they want to invest each pay period and where they want their money invested, they cannot know what their account value will be in the future because of various investment risks and market vagaries. As such, a 401(k) is a *defined-contribution* plan. Again, we can clearly define and quantify what we're contributing, but we can't say exactly how big a benefit our account will provide.

Some employers offer their employees what is known as a *defined-benefit* plan. In this case, the employer sets aside money to pay the employee a specified amount upon retirement. Hence, the term "defined benefit." This sought-after *pension* plan begins paying an employee a fraction of his or her salary upon retirement and ends when he or she dies. The longer the employee works for the employer, the greater the promised payments. It is the employer's responsibility to do whatever is required to ensure that it can continue to pay the defined benefit. No longer wanting (or being able) to carry this burden, more and more employers have ended this type of retirement plan.

### *The 401(k) match*

One way employers are making real contributions toward their employees' retirement goals is to *match* the contributions they make to their 401(k) accounts. Let's say Kirby receives a written offer for a position at CCF Corporation with a salary of $100,000. The offer explains that one of the benefits the corporation provides is a "dollar-for-dollar" 401(k) match for the first 3% of Kirby's salary. If he accepts the position and directs $3,000 of his pre-tax income into his 401(k) over the course of his first year, CCF will match his savings 100% by adding $3,000 to his account. For employees struggling to save, a match is just what the doctor ordered. Everyone should take advantage of this opportunity. It's found money.

## Saving for college and health care costs

Higher education can be expensive. The same is true for health care, even if we are insured! Thankfully, Congress allows their costs to be paid with tax-advantaged income.

Your employer can help you set up a *529 plan* whereby you save after-tax income that can grow tax free until it's withdrawn to pay for higher education expenses. Similarly, a *Health Savings Account (HSA)* or *Flexible Spending Account (FSA)* may be offered to allow payment of deductibles, co-pays, co-insurance and prescriptions with pre-tax income.

# The stock market

It's surprisingly difficult to get a bead on the total number of corporations that have their shares *listed* on a U.S. exchange, making them available for purchase by the investing public. A study by Credit Suisse in 2016 pegged that number at 3,671.[cxxxii] To demonstrate the breadth of industries in which these corporations operate, following is a classification list by *supersector:*[cxxxiii]

| FTSE Russell Industry Classification Benchmark (ICB) | | | |
|---|---|---|---|
| 1 | Technology | 2 | Telecommunications |
| 3 | Health Care | 4 | Banks |
| 5 | Financial Services | 6 | Insurance |
| 7 | Real Estate | 8 | Automobiles and Parts |
| 9 | Consumer Products and Services | 10 | Media |
| 11 | Retail | 12 | Travel and Leisure |
| 13 | Food, Beverage and Tobacco | 14 | Personal Care, Drug and Grocery Stores |
| 15 | Construction and Materials | 16 | Industrial Goods and Services |
| 17 | Basic Resources | 18 | Chemicals |
| 19 | Energy | 20 | Utilities |

In browsing these classifications, you may have realized that you can achieve a significant measure of diversification within your stock holdings by owning shares of corporations in different sectors.

## The Dow Jones Industrial Average

In 1882, financial journalists Charles Dow and Edward Jones formed Dow Jones & Co. with the goal of bringing unbiased information to investors in what was the relatively new and largely unregulated arena of stock trading. They started by publishing the daily *Customer's Afternoon Letter.* This two-page summary of the day's financial news was the precursor of *The Wall Street Journal,* which launched in 1889.

In 1896 a new feature was added: a list of the largest corporations in each of 12 sectors of the economy, their closing share prices,[126] and the average of their share prices. This *Dow Jones Industrial Average (DJIA)* gave investors the first indicator (or *index)* of the direction of stocks overall.[cxxxiv] [127]

Over the more than 100 years since its creation, the DJIA has undergone many changes. Also known as the *Dow Jones* or simply the *Dow,* it is now made up of 30 leading corporations. Because of its long history, the Dow holds a special place in the psyches of average investors. This is reinforced by financial news reporting, which often leads with changes in the value of the Dow.

---

[126] The existence of a *closing* price affirms that stocks, at least at this point, do not trade around the clock. Markets officially open at 9:30 AM EST and close 4:00 pm EST. The price of the last trade that occurs on or before 4:00 PM is the closing price. We note as well as that technology advances markets are allowing "extended hours" trading before 9:30 AM EST and after 4:00 PM EST.

[127] For simplification we're referring to the Dow *average* as an *index* to recognize its use as an indicator of the overall market.

### The Standard and Poor's 500

In 1923, the Standard Statistics Company created an index of 223 corporations that it published weekly. In 1926, it cut the number of corporations in the index back to 90, but tracked their values daily.[cxxxv] The 1941 merger of Standard Statistics with Poor's Publishing Company set the stage for Standard and Poor's 1957 launch of the *S&P 500 Stock Index*.[cxxxvi]

As its name implies, the index tracks the market values of 500 corporations. Right off the bat, we see that its sample of the overall market of stocks is much greater than that of the Dow, which is comprised of only 30 corporations. The *S&P 500* has another advantage over the Dow in that it uses company market values, not just their share prices, in its calculation.[128] Therefore, the value of the index is influenced more by the larger firms (i.e., those with higher market values) in the index.

Because it uses a larger sample of companies and is market-value weighted, the S&P 500 is the index professionals use as a truer representation, a *proxy*, of the overall stock market.

## Diversification and asset classes

When Grandma told you not to put all your eggs in one basket, she was telling you to *diversify*. Applied to investing, this means distributing your money among *asset classes* such as *stocks* and *bonds*. An asset class is comprised of investments that share unique characteristics, causing them to respond similarly to changing economic conditions.

### Common stock (aka Equities)

Corporations issue *common stock*, in units called *shares*, to

---

[128] Market value is determined by multiplying the number of shares of the corporation that are outstanding by the current price per share. This measure is also known as *market capitalization*, or market "cap."

raise money.[129] Shareholders are the owners of the corporation. Each share of common stock provides the holder the right to vote annually for candidates seeking to fill open seats on the *Board of Directors (BOD)*.[130] The right to vote for board members provides shareholders *indirect control* of the corporation. How? It is the BOD that hires, supervises and, if need be, fires the Chief Executive Officer (CEO). Equity is synonymous with ownership, and for this reason financial professionals refer to shares of common stock as *equities*.[131]

Corporations that have chosen to "go public" by making their shares available to the broad investment community must comply with extensive rules that ensure investors have accurate and current information on which to make informed decisions. Our largest *publicly-held* (also known as *publicly-traded*) corporations include Apple, Microsoft, Amazon and Alphabet (the parent of Google). Most, but not all, big corporations are publicly traded. Albertsons, Publix and Mars are businesses that have managed to grow without needing to raise money through a public offering of their shares.

Successful corporations often find themselves earning more in profits than they need to fund their operations, invest in *research and development* (R&D), and set aside for a rainy day. This excess cash invariably catches the eyes of shareholders who argue that, instead of sitting in the bank doing nothing, it should be paid out to them. Dividends, which we touched on in our taxes chapter, are one of two ways that stock investors earn money. The other is share price appreciation.

---

[129] We use the terms *stockholder* and *shareholder* interchangeably.

[130] Shareholders can also vote on major corporate decisions such as acquisitions and mergers.

[131] A person who owns an asset is said to have equity in it. A more sophisticated way to express that you invest in and own shares of corporations is to say that you invest in "equities."

Let's say that you buy one share of PPL Corporation for $100. A year later, you have received $2 in dividends and watched approvingly as the share price rose to $108. You decide to sell it, realizing a gain of $8 ($108 minus $100). Your *total return,* however, is $10 because we must include the $2 in dividends received.

Possessing common stock in a corporation makes the holder an owner in a real sense. Should the corporation thrive, stockholders will *go big*. There is literally no limit to how successful a corporation can be and, therefore, no upper limit on how much the dollar value of its shares may rise.

There is a downside to stock ownership as well. Many times a new technology or paradigm displaces an existing one. We referred to this earlier as creative destruction. In some cases, a corporation that is using the displaced technology or paradigm is forced into bankruptcy. The stockholders of a corporation that falls from grace and goes bankrupt will *go home.* When a business closes, it *liquidates* its assets. Shareholders are last in line to receive any cash from the "everything must go" sale. Because there's a good chance that there won't be enough cash raised to pay the company's debts, shareholders are likely to get nothing. Corporations that have recently gone bankrupt include Sports Authority, Toys 'R' Us, RadioShack, Payless Shoesource and Gymboree.

## Bonds (aka Fixed-income)

A bond is a remarkable invention in that it is at once simple, effective and… complex. A sample bond is shown next.

*"What good does it do to be well versed in investment opportunities when one has little or no money to invest?"*
– Thomas J. Stanley

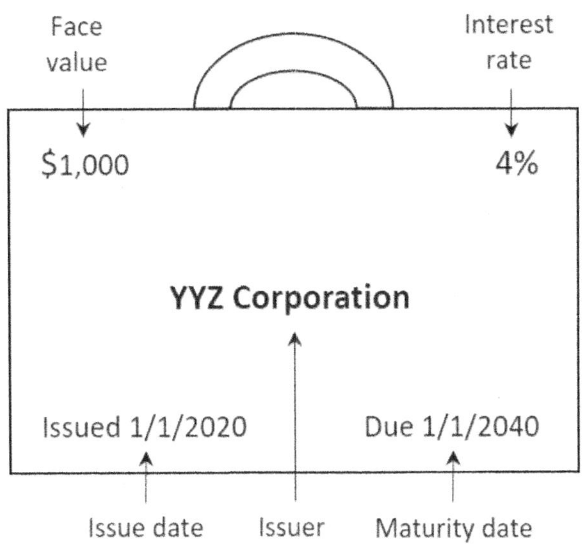


The illustration represents a certificate with a handle. YYZ Corporation is borrowing money in $1,000 increments. For each $1,000 lent, the investor receives one bond as evidence of YYZ's indebtedness. Each year the bondholder will be paid 4% of the $1,000 *face value,* or $40, in interest. This consistent payment is the reason professionals refer to bonds as *fixed-income* investments. In 2040, 20 years after issue, the bond is *redeemed* when the investor turns it in and receives $1,000.

The interest rate at which a corporation can borrow money is determined by its creditworthiness and the prevailing interest rate at the time it wants to borrow. Why the handle? The term of a bond, as in our example, can be decades. There is good news for investors whose circumstances change and who are unable or unwilling to hold their bond to maturity. While they can't force the issuer to take it back early,[132] they can sell it to another investor. They basically pass it off, like a

[132] This is not entirely true, as the rare bond with a *put provision* does allow the investor to force the issuer to take the bond back.

baton, to a buyer who wants to receive the remaining interest payments and the face value at maturity.

Let's say its 2030. The original investor in this bond, after holding it a decade (from 2020 to 2030), wants to sell it. An investor with an 8-year-old at home sees that it has 10 years (from 2030 to 2040) until maturity. She can purchase it, knowing it will mature when her child is 18 and about to attend college.

What's so complex? The price the buyer pays the seller for the bond is unlikely to be the face value. If interest rates have fallen, say, to 3% between 2020 and 2030, then corporations borrowing money in 2030 will issue new bonds with a 3% annual interest rate. This makes the 4% YYZ bond with a decade of life left more attractive and thus more valuable. After all, which would you rather have, a bond that pays you $40 in interest every year or one that pays $30? This demonstrates the famous axiom that *when interest rates fall, the value of a previously existing bond increases, and vice versa.*

It may have occurred to you that as a bondholder you receive your investment back with interest. As long as you invest in bonds that have little risk of default, you don't lose money. You only earn it. That can be a welcome relief to stock investors who have been burned by one too many promising corporations whose share prices later cratered. Since bonds represent less risk than stocks, their expected returns are lower, all else equal. In other words, a bond issued by the Hypothetical Corporation will offer a lower expected return than its common stock.

Finally, corporations aren't the only issuers of bonds. Governments borrow in a big way. We have one federal government, fifty state governments, thousands of counties and even more local authorities, most of which borrow money by issuing bonds.

## Real estate

The land and buildings that provide homes to people and businesses is referred to as real property. An intrepid investor may purchase land, construct apartments and then rent them to local residents. Another investor may build offices that can be rented to local businesses. In both cases, the investment is the cost of the land and the building. The income from the investment is the rent collected from the tenants. We can already see that real estate functions differently from stocks and bonds, making it its own asset class.

The good news is that we don't have to be able to pull off ambitious projects like those described above to gain *exposure* to real estate. There are many specialized publicly-traded corporations, called Real Estate Investment Trusts (REITs), whose sole purpose is to own and operate real estate for the benefit of their shareholders. This allows us to invest as little as or as much in real estate as we desire.

## Commodities

An app called GasBuddy helps drivers find nearby stations with the cheapest gas. Its users view gasoline as a commodity. That is, they believe a gallon of gas is a gallon of gas is a gallon of gas. No matter the source, it's all the same. Ditto for a bushel of corn and an ounce of gold. Where commodities are concerned, the law of supply and demand is key. If we believe that forces are coalescing to drive demand higher, we can purchase a commodity today and benefit as its price rises.

We have Wall Street to thank for not having to worry about taking actual delivery of the gas, corn or gold that we purchase. Banks and investment companies have created financial equivalents of the major commodities, giving us an extraordinarily simple way to speculate on them. For example, State Street Global Advisors offers an investment with the *symbol* GLD that rises and falls with the increases and decreases in the value of gold.

## Cash

Imagine you have a significant amount of cash in a tax-deferred investment account. One day a finance guru friend looks over your account statement and asks why you aren't "putting those dollars to work." She's asking why you keep cash on the *sidelines* instead of investing it in one or more of the asset classes discussed above. Your response is that if the definition of an asset class is its unique response to different market conditions, then cash would appear to be one. Indeed, it is one of the rare few assets whose value will remain intact when markets are getting crushed.

# Portfolios

Knowing the wisdom of diversification and having learned about asset classes, we should set a goal to create a *portfolio* of investments we can ride over decades through good and bad times. Finally, we have an excuse to include a pie chart, which is the way that asset *allocation* is usually illustrated:

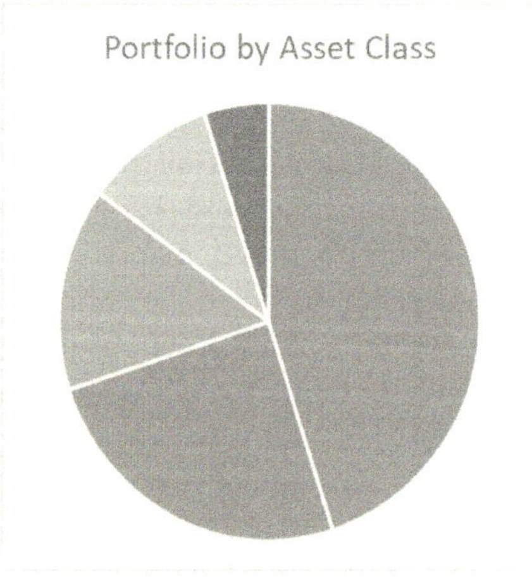


Why aren't any of the wedges labelled? Because the ideal portfolio is a matter of debate, and of circumstance. No two investors are identical with regard to their risk tolerance, contribution level, time horizon or retirement objectives. Further, comparing the results of different portfolios is backward looking. A portfolio that may have soared in recent decades is not guaranteed to continue outperforming.

## A simple portfolio of stocks and bonds

The two largest asset classes are stocks and bonds, so let's create a portfolio that divides the pie between only those two. For guidance we're going to turn to the point in life the investor finds him or herself.

Above, we learned that bonds are safer investments than stocks. It stands to reason that as a person approaches retirement, the overall risk of his or her portfolio should diminish. Stock markets do have a way of crashing every so often, something a person nearing retirement may ill afford. The less a portfolio is invested in stocks, the less it will be hurt by a decline in stock prices.

Keeping this in mind, some financial advisors provide a simple guideline that may spark your interest in portfolio composition: *the percentage of your portfolio that should be invested in bonds is equal to your age.*

At age 25, Santo is hired out of grad school by a big corporation. Working with its human resources (HR) department, he enrolls in its 401(k) plan and chooses a mix of investments that is 25% bonds and 75% stock. With $3 out of every $4 exposed to stock markets, this is an *aggressive* allocation. With each passing year, he tweaks his portfolio so that one less percent is invested in stocks and one additional percent is invested in bonds. By age 40, Santo's asset allocation is 40% bonds and 60% stock. By age 65, his asset allocation is 65% bonds and 35% stock. Over time, Santo's allocation changed from aggressive to *moderate*. By the time Santo reaches 75, only 25% of his portfolio will consist of stocks, making it *conservative*.

## Common portfolio components

Having introduced asset classes, it's time to categorize the investments within them. For example, the equity slice of a portfolio may hold common stock of:

- *large-cap U.S. corporations* because they are stable and better able to withstand economic downturns;[133]
- *mid-cap U.S. corporations* because they have the stability to weather downturns, but aren't so large that they can't achieve appreciable growth.
- *small-cap U.S. corporations* because they have the potential to grow rapidly.
- *international corporations* because the United States isn't the only game in town. When our economy is not doing well, others around the world may be.
- *emerging-markets* corporations. This is a way to "get in on the ground floor" in regions that are just starting to install the governance and policies that will allow them to attract investment and flourish in the future.

The fixed income slice of the portfolio may consist of bonds issued by:

- our *federal* government. Called *treasuries* because the U.S. Treasury issues them, these bonds do well in times of panic. A special version of treasuries called *TIPS* protects investors against inflation.[134]
- *state* and *local* governments. Called *municipal bonds* (or simply *munis*), the interest they pay is exempt from federal income taxes and may also be exempt from taxation by the issuing state or local government. For

---

133 As noted earlier, "cap" is short for capitalization and is a measure of the total market value of a corporation.

134 TIPS stands for Treasury Inflation Protected Securities.

example, the interest earned on a municipal bond issued by Orange County, California is exempt from federal income taxes and also from California and Orange County income taxes when purchased by a California resident. However, an Ohioan who invests in the same bond must declare the interest received as income when he files his Ohio income tax form. This approach encourages us to support public works in our own states by investing in the bonds issued to finance them.

- stronger corporations, making them *investment grade.*
- weaker corporations, which offer investors the chance to earn a *high yield* when compared to the interest paid on safer bonds.[135]
- *foreign* issuers, including those of emerging-market governments and corporations.

We need not dive into the nitty-gritty of real estate, commodities and cash to realize that it would be very easy to drown in the plethora of components from which to build a portfolio. So, we're not going to. Instead, we'll introduce a high-profile portfolio as one example of the many ways we can distribute our investments.

## The Ivy League endowment portfolio

An endowment is a sum of money that a university receives from donors. The money is then invested so that it can fund scholarships, research, and facility upgrades. If an endowment fund is successful, the sum of the donations it receives and the investment returns it achieves will exceed the cost of the projects it funds. This allows it to pay for important undertakings while simultaneously growing in value. Ivy

---

[135] These bonds are also referred to as *non-investment grade, speculative* and *junk.*

League universities have the largest endowments with Harvard, at $38.3 billion,[cxxxvii] leading the way. Translated into asset classes to which the ordinary investor has access, the average asset allocations of Harvard, Yale ($29.3 billion) and Stanford ($26.4 billion) is:[cxxxviii]

- o 35% U.S. equity (stocks)
- o 28% Bonds
- o 15% Foreign equity (stocks)
- o 11% Real estate
- o 11% Commodities

So, there it is, a mix of assets that is intended to protect and grow their endowment funds over the long term. What about us individual investors? Thankfully the cavalry has again arrived in the form of technology, which we will discuss later.

*Who is or was?* Ryan White.

## Investment companies and mutual funds

We live in the age of specialization. If a water pipe has broken, you're going to call a plumber. If you run screaming from the pantry because a roach poked his creepy head out from behind a box of cereal, it won't be but a minute before you've got the exterminator on the line. We hire specialists to address legal issues, taxes, auto repair, landscaping and more because they have the expertise and experience needed to solve the problem at hand. Is it any wonder that adults with careers in farming, medicine, manufacturing, technology, education, entertainment, sports, transportation, hospitality, law, food service, logistics—really any career except finance—turn to investment professionals to manage their money? I mean, things were starting to get a little complicated when we discussed diversifying across and within asset classes.

The average person brings in the professionals by using retirement account funds to purchase shares in *mutual funds* that are offered by *investment companies.* Mutual funds sell shares to investors. Most are *actively managed,* employing a skilled team to invest in the shares of an array of carefully selected corporations. To that end, the fund can sell *holdings* and buy new ones whenever it wishes. A study conducted in 2013 showed that the average equity mutual fund held 90 corporations, although the 20% that were the most diversified owned shares in an average of 228 corporations.[cxxxix]

Note that investors own shares in mutual funds that in turn own shares in publicly-traded corporations. This gives them *indirect ownership* of those corporations.

A mutual fund's investment selection team is headed by an experienced *fund manager* whose reputation alone may attract investors. These professionals charge fund shareholders a *management fee* for their services.

As employees have fed money into mutual funds through their 401(k)s for the last several decades, the industry has become enormous. At the end of 2018, 846 U.S. registered investment companies held $17.7 trillion in mutual funds belonging to 99.5 million Americans.[cxl] [cxli] That's trillion with a "t"!

Investment companies frequently offer a *family of funds,* enabling them to provide investors one-stop shopping. Fidelity Investments is the largest sponsor of funds, with 260 stock funds from which investors can choose.[cxlii] This number is difficult to fathom until you realize that Fidelity provides a stock fund to meet just about any objective an investor may have.

For starters, there are *sector* funds that allow you to direct your money to areas of the economy you believe are poised for success. We identified 20 of them a few pages ago. Over the last several decades telecommunications has experienced tremendous growth. With 5G wireless here, another cycle of equipment upgrades is in the offing. You'd like to take advantage of this unfolding scenario. Good news. There are several funds that will enable you to do just that, including Fidelity Select Communication Services Portfolio, Fidelity Select Telecommunications Portfolio and Fidelity Select Wireless Portfolio.

Then, there are funds that divvy up the world of corporations by their size. Perhaps you believe the sweet spot for stock investing is medium-sized (aka mid-cap) U.S. corporations. There's a fund for that, as well as funds that invest exclusively in small corporations and others that invest only in large corporations. Drilling down further, there are funds that invest in corporations that are expanding rapidly, called *growth* funds. There are funds whose management teams search for corporations that are currently being overlooked by investors, making them an attractive *value*. Mixing these, we can invest in *large-cap growth* funds as well as a *large-cap value* funds.

Businesses that deliver electricity, water and natural gas (otherwise known as *utilities)* are a unique breed. Being well protected, they are able to pay out dividends that are especially high when compared to their share prices. These cash payments can be spent by shareholders; thus, they are income. Not surprisingly, *income funds* own a collection of high-dividend paying stocks and are suitable for retirees who need a steady stream of cash coming in.

Hold on, because we're not done. Let's say that after reading up on investing, you decide that the U.S. equity portion of your portfolio should be split between large-cap growth and large-cap value. So, you work with your 401(k) plan administrator to identify a fund for each. Understanding what you are trying to accomplish, she explains that you can achieve your objective by purchasing a single fund. She tells you that there are funds that split their investments between the two. If such a fund's holdings consist of the shares of 100 corporations, 50 may be large growth corporations and 50 large value corporations. Combining these two categories of corporations within one fund makes it a *blend* fund. Here, we've described a *large-cap blend* fund.

Lastly, there are even *funds of funds*, wherein a mutual fund can invest in other mutual funds. This may seem absurd, but it's actually kind of neat. Imagine that Ivy Fo Fund's manager puts 35% of investor money into a U.S. equity mutual fund, 28% into a bond mutual fund, 15% into a foreign equity mutual fund, 11% into a real estate fund and 11% into a commodity mutual fund. Ivy Fo Fund has just replicated the Ivy League endowment portfolio. By purchasing shares of this single mutual fund, Ivy Fo Fund, you are investing like the Ivy League endowment managers![136]

## How it was supposed to work

So, we get on with our lives and careers, secure in the knowledge that no matter the funds we've chosen, our money is being professionally invested. Let's say that Wilmer has the U.S. stock portion of his portfolio invested in a broad equity mutual fund. Shortly after the year ends, he receives a statement indicating that the holdings of the fund rose 14% in the year just ended. Upon learning that the S&P 500 rose 10%, he's very pleased. Even with fees of 2% subtracted from the fund, he's still up 12% (14% minus 2%). With holdings of a similar risk to the S&P 500, the fund has beaten the overall market. The investment managers are earning their keep.

## How it has worked

Earlier, we mentioned a book titled *A Random Walk Down Wall Street* and its example of twin brothers, one who begins saving early and the other, late. Published in 1973, the title of the book hints at a larger issue. Author and economist Burton Malkiel asserts that stock prices move randomly over most

---

[136] The drawback of investing in a fund of funds is that they are likely to charge investors higher fees.

time frames, except for very long term periods of at least a decade. Commonly used evaluation techniques, known as *fundamental analysis* and *technical analysis,* don't reliably tell us, even in the hands of professionals, in what direction a stock will go.

It doesn't help that all those teams of experts from all those investment companies must pore over the shrinking universe of publicly-traded corporations, exchanging the shares of ones they think will fall for ones they think will rise. I've had the following conversation with students over the years when they participate in our fantasy stock market challenge:

Student: Mr. Barrella, let me show you the trade I'm making this morning. I'm buying 100 shares of BTNB Corporation.

Teacher: Why did you make the decision to buy?

Student: Because I did a lot of research, and I think that BTNB is going to do well in the future.

Teacher: We just finished looking at how stocks trade. From where or whom will you get your shares?

Student: From an investor selling them.

Teacher: Let's say that investor is equally as educated, motivated and thorough as you. Why would the investor sell?

Student: Because he or she thinks the stock is going down. (Long pause). Oh.

This conversation seems a little simplistic until you learn that there are 3,419 actively managed equity mutual funds whose investment teams choose from among 3,671 publicly-held U.S. corporations (as of 2016).[137] [cxliii]

---

[137] A screen was run at Zacks.com on funds with 0% invested in bonds, 0% in foreign stocks, and an expense ratio of 0.25% or higher.

### *The first little secret*

The studies are in, and they're not pretty. The vast majority of actively managed mutual funds fail to beat the overall stock market. For example, the SPIVA U.S. Scorecard published in 2015,[cxliv] shows that during the prior decade over 80% of actively managed small-, mid- and large-cap mutual funds did not outperform the overall market.

What do we mean by "beat" the market? Well, the S&P 500 is a stable group of 500 large U.S. corporations. The index's value at the start of 2006 was 1,268.80. At the end of 2015, the index's value was 2,058.20.[cxlv] This represents a 62.2% increase.[138] Despite the ample training and skills of team members, despite having access to extensive amounts of data and computing resources, despite their finely honed evaluation methods and the freedom to buy and sell their holdings whenever they wish, the managers of four out of five actively managed equity funds were unable to select investments that increased in value as much as the S&P 500 Index.

Critics will add that over the *following* decade, the one out of every five funds that beats the market is unlikely to be the same fund that beat the market the prior decade.

### *The second little secret*

The PBS Frontline documentary *The Retirement Gamble* follows economist Robert Hiltonsmith as he does a deep dive into the fees charged by the fund industry. His catalyst for doing so was him noticing that, despite a positive investing environment wherein the overall market was rising, the value of his 401(k) never seemed to increase. The documentary shows Hiltonsmith sitting at his computer and scanning an on-screen fund report. The camera zooms in on one of the

---

138 (2,058.80 – 1,268.80)/1,268.80 = 789.40/1,268.80 = 0.622 = 62.2%.

column headings, which reads **EXP** on the first heading line and **Ratio** underneath it. When I'm watching this movie with my classes, I will pause it and ask what they think EXP Ratio stands for. "Exponent" is a common answer. Other suggestions are offered, but none of them ever happen upon what it is, "Expense Ratio."

There are plenty of reasons for the industry to be coy about the annual cost of being a mutual fund investor. Mr. Hiltonsmith found more than a dozen types of fees, including asset management fees, marketing fees, distribution fees, administrative fees and redemption fees. The documentary, which aired in 2013, states that the average actively managed mutual fund has an *expense ratio* of 1.3%.[139]

So, I was surprised when, later in the documentary, a certain industry legend used an expense figure of 2% to illustrate the drag that fees place on an investment account. The scenario is this: At age 20, friends Gary and Shari have each saved the curious sum of $3,394.78. Shari invests it herself (thus paying no fees), earning 7% per year. At the end of 50 years, she will have $100,000, as shown in the year-by-year wealth accumulation table on the next two pages.

*"Our favorite holding period is forever. We are just the opposite of those who hurry to sell and book profits when companies perform well but who tenaciously hang on to businesses that disappoint. Peter Lynch aptly likens such behavior to cutting the flowers and watering the weeds."*
- Warren Buffett

139 Expense ratio = $ amount of expenses/$ amount of fund assets. Example: $100 million in expenses/$10 billion in assets is 0.01, or 1%.

| Shari's Growth of Initial Sum over 50 Years | | | | | |
|---|---|---|---|---|---|
| | A | B=Ax7% | C=A+B | D=Cx0% | E=C-D |
| Age | Beginning balance | 7% earned | Year-end balance | 0% fee taken | After-fee balance |
| 20 | $3,394.78 | $238 | $3,632 | $0 | $3,632 |
| 21 | $3,632 | $254 | $3,887 | $0 | $3,887 |
| 22 | $3,887 | $272 | $4,159 | $0 | $4,159 |
| 23 | $4,159 | $291 | $4,450 | $0 | $4,450 |
| 24 | $4,450 | $311 | $4,761 | $0 | $4,761 |
| 25 | $4,761 | $333 | $5,095 | $0 | $5,095 |
| 26 | $5,095 | $357 | $5,451 | $0 | $5,451 |
| 27 | $5,451 | $382 | $5,833 | $0 | $5,833 |
| 28 | $5,833 | $408 | $6,241 | $0 | $6,241 |
| 29 | $6,241 | $437 | $6,678 | $0 | $6,678 |
| 30 | $6,678 | $467 | $7,146 | $0 | $7,146 |
| 31 | $7,146 | $500 | $7,646 | $0 | $7,646 |
| 32 | $7,646 | $535 | $8,181 | $0 | $8,181 |
| 33 | $8,181 | $573 | $8,754 | $0 | $8,754 |
| 34 | $8,754 | $613 | $9,366 | $0 | $9,366 |
| 35 | $9,366 | $656 | $10,022 | $0 | $10,022 |
| 36 | $10,022 | $702 | $10,723 | $0 | $10,723 |
| 37 | $10,723 | $751 | $11,474 | $0 | $11,474 |
| 38 | $11,474 | $803 | $12,277 | $0 | $12,277 |
| 39 | $12,277 | $859 | $13,137 | $0 | $13,137 |
| 40 | $13,137 | $920 | $14,056 | $0 | $14,056 |
| 41 | $14,056 | $984 | $15,040 | $0 | $15,040 |
| 42 | $15,040 | $1,053 | $16,093 | $0 | $16,093 |
| 43 | $16,093 | $1,127 | $17,220 | $0 | $17,220 |
| 44 | $17,220 | $1,205 | $18,425 | $0 | $18,425 |
| 45 | $18,425 | $1,290 | $19,715 | $0 | $19,715 |
| 46 | $19,715 | $1,380 | $21,095 | $0 | $21,095 |

| Shari's Growth of Initial Sum over 50 Years (cont.) | | | | | |
|---|---|---|---|---|---|
| | A | B=Ax7% | C=A+B | D=Cx0% | E=C-D |
| Age | Beginning balance | 7% earned | Year-end balance | 0% fee taken | After-fee balance |
| 47 | $21,095 | $1,477 | $22,571 | $0 | $22,571 |
| 48 | $22,571 | $1,580 | $24,151 | $0 | $24,151 |
| 49 | $24,151 | $1,691 | $25,842 | $0 | $25,842 |
| 50 | $25,842 | $1,809 | $27,651 | $0 | $27,651 |
| 51 | $27,651 | $1,936 | $29,586 | $0 | $29,586 |
| 52 | $29,586 | $2,071 | $31,657 | $0 | $31,657 |
| 53 | $31,657 | $2,216 | $33,873 | $0 | $33,873 |
| 54 | $33,873 | $2,371 | $36,245 | $0 | $36,245 |
| 55 | $36,245 | $2,537 | $38,782 | $0 | $38,782 |
| 56 | $38,782 | $2,715 | $41,496 | $0 | $41,496 |
| 57 | $41,496 | $2,905 | $44,401 | $0 | $44,401 |
| 58 | $44,401 | $3,108 | $47,509 | $0 | $47,509 |
| 59 | $47,509 | $3,326 | $50,835 | $0 | $50,835 |
| 60 | $50,835 | $3,558 | $54,393 | $0 | $54,393 |
| 61 | $54,393 | $3,808 | $58,201 | $0 | $58,201 |
| 62 | $58,201 | $4,074 | $62,275 | $0 | $62,275 |
| 63 | $62,275 | $4,359 | $66,634 | $0 | $66,634 |
| 64 | $66,634 | $4,664 | $71,299 | $0 | $71,299 |
| 65 | $71,299 | $4,991 | $76,290 | $0 | $76,290 |
| 66 | $76,290 | $5,340 | $81,630 | $0 | $81,630 |
| 67 | $81,630 | $5,714 | $87,344 | $0 | $87,344 |
| 68 | $87,344 | $6,114 | $93,458 | $0 | $93,458 |
| 69 | $93,458 | $6,542 | $100,000 | $0 | $100,000 |

We've included a column for fees which, in Shari's case, are 0%. Gary invests in a mutual fund that also earns 7% per year, but which charges fees totalling 2% per year. The next table shows Gary's wealth accumulation.

| Gary's Growth of Initial Sum over 50 Years | | | | | |
|---|---|---|---|---|---|
| | A | B=Ax7% | C=A+B | D=Cx2% | E=C-D |
| Age | Beginning balance | 7% earned | Year-end balance | 2% fee taken | After-fee balance |
| 20 | $3,394.78 | $238 | $3,632 | $73 | $3,560 |
| 21 | $3,560 | $249 | $3,809 | $76 | $3,733 |
| 22 | $3,733 | $261 | $3,994 | $80 | $3,914 |
| 23 | $3,914 | $274 | $4,188 | $84 | $4,104 |
| 24 | $4,104 | $287 | $4,392 | $88 | $4,304 |
| 25 | $4,304 | $301 | $4,605 | $92 | $4,513 |
| 26 | $4,513 | $316 | $4,829 | $97 | $4,732 |
| 27 | $4,732 | $331 | $5,064 | $101 | $4,962 |
| 28 | $4,962 | $347 | $5,310 | $106 | $5,204 |
| 29 | $5,204 | $364 | $5,568 | $111 | $5,456 |
| 30 | $5,456 | $382 | $5,838 | $117 | $5,722 |
| 31 | $5,722 | $401 | $6,122 | $122 | $6,000 |
| 32 | $6,000 | $420 | $6,420 | $128 | $6,291 |
| 33 | $6,291 | $440 | $6,732 | $135 | $6,597 |
| 34 | $6,597 | $462 | $7,059 | $141 | $6,918 |
| 35 | $6,918 | $484 | $7,402 | $148 | $7,254 |
| 36 | $7,254 | $508 | $7,762 | $155 | $7,606 |
| 37 | $7,606 | $532 | $8,139 | $163 | $7,976 |
| 38 | $7,976 | $558 | $8,534 | $171 | $8,364 |
| 39 | $8,364 | $585 | $8,949 | $179 | $8,770 |
| 40 | $8,770 | $614 | $9,384 | $188 | $9,196 |
| 41 | $9,196 | $644 | $9,840 | $197 | $9,643 |
| 42 | $9,643 | $675 | $10,318 | $206 | $10,112 |
| 43 | $10,112 | $708 | $10,820 | $216 | $10,603 |
| 44 | $10,603 | $742 | $11,346 | $227 | $11,119 |
| 45 | $11,119 | $778 | $11,897 | $238 | $11,659 |
| 46 | $11,659 | $816 | $12,475 | $250 | $12,226 |

| Gary's Growth of Initial Sum over 50 Years (cont.) | | | | | |
|---|---|---|---|---|---|
| Age | Beginning balance | 7% earned | Year-end balance | 2% fee taken | After-fee balance |
| 47 | $12,226 | $856 | $13,082 | $262 | $12,820 |
| 48 | $12,820 | $897 | $13,717 | $274 | $13,443 |
| 49 | $13,443 | $941 | $14,384 | $288 | $14,096 |
| 50 | $14,096 | $987 | $15,083 | $302 | $14,781 |
| 51 | $14,781 | $1,035 | $15,816 | $316 | $15,500 |
| 52 | $15,500 | $1,085 | $16,585 | $332 | $16,253 |
| 53 | $16,253 | $1,138 | $17,391 | $348 | $17,043 |
| 54 | $17,043 | $1,193 | $18,236 | $365 | $17,871 |
| 55 | $17,871 | $1,251 | $19,122 | $382 | $18,740 |
| 56 | $18,740 | $1,312 | $20,052 | $401 | $19,651 |
| 57 | $19,651 | $1,376 | $21,026 | $421 | $20,606 |
| 58 | $20,606 | $1,442 | $22,048 | $441 | $21,607 |
| 59 | $21,607 | $1,512 | $23,120 | $462 | $22,657 |
| 60 | $22,657 | $1,586 | $24,243 | $485 | $23,758 |
| 61 | $23,758 | $1,663 | $25,421 | $508 | $24,913 |
| 62 | $24,913 | $1,744 | $26,657 | $533 | $26,124 |
| 63 | $26,124 | $1,829 | $27,952 | $559 | $27,393 |
| 64 | $27,393 | $1,918 | $29,311 | $586 | $28,725 |
| 65 | $28,725 | $2,011 | $30,735 | $615 | $30,121 |
| 66 | $30,121 | $2,108 | $32,229 | $645 | $31,585 |
| 67 | $31,585 | $2,211 | $33,795 | $676 | $33,120 |
| 68 | $33,120 | $2,318 | $35,438 | $709 | $34,729 |
| 69 | $34,729 | $2,431 | $37,160 | $743 | $36,417 |

The 2% fee would not appear to be that big of a deal. Yet, Gary's final account balance is just $36,417, or 36.4% of Shari's $100,000! Where did the rest of the money go? To the management company! The unnamed gentleman in the documentary asks, "Do you really want to invest in a system where you put up 100% of the capital—you, the mutual fund shareholder—you take 100% of the risk, and you get 30% of the return?"

When he says "100% of the risk," the man is pointing out that if the value of the holdings of the fund drop, it's your money that's being lost. Let's say you're invested in a mutual fund and one year the fund's holdings decrease in value by 15%. Perhaps the economy slowed and the market overall lost value. It's to be expected that the fund will also suffer losses. The problem, though, is that you didn't lose 15%. You lost 17% because the mutual fund continues to charge its 2% fee no matter how the fund or the market performs.

We should note that while this pioneer (who we'll introduce shortly) makes his point with a dramatic example, we are unlikely to enjoy the good fortune of having a single sum dropped in our laps early in our investing lives. Instead, we save a portion of our earnings methodically over decades, which results in fees being less impactful than our example illustrated. On the other hand, it just lessens the percentage lost to fees from "that can't be" to simply "dreadful."

It also appears that the 2% annual fee used in the example is too high, padded to exaggerate the difference in the outcomes for Shari and Gary. Again, the 2013 documentary states that the average expense ratio is 1.3%. That's not half the story, however. The expense ratio is a *disclosed* fee. You would be forgiven if you walked around, as I did, thinking that this readily available data point represented the actual cost of being a mutual fund investor. It turns out that there is also an array of hidden fees. An example is *transaction costs,* which alone can run higher than the expense ratio! The frightening reality: Total fees can reach 3%, 4%, or more per year.[cxlvi] [cxlvii] The second little secret, then, is that the cost of investing in an actively managed mutual fund is higher than we're being told.

### *More secrets*

Let's say you are a big muckety-muck at investment company StoneRockBoulder Funds, a name chosen to convey solidity. You've watched as the country of Genovia has experienced a political revolution that promises to make it more open to investment and free markets. Wanting to offer investors an opportunity to benefit from these exciting developments, you create not just one fund that will invest in corporations in and around Genovia, but three. That's three investment teams led by three fund managers, all crawling around the area looking for investment opportunities. Fast forward five years, at which point your funds post the following results:

| | Average return per year | | |
|---|---|---|---|
| Fund Name | 1-year | 3-years | 5-years |
| Genovia Region A | 5% | 6% | 4% |
| Genovia Region B | 12% | 10% | 9% |
| Genovia Region C | -2% | 5% | 6% |

Fund B clearly achieved the best results. At this point, you fold funds A and C into Fund B. Next, you drop B from the name. Going forward, the company offers a single fund, StoneRockBoulder Genovia Region, complete with a darned impressive track record. In the process you've also relegated the others to the dust bin of history, where they're out of the reach of studies on mutual fund performance.

Then, there is the issue of the accuracy of the rates of return reported by the industry in tables like the one above. Because they are *simple* or *arithmetic* averages (as opposed to compound growth rates), they're not the actual rates of return achieved for investors! To illustrate, we'll turn to and extend an example from Tony Robbins' 2014 book *MONEY Master the Game*. A mutual fund achieves wildly different results over the course of five years, as shown below. Alongside the returns, we show how $10,000 invested at the beginning is impacted by the ups and downs of good years followed by bad years.

| Roller Coaster Mutual Fund | | | |
|---|---|---|---|
| | A | B | A+AxB |
| | Starting value | Return achieved | Ending value |
| Year 1 | $10,000 | 50% | $15,000 |
| Year 2 | $15,000 | -50% | $7,500 |
| Year 3 | $7,500 | 50% | $11,250 |
| Year 4 | $11,250 | -50% | $5,625 |
| Year 5 | $5,625 | 50% | $8,438 |
| 5-year avg return | | 10% | |

Adding up the returns for all five years, we get a total of 50%. Dividing this total by the fund's five years in operation, we calculate that the fund has achieved a solid 10% arithmetic average annual return. That's news to a person who invested $10,000 in the fund at the start of the first year and found that her account value had shrivelled to $8,438 five years later.

While the above example is extreme, reporting returns arithmetically as the industry does gives investors the impression they are earning more than they are. For example, the S&P 500's arithmetic annual return from 2000 to 2016 was 6.16%. Its true compound annual return? Only 4.51%.[cxlviii]

## Being, not beating, the market

There must be a better way. There actually has been—for several decades—a better way. It's just that most people didn't know about it. Or, they refused to believe it really was better.

In a Terminator-like move, the investing resistance sent the parents of John Clifton "Jack" Bogle back to Montclair, New Jersey in 1928, so that he could arrive on this earth in 1929. Showing an aptitude for math, Jack attended the Blair

Academy. Graduating in 1947, he enrolled at Princeton University. Four years later, young Mr. Bogle wrote his final year thesis on the relatively obscure business of investment companies. It caught the attention of Walter L. Morgan, founder of the Wellington Fund, who hired him.

In the 1950s, Bogle helped the company expand by offering additional funds. In 1965, at age 35, Bogle was appointed executive vice president of the company, effectively putting it under his leadership. In 1966, Jack led a merger with a Boston-based asset management company. However, the economy tanked in the early 1970s, and in 1974, Bogle was fired from the company. Perhaps he was not the investor's savior, after all. Maybe, but let's keep the faith a little while longer.

Forming The Vanguard Group in 1975, he hit the ground running by providing administrative and asset management services to his former employer. Bogle's biography on Vanguard.com notes that these services were provided "on an at-cost basis." Make a mental note of that. The following year the company introduced the First Index Investment Trust. All the pieces were in place, but for what? [cxlix] [cl]

At the time, investment companies had stockholders who expected them to earn profits. The companies did so by creating and promoting mutual funds, enticing investors to purchase shares in the funds, and charging them fees for managing their money. This creates a troubling dynamic.

Let's say that the manager of StoneRockBoulder Genovia Region fund approaches the CEO of the StoneRockBoulder investment company explaining that because he and his team have adopted a new technology platform, costs have decreased. He suggests lowering the fees charged to the *fund's* shareholders. The CEO, however, resists. Why? She realizes that if actual costs are lower while the same fees continue to be charged, this will result in higher profit for the *investment company's* shareholders. It begs the basic question, for whose benefit is the mutual fund actually being run? Jack Bogle answered this question loudly and clearly by structuring The Vanguard Group such that it is owned by its funds' shareholders. If this seems familiar, that's because it's similar to how credit unions are owned—i.e., by their account holders.

Even if the goings-on in the stock market are just background noise to you, you probably believe that it has done well over time, and that wealth can be built by investing in it. You would be correct. Over the 50 years between 1965 and 2015, the compound annual growth of stocks, including re-invested dividends, was 9.75%.[cli] This is a substantial rate of return that investors should be happy to sign up for, if only they could.[140] Enter the aforementioned First Index Investment Trust, which was created to hold a variety of stocks representing the overall market. We learned earlier that groups of stocks that are a fair representation of a market, like the S&P 500, are known as *indexes.* This fund, managed at a low cost, was the first *index fund* available to us *retail* investors.

Its launch was anything but auspicious, raising only $11 million, a small fraction of Bogle's goal of $150 million. There were early struggles to match the S&P 500 index.[clii] Then came the go-go markets of the 1980s and 1990s, wherein even actively managed mutual fund investors were earning too much to care about fees.

Perhaps due to the dot.com crash of 2000, the housing debacle of 2008, the growing awareness that actively managed funds weren't earning their fees—or all three—Jack Bogle was finally welcomed in from the cold. The man who had for decades preached the idea of giving investors a "fair shake," a chance to buy and own American businesses at a low cost, found his audience. Investors came over to Mr. Bogle's way of thinking: *It is better to be, than try to beat, the market.*

---

140 Past performance, however, is not a guarantee of similar future results.

They began voting with their money, redeeming their actively managed mutual fund shares and buying shares in the renamed Vanguard 500 Index Fund. Today, investors have $500 billion invested in the Vanguard 500 Index Fund,[cliii] and The Vanguard Group manages $5 trillion of assets.[cliv] [141]

Jack Bogle's idea not only established Vanguard as a pioneer, it transformed an entire industry. A 2019 Bloomberg article bearing a headline that includes the phrase "epic shift" explains how the total dollars invested in passively managed equity index funds, at $4.271 trillion, had surpassed the $4.246 trillion invested in actively managed equity mutual funds.[clv] And, yes, the unnamed gentleman from *The Retirement Gamble* documentary is indeed Jack Bogle.

## The conventional retirement

It's the dream of many to enjoy a retirement of leisure one day, with the time to pursue long-held dreams. Early retirement would be nicer. The younger you are, the more likely you are to continue to have, as my colleague Jason likes to say, the "giddy-up" to tackle demanding pursuits. The goal of most people is to accumulate an amount of wealth that can support them until they pass away, as illustrated below:

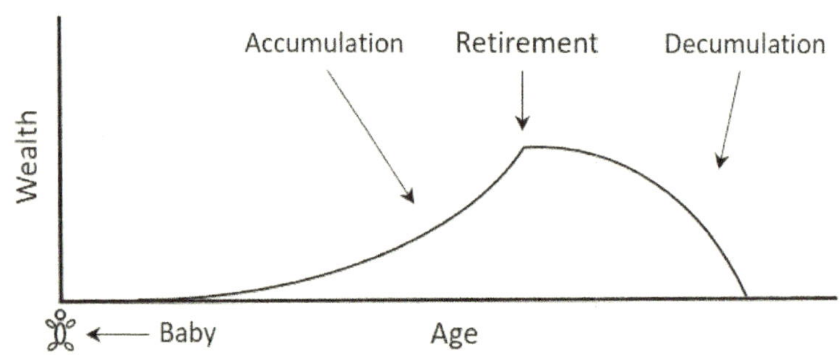


[141] It is only fitting that Mr. John Clifton Bogle, humble and lucid until his passing in 2019 at age 89, lived long enough to witness his once heretical proposition be widely embraced.

The building up of wealth is called the *accumulation* phase of one's life. Upon retirement, the *decumulation* phase starts. We expect the build-up of wealth to follow an exponential path. Unfortunately, in decumulation wealth accelerates downward because the dollars withdrawn each year are no longer around to produce future income.

### The careful

Let's look at the situation of Hubert, who barely held it together long enough to get out of high school. He began working in a trade and never looked back. His great-great-great uncle on his mother's side lived until he was 95. So, Hubert plans to work and save for 50 years to be sure his wealth will last him at least until age 90. His accumulation phase doesn't go quite as planned, but Hubert figures that he can still retire at 68 as long as he is careful with his spending. His lifetime wealth profile:

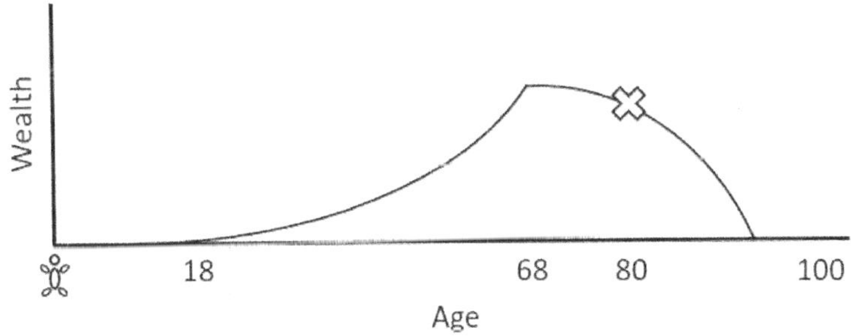


What spot is X marking? After eating macaroni and cheese from age 68 to 80, Hubert passes away. Having spent only a fraction of his accumulated wealth, he leaves the rest to his kids, who never called.

### The rebel

Hard-charging, chopper-riding, bourbon-shooting, rough neck Conrad retires from his job at age 60. A collection of scars, broken bones, and comorbidities, Conrad has an oft-repeated mantra: "I'm not here for a long time; I'm here for a good time." Still, owing to humble beginnings, he scrimped and saved, and has $402,605 in his retirement account. Conrad believes he'll never see age 65. Just in case, though, he wants his savings to provide for him until age 70.

The following table illustrates how Conrad will completely "draw down" his retirement account over 10 years, assuming he can earn 8% annually on his Roth IRA investments.

| | A | B=Ax8% | C=A+B | D | C-D |
|---|---|---|---|---|---|
| Age | Beginning balance | 8% earned | Year-end balance | Annual with-drawal | Ending balance |
| 60 | $402,605 | $32,208 | $434,813 | $60,000 | $374,813 |
| 61 | $374,813 | $29,985 | $404,798 | $60,000 | $344,798 |
| 62 | $344,798 | $27,584 | $372,382 | $60,000 | $312,382 |
| 63 | $312,382 | $24,991 | $337,373 | $60,000 | $277,373 |
| 64 | $277,373 | $22,190 | $299,563 | $60,000 | $239,563 |
| 65 | $239,563 | $19,165 | $258,728 | $60,000 | $198,728 |
| 66 | $198,728 | $15,898 | $214,626 | $60,000 | $154,626 |
| 67 | $154,626 | $12,370 | $166,996 | $60,000 | $106,996 |
| 68 | $106,996 | $8,560 | $115,556 | $60,000 | $55,556 |
| 69 | $55,556 | $4,444 | $60,000 | $60,000 | $0 |

The table shows that Conrad can withdraw $60,000 to live on each year. The remaining account value continues to earn 8%. Conrad's wealth profile:

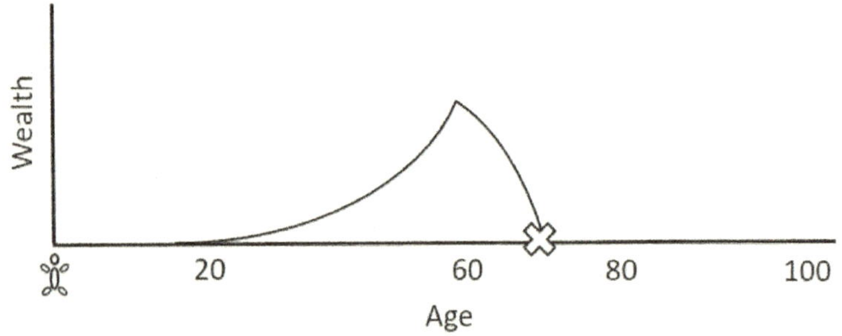

At point X, Conrad walks out of his doctor's office in dismay. Later on, he meets a friend for a beverage. Seeing that Conrad is out of sorts, his friend asks him what's going on. Conrad replies, "My doctor just hit me with something I wasn't expecting." Leaning forward his friend deadpans, "What did he tell you?" "He said that, all things considered, I'm in pretty good shape." "Isn't that a good thing?" his confused friend replies. "Not really. I'm flat broke."

Graduates of my investing course are apt to recall several of the Dirty Dozen risks we explore in great depth. When it comes to retirement, the biggest uncertainty, the wild card, is how long we will live. Not being able to know brings *longevity risk*, the possibility we will outlive our money, front and center. Conrad outlived his money, but Hubert's situation is tragic in its own right. Being so concerned about falling victim to longevity risk, he traveled rarely, indulged sparingly and didn't allow himself to enjoy the fruits of a lifetime of delayed gratification.

How did Conrad's money go away so quickly? In the first year of his 10-year wealth drawdown table, we see that his $400,605 in investments earned $32,208. But, with annual withdrawals of $60,000, he not only withdrew all of the first year's earnings, but also $27,792 ($60,000 minus $32,208) of investment principal. The following year there is less money in the account, so it earns less. This means he must withdraw even more of the principal the following year, until it's all gone in just 10 short years.

## How much is enough?

Because most people, financial professionals and systems approach retirement using this conventional paradigm of accumulation and later decumulation, let's stay with it a little longer.

In our budgeting chapter, we saw that Justine and Alberto got on track—we'll assume at age 30—saving $600 per month toward their retirement. It's a late start, but not uncommon. Justine graduated college, secured a job, moved into an apartment, got a roommate, dated, got married and purchased a home. It is what it is. At age 30, they sit at their kitchen table with a retirement calculator open on their laptop. Assuming the couple saves for 37 years, at their retirement age of 67 their sizable accumulated wealth possibilities are (column B):

| $600 saved per month for 37 years[142]... | | |
|---|---|---|
| A | B | B/2.99 |
| earning a rate of ... | will accumulate to ... | but will be able to buy as much as ... does today |
| 6% | $916,330 | $306,955 |
| 7% | $1,154,429 | $386,714 |
| 8% | $1,462,106 | $489,781 |
| 9% | $1,860,307 | $623,171 |
| 10% | $2,376,284 | $796,015 |

This is the good news. The bad news is that if the rate of inflation is 3% per year, the price of an item that costs $1 today will be $2.99 in 37 years.[143] Basically, the price of everything will have tripled by the time they retire. By taking a third of these sums (column C), we get a sense for their current purchasing power.

Is it enough? One of the reasons you may be reading this book is because you suspect the answer is "that depends." It depends on what rate of return they can achieve. If it's close to 6%, it's not looking like a retirement full of tropical sunsets. If it's close to 10%, their situation will be much brighter. Will they have a supplemental source of income, such as Social

---

142 For simplicity, we are compounding annually using $600 x 12 months = $7,200 saved per year.

143 $\$1 \times (1+0.03)^{37} = \$2.99$.

Security, carrying some of the load? If their wealth accumulation occurs in traditional IRAs and 401(k)s (as opposed to their Roth alternatives), the couple will have to assume a certain percentage of their withdrawals will be lost to income taxes. We say "certain percentage" because we don't know what personal income tax rates will be several decades in the future. Will the couple be adventurous in retirement, spending as much as or more than they did when they worked? After all, they'll have a lot of newly found free time to fill. Will they realize that they want to stay engaged by working a few days each week? Will one or the other require long-term care? If so, are they adequately insured for the costs?

And, of course, we have the issue of how long the couple will live. With two adults in the mix, we now have to be concerned with a whole new set of probabilities. Assuming they both reach age 67, there is a 90% chance that one will live to age 84. That sounds about right. But there's a 67% chance that one will live to age 90! There's even a 36% chance, more than one in three, that one of them will live to age 95.[clvi]

## The unconventional retirement

The holy grail of retirement is to generate a never-ending stream of income that can't be outlived. Based on the statistics we just saw, it would be wise to set our sights on ways to achieve this.

### Living off investment earnings

Early on, we briefly described winning the financial game of life. We said that the game was won when a person or couple could live off the earnings of their investments and never need to "eat into" the principal. The final figure in the last table was $796,015. This is the amount Justine and Alberto will have accumulated in wealth in today's dollars at an annual 10% rate of return. If they can continue to achieve that rate, they will earn $79,602 each year. If they can support themselves on that sum (and other sources of recurring income, such as Social Security), they will be able to avoid touching their investment principal and can look forward to generating the same annual income indefinitely.

What's the downside here? Let's say that Justine and Alberto are able to earn a substantial, but not quite as impressive, rate of return of 8%. By retirement age, they'll have $489,781 in today's dollars. At a continued 8% rate of return, they can look forward to it earning $39,182 each year, which may not be enough.

We see that living off one's investment income requires that the investment principal be substantial and that it be able to continue earning an appreciable rate of return in retirement.

## Turning accumulated wealth into a pension

We dedicated a chapter to explaining ways we can transfer common risks over to insurance companies that have the resources to handle them. Thankfully, they can even handle longevity risk. Upon retirement, a couple can transfer their wealth (or as much of it as they wish) to an insurance company in return for the right to be paid a fixed sum of money each month until they pass away. This appears to be a dangerous proposition for the insurance company because it doesn't know how long a person will live. That's true, but because of another important concept we discussed—the law of large numbers—they don't have to know. If they make this deal with not one retiree, but thousands of them, for every person who lives five years past average life expectancy, there will be one who dies five years short of it. Collectively, everyone will pass away right on schedule.

This insurance is called an *annuity*. Annuities come in many types and with enough bells and whistles as to make them indecipherable. The simplest form, which we just described, has the retiree depositing a lump sum upon retirement in return for payments that begin right away. Let's look at an example of this Single Premium Immediate Annuity (SPIA) in the amount of $489,781, with the help of online quotes.

One *joint life* quote estimated a payment of $2,127 and another $2,143, for an average of $2,135 per month.[144] This equates to a scant $25,620 per year. Why is the annual income so low? Well, we just saw that there is a significant chance that at least one person in the couple will live to a very ripe old age. That possibility must be incorporated into the payment calculation. Second, the insurance company cannot be reckless with the lump sum, the single premium, it has been given. It's all well and good to talk about how stocks can do really well over time. But they are risky. The pile of cash that *annuitants* pay the insurance company is primarily invested in safer bonds instead. As we will discuss in our next (and last) chapter, interest rates are at historic lows. This means that bonds, with yields that reflect current interest rates, earn investors very little. It follows that if the insurance company can't earn much with the annuitant's premium, it's not able to pay much.

Let's also stress the stark consequences of the annuity arrangement. It's a non-cancellable deal, so once the premium check is cashed by the insurance company, it's gone.[145] We said earlier that the nature of an annuity is an exchange of a lump sum of cash for a right to receive payments until death. What if Justine and Alberto enter into an annuity by paying an insurance company their hard-earned $489,781, only to pass away in an accident a year later? In hindsight, the insurance company will have benefited greatly because its obligation to

---

[144] The sites sampled were immediateannuities.com and schwab.com. Information includes one male, one female, both age 67, living in NY.

[145] This is not really true, but was phrased this way for dramatic effect. In reality, acquirers of life insurance are entitled to a *free-look* period that gives them 10 or more days to cancel the policy.

pay ended earlier, much earlier, than it had planned. Notice as well that with an annuity there is no wealth for the couple to pass on to their children.

Lest you vow to swear off the SPIA forever, there is a way to recapture a portion of the premium. When the SPIA's "cash refund" option is checked, the remaining premium principal will be refunded to the annuitant's heirs upon the death of the last spouse, in return for a slightly lower monthly payment. By how much does this option reduce the monthly payment? The same annuity with the refund option will pay $2,056 at one site and $2,098 at another, for an average of $2,077. This compares to an average monthly payment of $2,135 without the refund provision. The $58 decrease is a reduction of 2.7%,[146] which appears to be a small price to pay to insure against the annuitants' early passing.

Again, however, the small reduction in the monthly payment is not the issue. The real issue is still how low the payment is. We tried to pull a rabbit out of a hat with the Single Payment Immediate Annuity, but it got stuck.

Let's not give up on our dream of substantial lifetime income just yet. What if there was a way to combine the higher rates of return the stock market is capable of generating with the guaranteed lifetime income of an annuity? Actually, there is. It was imagined and invented a long time ago and is called a *variable annuity.* Researching this Frankensteinian creation will make you aware of its high fees, serious tax implications and degree of complexity that leaves even variable annuity owners with little understanding of what they're actually holding. Investigate variable annuities and let me know what you learn.

---

[146] ($2,135 - $2,077)/$2,135 = $58/$2,135 = 0.027 = 2.7%.

## Improving retirement illustrations

Earlier we said that Justine and Alberto planned to retire at age 67 by saving $600 per month, beginning at age 30. We saw that by earning 8% annually this savings plan enables them to accumulate $489,781, in today's dollars, by age 67. Let's say they want to ensure that their money holds out until age 92.[147] That's 25 potential years of retirement! The following is their *amortization* table:

| Retirement Amortization with Fixed Withdrawal | | | | | |
|---|---|---|---|---|---|
| | A | B=Ax8% | C=A+B | D | C-D |
| Age | Beginning balance | 8% earned | Year-end balance | Annual with-drawal | Ending balance |
| 67 | $489,781 | $39,182 | $528,963 | $45,882 | $483,081 |
| 68 | $483,081 | $38,647 | $521,728 | $45,882 | $475,846 |
| 69 | $475,846 | $38,068 | $513,913 | $45,882 | $468,031 |
| 70 | $468,031 | $37,443 | $505,474 | $45,882 | $459,592 |
| 71 | $459,592 | $36,767 | $496,359 | $45,882 | $450,477 |
| 72 | $450,477 | $36,038 | $486,515 | $45,882 | $440,633 |
| 73 | $440,633 | $35,251 | $475,884 | $45,882 | $430,002 |
| 74 | $430,002 | $34,400 | $464,402 | $45,882 | $418,520 |
| 75 | $418,520 | $33,482 | $452,001 | $45,882 | $406,119 |
| 76 | $406,119 | $32,490 | $438,609 | $45,882 | $392,727 |
| 77 | $392,727 | $31,418 | $424,145 | $45,882 | $378,263 |
| 78 | $378,263 | $30,261 | $408,524 | $45,882 | $362,642 |
| 79 | $362,642 | $29,011 | $391,653 | $45,882 | $345,771 |
| 80 | $345,771 | $27,662 | $373,433 | $45,882 | $327,551 |

[147] The odds of one of them being alive at age 92 is still a staggering 55%! Age 97? 24%! One way to solve this persistent "problem" of living too long is to purchase a *longevity annuity* that begins at an advanced age, and which, because it has significant odds of never paying, can be purchased at an attractive premium.

| Retirement Amortization with Fixed Withdrawal (cont.) | | | | | |
|---|---|---|---|---|---|
| | A | B=Ax8% | C=A+B | D | C-D |
| Age | Beginning balance | 8% earned | Year-end balance | Annual with-drawal | Ending balance |
| 81 | $327,551 | $26,204 | $353,755 | $45,882 | $307,873 |
| 82 | $307,873 | $24,630 | $332,502 | $45,882 | $286,620 |
| 83 | $286,620 | $22,930 | $309,550 | $45,882 | $263,668 |
| 84 | $263,668 | $21,093 | $284,761 | $45,882 | $238,879 |
| 85 | $238,879 | $19,110 | $257,989 | $45,882 | $212,107 |
| 86 | $212,107 | $16,969 | $229,076 | $45,882 | $183,194 |
| 87 | $183,194 | $14,656 | $197,849 | $45,882 | $151,967 |
| 88 | $151,967 | $12,157 | $164,125 | $45,882 | $118,243 |
| 89 | $118,243 | $9,459 | $127,702 | $45,882 | $81,820 |
| 90 | $81,820 | $6,546 | $88,365 | $45,882 | $42,483 |
| 91 | $42,483 | $3,399 | $45,882 | $45,882 | $0 |

As we can see from the value in column D, based on our assumptions, the couple can withdraw $45,882 annually. It is likely to be supplemented by Social Security and perhaps the sale of, or a loan secured by, their fully paid-off home. There is a big issue with this illustration. Can you guess what it is?

Well, just because the couple is retiring doesn't mean that inflation will call it quits as well. Look down the table again. With each passing year that $45,882 will buy less and less. We discussed how prices will double in 24 years at an inflation rate of 3%. We're illustrating a 25-year retirement. By the time Justine, Alberto—or both—reach age 90, their annual withdrawal will buy half of what it purchased at the start!

If you're going to sit down at a computer and mess around with different scenarios, the better way to model retirement is to ensure that whatever dollar amount is to be withdrawn increases 3% each year while still allowing for withdrawals until the desired age. This is called a *graduated,* or *growing, annuity*. Following is their illustration with such an annuity:

| Retirement Amortization with Increasing Withdrawal | | | | | |
|---|---|---|---|---|---|
| | A | B=Ax8% | C=A+B | D=D+3% | C-D |
| Age | Beginning balance | 8% earned | Year-end balance | Annual with-drawal | Ending balance |
| 67 | $489,781 | $39,182 | $528,963 | $35,273 | $493,690 |
| 68 | $493,690 | $39,495 | $533,186 | $36,331 | $496,854 |
| 69 | $496,854 | $39,748 | $536,603 | $37,421 | $499,182 |
| 70 | $499,182 | $39,935 | $539,116 | $38,544 | $500,572 |
| 71 | $500,572 | $40,046 | $540,618 | $39,700 | $500,918 |
| 72 | $500,918 | $40,073 | $540,991 | $40,891 | $500,100 |
| 73 | $500,100 | $40,008 | $540,108 | $42,118 | $497,990 |
| 74 | $497,990 | $39,839 | $537,830 | $43,381 | $494,448 |
| 75 | $494,448 | $39,556 | $534,004 | $44,683 | $489,321 |
| 76 | $489,321 | $39,146 | $528,467 | $46,023 | $482,444 |
| 77 | $482,444 | $38,595 | $521,039 | $47,404 | $473,635 |
| 78 | $473,635 | $37,891 | $511,526 | $48,826 | $462,700 |
| 79 | $462,700 | $37,016 | $499,716 | $50,291 | $449,425 |
| 80 | $449,425 | $35,954 | $485,379 | $51,800 | $433,579 |
| 81 | $433,579 | $34,686 | $468,266 | $53,354 | $414,912 |
| 82 | $414,912 | $33,193 | $448,105 | $54,954 | $393,151 |
| 83 | $393,151 | $31,452 | $424,603 | $56,603 | $368,000 |
| 84 | $368,000 | $29,440 | $397,440 | $58,301 | $339,139 |
| 85 | $339,139 | $27,131 | $366,270 | $60,050 | $306,220 |
| 86 | $306,220 | $24,498 | $330,718 | $61,851 | $268,866 |
| 87 | $268,866 | $21,509 | $290,375 | $63,707 | $226,668 |
| 88 | $226,668 | $18,133 | $244,802 | $65,618 | $179,184 |
| 89 | $179,184 | $14,335 | $193,518 | $67,587 | $125,931 |
| 90 | $125,931 | $10,075 | $136,006 | $69,614 | $66,392 |
| 91 | $66,392 | $5,311 | $71,703 | $71,703 | $0 |

Scan down column D, which is growing 3% each year. What a difference! For the couple to withdraw an amount that will continue to preserve their purchasing power, the amount withdrawn in the first year must be only $35,273. In the last year, a withdrawal of $71,703 is required to buy what the initial withdrawal was able to purchase 25 years prior.

Note that this idea also applies to the "unconventional" retirement scenario. The amount withdrawn there must actually be less than the annual earnings of the retirement account so that it can continue to grow and support even greater withdrawals in the future. To reiterate, if you are going to tinker around with retirement scenarios, incorporate an increasing annual withdrawal. Old age has enough challenges. The last thing you want to do is go broke slowly.

## The rise of the machines (robo advisors)

In some ways saving for retirement, as daunting as it appears, is simple. Saving X dollars for Y years earning a Z% rate of return will result in our sitting on a mountain of wealth one day. However, the never-ending array of choices, voices, opinions, studies and headlines leave us wandering aimlessly in a cloud of indecision. With so many options flying this way and conflicting viewpoints zooming that way, we descend into analysis paralysis. That's a shame because the longer we remain frozen, the more we miss out on the extraordinary power of compound growth.

Slashing through the mire is a growing army of new financial firms that harness the latest technology to simplify and streamline the investing process. In so doing, they make it approachable and affordable for the average investor. Their automated online platforms have become known as *robo advisors.* Engaging with a robo advisor is as simple as answering a few questions about your age, current financial position, income, risk tolerance, and savings goals. Based on this information, the advisor will tell you how much you'll need to invest each month in an index fund portfolio that it also constructs. Besides the ubiquitous retirement, common goals include saving for a down payment on a home, higher education and the elusive dream vacation.

Some robo advisors even formalize important personal finance practices, such as saving first for an emergency fund before directing money toward less critical savings objectives. Banking, insurance and estate planning are among other financial services they may offer.

## The robo advisor value proposition

After setting up a portfolio for each savings goal, the robo advisor will monitor the portfolio's growth against expectations. Should an issue arise, your robo friend will tap you on the shoulder and let you know in a visual manner, as follows:

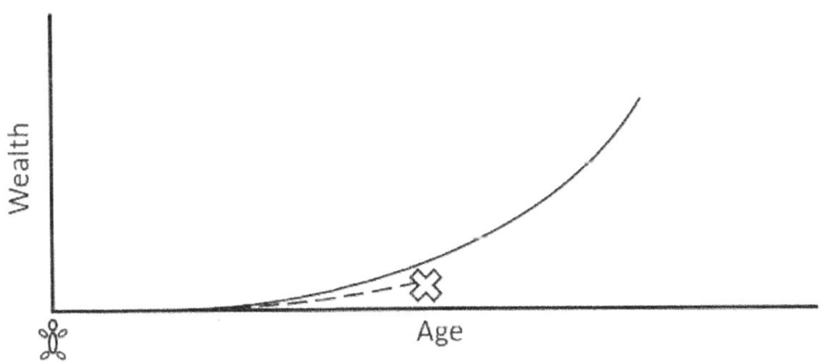


With your wealth growing along the path of the dashed line (when it was supposed to follow the solid line), you find yourself at point X. It's clear you're falling behind. Perhaps you missed a monthly contribution here or there. Perhaps the investments haven't performed as expected. What to do? The advisor will offer some options. It will let you know by how much you should increase your monthly contribution to get back on track. Another option is to extend the projected attainment of your goal. You might have dreamed of retiring at age 55, but in the overall scheme of things, if you have to wait until age 58, this should not be crushing news. A third option is to lower the dollar amount of your wealth accumulation goal. This may sound irresponsible, but if circumstances have changed, such as your developing an unanticipated income stream or inheriting an income-producing asset, you may not need your financial investments to carry as much of the load.

The cost of a robo advisor is in the vicinity of 0.25% to 0.30% of the account value per year. That's one-fourth of one percent to three-tenths of one percent. If your account has a value of $100,000, the fee is $250. For a $500,000 account, the annual fee would be $1,250. The costs incurred to manage the Exchange Traded Funds (ETFs) that make up your portfolio represent additional costs.[148] Thankfully, ETFs carry low fees. How low? In 2018, leading robo advisor Betterment reported that the ETF fees for its recommended portfolios ranged from 0.07% to 0.15%.[clvii] The bottom line is that it is possible to have one's investment assets effectively invested and managed for an all-in cost of less than one half of one percent.

### *Portfolio rebalancing*

There are additional benefits your robo buddy provides to keep your portfolio fine-tuned. Consider that over time some of the asset classes in your portfolio will rise in value more than others. They may rise in value as others fall. This results in the wedges of the pie chart, the distribution of your wealth across asset classes, drifting away from the carefully planned allocations with which you began. To reset your portfolio to

---

[148] An Exchange Traded Fund, or ETF, is an index fund that, because it can be bought and sold during the trading day, is the best vehicle for advisors to build and maintain portfolios. Individual investors are also able to invest directly in ETFs.

the ideal—the *model*—allocation, requires you to sell a certain amount of assets in classes that are now overrepresented (because they've increased in value) and use the cash raised to buy more assets in classes that are now underrepresented.

Let's say that one dreamy day you inherit $200,000. You open an investment account and invest it in a simple portfolio that's evenly split between stocks and bonds. A year later, your stocks have gone up 8% in value, and your bonds have gone up 2% in value. The following illustrates your year:

| Asset class | Planned allocation | Starting value | First year's return | Ending value | Ending allocation |
|---|---|---|---|---|---|
| Stocks | 50% | $100,000 | 8% | $108,000 | 51.43% |
| Bonds | 50% | $100,000 | 2% | $102,000 | 48.57% |
| | Total | $200,000 | Total | $210,000 | |

At the end of the year, your stocks are worth $108,000 and your bonds are worth $102,000. The success of your equity investments caused your portfolio to be overrepresented in stocks. How do you *rebalance* this simple portfolio that is now worth $210,000? Going into the next year, you want half of this value, $105,000 ($210,000 divided by 2), invested in stocks and the same in bonds. With $108,000 in stocks and $102,000 in bonds, the solution is to sell $3,000 of your stocks and purchase $3,000 more in bonds. It should be comforting for investors to know that the robo advisor is on the job and rebalancing the portfolio automatically without them having to do or say a thing.

### *Tax loss harvesting*

In our chapter on taxes we explained that for a profit on an investment in a non-tax-preferenced account to be considered taxable, the investment has to be sold. Selling the investment at a price higher than the price at which it was bought locks in the profit and makes it real. We just provided an example, portfolio rebalancing, wherein investments are sold at a profit. Of course, we would expect to pay income tax on the realized gains. We also learned that if we sell an asset in a portfolio at a loss, the realized loss can be subtracted from the realized gain, thereby reducing or even fully negating the gain.

Here is an interesting twist: It is possible to hit the "sell" button to realize the loss on an investment that is down, after which we can repurchase the same investment moments later at virtually the same price. By doing so, we would get the benefit of the realized loss. We would also have practically continuous ownership of the investment, so we wouldn't miss out if its value recovers by moving higher.

Alas, this is literally too good to be true. The IRS has established the *wash sale* rule, which says that in order for a realized loss to be used to offset a realized profit or gain, the asset cannot be repurchased for at least 30 days after it has been sold.[149] The idea is that if you want the benefit of the tax loss that comes from selling the losing investment, you have to risk missing out on any recovery the investment may stage in the month after you sell it.

However, savvy investors can skirt this rule by selling a losing investment and then purchasing an investment that is in the same asset class and that behaves similarly to the investment that was sold. Purchasing the similar investment ensures that the portfolio remains properly balanced while taking advantage of the realized loss that's only available by selling a losing position. This portfolio maximization strategy is known as *tax-loss harvesting* and is another benefit provided automatically by the robo advisor.

---

[149] The rule also applies to the investor doubling up on the investment, buying shares at a low price, and then selling the originally-purchased shares at a loss within 30 days of the second purchase.

### *The personal touch*

While it is the hope of all robo advisory firms that you can get all of your financial needs met through their online interfaces (both to keep costs low and affirm that they've designed their systems well), there are just those times when it would be nice to speak to a human being. A physical setback might have you thinking that it would be better to begin taking Social Security early. Perhaps you've lost a lawsuit and need to come up with a certain amount of cash. More likely, it's the dreaded divorce.

To respond to these situations, many robo advisory firms offer a second tier of service to their clients that we will call "robo plus." While the regular robo advisor-only service is available for, say 0.25% of the value of your assets per year, robo plus, which gives you the ability to speak with the firm's certified financial professionals, may be priced at 0.40% of assets per year.

We should also note that while in the last decade several firms, such as Betterment and Wealthfront, have sprung from the ground up to be robo advisors, established investment firms now offer their own robo advisor services. An example is Charles Schwab, which calls its service "Intelligent Portfolios." Fidelity calls its robo advisor "Fidelity Go." Another is Vanguard's "Personal Advisor Services," which includes access to the company's investment professionals, for 0.30% per year.

In retrospect, it seems the robo advisor is the next logical step to fulfill Vanguard's mission, finally providing its investors a low-cost, comprehensive investment plan, not just a collection of low-cost funds. Vanguard's Personal Advisor Services has quickly jumped to the head of the robo advisor field, with over $100 billion of *assets under management*.[clviii]

## Standards of care

If you've been paying attention, there are several times in this chapter wherein it appears that the company or firm with which you are investing is not looking out for you. That's because there's a good chance it's not. Seriously. The most basic level of care that an investment advisor or firm must adhere to is the *suitability* standard. This means what it says: that the investment that's recommended to you must be suitable for your situation. For example, if you're about to retire and will need to replace a significant portion of your salary, a suitable investment is an income mutual fund.

The investment advisor has the ability to choose among several income funds from several investment companies, all of which are suitable. How to decide? Remember those mutual fund fees, some stated and some hidden? Well, some find their way back to the investment advisor in the form of annual *trailer fees,* which can vary from fund to fund. For example, one mutual fund may pay a trailer of 0.50% per year of the amount invested in the fund for as long as the retiree's money remains invested in it. Would it surprise anyone to learn that the fund into which the financial advisor places the retiree's money is the one that promises the largest trailer fee? With this scenario we begin to see the limits of the suitability standard.

Thankfully, there is a higher standard of care that many firms and advisors pledge to uphold, the *fiduciary* standard. Under the standard, the financial advisor is obligated to show the utmost loyalty to the investor and to put the best interests of the investor ahead of his or her own.

To shed light on the disparity between the guidance given by advisors in the two camps, let's highlight a key finding of the 2015 President's Council of Economic Advisors study. It estimated the nationwide annual cost of what it termed "conflicted" advice to be $17 billion.[clix]

Advisors with the Chartered Financial Analyst (CFA) or Certified Financial Planner (CFP) credential are fiduciaries. If there's ever a doubt as to whether the person you are considering engaging to help create and implement a financial plan is a fiduciary, simply ask, "Are you a fiduciary? Are you acting in my best interest?" If the advisor is not, he or she will be hard-pressed to answer the question to your satisfaction.

*Who is or was?* Aaliyah.

## Exercises on investing

1. You purchased one share of stock for $50 per share. One year after you bought it, you sell it for its current $53 price. You were also the recipient of $1 in dividends during the year you owned it. What is your total return? What is your total rate of return?
2. You own a bond with a 4% stated annual rate of interest. If inflation is 3% each year, what is your real annual rate of return?
3. Explain the relationship between the risk of an investment and its potential rate of return.
4. You inherit $100,000. If you can invest it at a rate of 5% per year for 40 years, how many dollars will you have after 40 years?
5. Research and describe the curious origin of provision 401(k) of the tax code.
6. Compare and contrast the traditional IRA with the Roth IRA.
7. Identify which significant personal expenditures the government allows to be paid with tax-advantaged income.
8. Identify two reasons why the S&P 500 is a better market indicator than the Dow Jones Industrial Average.

9. Explain how stocks and bonds, two major assets classes, are fundamentally different.
10. Besides stocks and bonds, identify two other asset classes that are part of the Ivy League endowment portfolio.
11. Identify the two main criticisms of actively managed mutual funds.
12. Research Peter Lynch. What actively managed mutual fund did he head? What annual compound rate of return did he achieve for the fund? To what extent did his success create goodwill toward the fund industry?
13. Identify two major contributions Jack Bogle made to the field of investing.
14. As it relates to actively managed mutual funds, research and explain "window dressing."
15. Identify the biggest risk related to retirement planning and two ways it can play out in real life. Hint: Review the stories of Hubert and Conrad.
16. Identify the insurance policy/product that can eliminate the risk you identified above, as well as its strengths and weaknesses.
17. Identify three services that a robo advisor provides that the average investor should find valuable.
18. Explain how a robo advisor can provide these services for a low fee.
19. Do an Internet search on the best robo advisors. What familiar names are there? Which are new to you? On what measures were they graded?
20. Research Regulation FD and Regulation BI. How do they impact the standard of care investment advisors provide to their clients?

# Chapter 10 Onward

We've covered a lot of ground. Now that we have so much content under our belts, let's see if we can make some larger sense of it. As well, there are several loose ends that did not fit snugly into any of the previous chapters, so here they are.

## Concerns

It's a big country. There's a lot going on, with much of it disconcerting. A smattering:

### Interest rates have fallen and they can't get up

Imagine you're watching an investing game show. The latest contestant is directed to the stage, where, behind her are two doors:

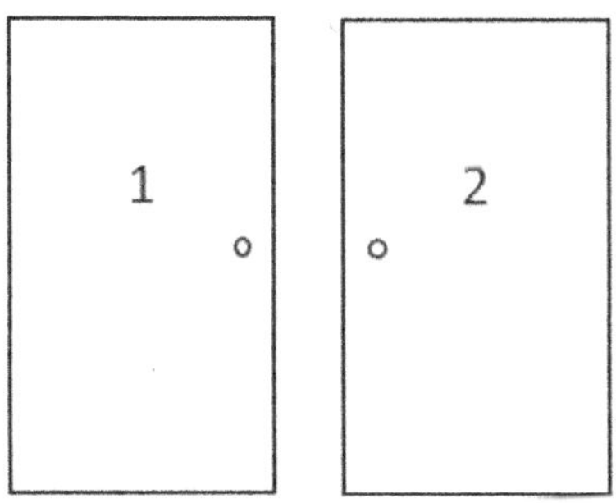


The host explains that if she places her money into the investment behind door 1, while there is risk, the investment provides her a good chance to achieve an appreciable rate of return. The host says that if she chooses the investment behind door 2, she will earn next to nothing. Turning back to the contestant, the host asks with bated breath, "So, which door do you choose?" This is not much of an exaggeration of the situation in which investors find themselves. The investment behind door 1 is equities—shares of common stock. The investment behind door 2 is bonds. Bonds are the stable, reliable portion of our portfolios. The interest rates they pay (and we earn) are dependent on prevailing interest rates in the economy. Following is a chart of one of the key interest rates from 1962 through the spring of 2020, courtesy of the Federal Reserve:[150]

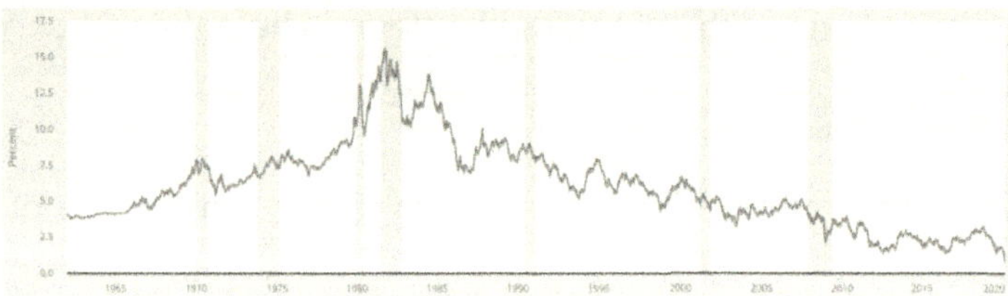

Rates, which had already been falling for decades, took a big step down in the aftermath of the Great Recession of 2008 (marked by the wide vertical band on the right). The coronavirus finished them off. Due to a host of reasons that must be left for another day, we are in a period of financial repression that is likely to see interest rates continue to lay helplessly on the floor.

One of the two major asset classes upon which investors have always built their portfolios is barely getting it done, if at all. Perhaps you have an idea. You'll just go and purchase the bonds of foreign issuers—in Europe, perhaps. Well, at the time of this writing, a 10-year German treasury bond will earn you a *negative* rate of interest. The 0% floor was always thought to represent absolute bottom. Somehow, it has been breached. Let's hope negative rates don't come to our shores.

The tragedy (a word not used lightly) of this new reality is that regardless of investors' risk tolerances or the vulnerable life stages in which they may find themselves, they are nonetheless herded into investing in the stock market. They simply have no choice.

One of the ways I've tried to recognize the fact that the

[150] Shown is the 10-year treasury constant maturity rate.

fixed-income portion of one's portfolio earns little is by using what seem like modest overall portfolio rates of return, such as 6%, 7% and 8%, in the illustrations of investment growth over time. It'd be much more exciting to assume you're going to earn 12% per year, accumulate millions and retire early. In this new age, I don't believe it would be responsible to do so.

## The all-consuming weight of the idyllic life

A recent survey revealed that more than 67%, two out of every three of us, are somewhat, or extremely, anxious over the state of our finances.[clx]

Knowledge is power, however, and by turning these pages you've now got a lot of both. By taking the positive steps discussed below, you will soon realize that the formidable challenge of successfully managing your personal finances can be met. Alas, you are among a small minority who have chosen to acquire the knowledge needed to face the issues head on.

Years ago, I watched a documentary by economist Robert Reich. In it he discussed how, as the last several decades unfolded, we gradually transitioned from one-income earning families to two-income earning families to preserve our lifestyles in the face of rising costs (and stagnant wages). As costs continued to rise (no doubt alongside our tastes and expectations), we began to work more hours. Finally, to maintain, we began taking on—and then going deep into—debt. All this in service of our lifestyles. But why? The cold truth is that it's better to have never achieved a status than to have had and lost it. No one wants to take a step down, to give up even one hard-fought-for rung, on the economic ladder. So, we hold on for dear life.

Being consumed with preserving our lifestyles means sometimes not being there for our kids. Even when we're physically present, we're emotionally absent. At least at some level we're aware of what it's costing them. A less urgent area that suffers from our living as we do is civic engagement. Assume a likeminded friend informs you that two Mondays from today there's a rally planned at the state capitol. She asks if you are interested in attending. Your response is a wry smile. With the new roll-out at the company, there's no way you can risk the bad optics of taking off that day. Perhaps you get paid hourly, and you literally can't afford to take a day off. Our republic only works when we have an informed citizenry that advocates for the causes in which it believes. When we are too exhausted to engage, to fight for what we believe in, we wind up living with critical policies that were crafted by others. Over time, we risk becoming citizens of a country we no longer recognize.

### What the coronavirus has laid bare

It began with a vague notice about a little understood virus in a far-off land. Then, like a tidal wave the coronavirus arrived here and wreaked the place. Tens of millions of citizens already leaning over their skis were faced with a prospect they never imagined: no job and no income until further notice.

Instead of having to pray that the government will come through with financial aid, instead of having to decide whether to pay the rent or the utilities, instead of having to forage around the house for things to sell on line, those who have adopted sound financial practices are secure in the knowledge that their emergency funds will get them through. This lesson will never be more stark nor the wake-up call more piercing.

## Advice

Disclaimer: The following is general advice. If it speaks to you and your current situation, act on it! If not, keep it in your memory bank for possible future use.

## Work on you

Instead of equipping our youth to navigate an increasingly challenging course, we've actually handicapped them. Quieted by electronic devices at too tender an age, iGens are addicted to social media; they draw their self-esteem from how many likes their posts receive. Their universe has been reduced to the 15-square-inch black mirror that is their cell phones. All the false intimacy that comes from spending five to six hours a day online has left them lonely, anxious and depressed.[clxi].

To boost your chances of living a satisfying life, it's more important than ever to work on you and become your best self. Put the phone down and see how long you can do without it. Spend stretches of time outside. Find your faith. Learn to be grateful. Be honest with yourself. Let go of people who are about nothing but drama. Meet your friends in person. Exercise. Eat well. Get enough sleep. Make time for the people you love and the pursuits that bring you joy.

Of time, there's only the past, the present and the future. The past has already happened and can't be changed. What's the point of fixating on it? Worry isn't going to help the future play out more favorably. Ultimately, we're left with the present. Learn how to make the most of it. Get out of your head and live in the moment. It's a place worth being.

## Start moving forward

The most difficult step in moving toward financial independence is the first one. Open a bank account and start building an emergency fund. Begin using a budgeting app to track your spending. Test-drive the online robo advisors by working through different "what if" scenarios. You can do all these, even as a student who is not yet self-supporting. The good news is that the time you spend contemplating and planning your adult life is preparing you to make sound decisions when it arrives.

## Don't be too proud to save

About a decade ago, there premiered a show on "extreme couponers," individuals who would present a combination of store- and manufacturer-provided savings to the cashier, resulting in their either paying a pittance or, although they'd paid nothing, receiving a refund! This has to take the prize: being paid to walk out of the grocery store with a cart full of food.

The most diabolical money-saving maneuver I've ever heard came from a show on cheapskates. One of the subjects explained that he once got a stain on his favorite shirt that he could not get out. He didn't want to pay the cost of dry cleaning. Instead, he donated the shirt to his local thrift shop. The shop presumably had a relationship with a local dry cleaner that would charitably clean its clothes. He watched for his shirt to show up on the rack and eventually was able to scoop it up for half of what it would have cost to dry clean.

It should go without saying, but there's no reason to spend any more money for a good or service than necessary. Whether it's using coupons, buying in bulk, patronizing off-price stores, comparison shopping, negotiating large ticket items, or bundling purchases, when it comes to which money saving strategy to adopt, the answer is "All the above."

## Get college credits in high school

The cost of a four-year education, with room and board, at some colleges is well in excess of the median $226,800 home price.[clxii] If you decide that college is for you, an effective way to keep costs down is to begin accumulating college credit while still in high school. The primary method for doing so is to take Advanced Placement (AP) courses and to score well on their year-end exams. The exam's sub-$100 fee is the only cost associated with an AP course, a tiny fraction of the charge for a three-credit course at the typical university.

A similar strategy is to take college-level courses taught in conjunction with local universities. While atypical, my high school's business education department offers students the ability to earn 36 college credits. Graduating business majors can actually roll up to their colleges as sophomores.

In both instances, the caveat is that each university has its own policy regarding the types of credits it will accept, and to what extent. It pays to research them. As could be expected, the more selective the college, the less likely it is to translate these courses into credits.

## Maximize workplace saving

Once you are situated in a solid, full-time job that will hopefully be the start of a rewarding career, make sure to take full advantage of its benefits.

### *Max out your employer's 401(k) match*

In our discussion of tax-advantaged saving and investing, we met Kirby. He earns $100,000 per year. His employer matches the first 3% of employee' contributions to their 401(k)s. Kirby's employer will match the first $3,000 of the salary he saves. By saving $3,000, he'll have $6,000. It is a no-brainer, an instant 100% return.[151] It is nothing less than a financial sin not to contribute up to the limit that one's employer will match!

### *Boost savings with each raise*

One of the vexing challenges adults continually face is "finding" extra money to save after the low-hanging fruit has been picked. An opportunity that will hopefully present itself from time to time is an outsized raise for superior job

[151] Unfortunately, some employers are taking to dangling the match over new employees' heads by establishing a *vesting period* during which employees forfeit some of the match if they leave the company.

performance.[152]

A significant raise is basically found money. If you're serious about reaching your financial goals, you'll know immediately what to do with the additional income. You're not going to upgrade your vehicle from an entry-level sedan to a luxury sedan. You're not going to add a man cave by blowing out the back of the house. You're not going to Vegas to stay a week in the Presidential Suite. You are not going to do any of these things because you will not allow yourself to become a victim of the awful scourge that fells too many, the aforementioned lifestyle creep. Instead, you will call the firm's HR department and promptly ratchet up your 401(k) contribution by the lion's share of your raise.

## Don't go it alone

Today, 46% of Americans report feeling alone sometimes or always.[clxiii] At the same time, median home prices are unaffordable for average wage earners in 319 of 483 counties.[clxiv] And yet, inexplicably, the number of Americans living alone has reached 35.7 million. This represents 28% of households, up from 13% in 1960.[clxv]

Although it may fall on deaf ears, I'll offer an idea that would solve a lot of problems: Get a roommate. Seriously, humans are social animals. Why be broke and lonely by living alone? Perhaps you consider yourself "particular," "fussy" or set in your ways. Perhaps you should get over yourself. Perhaps you should try to better yourself by finding the redeeming qualities in others. Perhaps that will have you building relationships and finding a roommate with whom you get along.

Young people, do you want a rewarding retirement for your

---

152 The reason we say "outsized" is that, as we've established previously, you need to receive raises of 3% per year just to keep pace with inflation.

parents who have sacrificed so much for you that they're now "below plan?" Do you really mean that? If so, then explore a *multigenerational house* with a layout that will allow your parents to have their privacy while you all live under one roof. Imagine how close a bond your children can form with your parents. Imagine how much you will save on babysitting.

People, we have talked about how living expenses are the single largest component of a budget. Here's your invitation to transform a vexing challenge into something wonderful.

## Continue exploring

If you want to continue this journey of financial literacy, following is a list of recommendations that should keep you busy for a while:

- Watch the PBS Frontline documentary *The Retirement Gamble,* which really personalizes the themes of this book.
- To be forewarned is to be forearmed, so why not watch *The Pension Gamble,* also from PBS Frontline, as well? If you are entitled to receive a pension, it's high time to learn what a canary in a coal mine looks like.
- The 2008 housing crisis wasn't just one of those things that happens from time to time. To learn how vulnerable we are to bad actors in our financial system, watch *Inside Job* by Charles Ferguson. Have your preferred stress management device nearby because it's going to be an infuriating ride.
- Read Dave Ramsey's *Total Money Makeover* and/or *Complete Guide to Money.* Dave, with a nationally syndicated radio show that has become a fixture over the last 25 years, is the guru of personal finance. His advice is especially valuable for adults who are in a financial bind. You'll learn about his "baby steps," getting the debt elimination "snowball" moving downhill, how to negotiate, and much more.

- o Read *MONEY Master the Game* by Tony Robbins. As the man who put life-improvement coaching on the map, Tony has the wealth and standing to dismiss reprisals that might have resulted from calling out the investment industry for its sins. Call it out, he does. The book has many compelling personal stories, even managing to introduce rarely talked about investments such as *structured notes*.
- o Read up on a guy named Alexander Green and his book *The Gone Fishin' Portfolio*. If you want to try your hand at creating your own investment portfolio, *Gone Fishin'* is worth a read. You'll have the benefit of a 0.00% advisory fee, unless, of course, you want to charge yourself for your services.
- o Evaluate, download and fire up mobile apps that facilitate budgeting, banking and investing. Knowing what's going on with your finances is empowering, and there's no more convenient way to do that than with a glance at your phone.

## Asks

This is no time to be bashful, so I ask for your help.

### *Support the cause*

Like sunshine, puppies, and ice cream, everyone loves financial literacy. We're confident that we can conquer the financial challenges of living a modern life by equipping ourselves with financial knowledge.

Actions haven't matched platitudes, however, since only six states have incorporated the gold standard in financial literacy education, a stand-alone course at the high school level.[clxvi] [153]

---

153 The states with a stand-alone high school course requirement are Alabama, Iowa, North Carolina, Tennessee, Utah and Virginia.

It's not a requirement in my own state, New York. Despite being a part of the twelfth best public school district in the nation,[clxvii] I am unable to report that it is a graduation requirement, because it isn't. To be sure, over the years I've dropped a few hints. But there's a problem with my advocacy. As an educator, I am not the district's "customer." That would be the parents living in the district. It is they that the school board and district administration rightfully listen to and serve. If you are a parent who believes that all young people graduating into adulthood should be financially literate, it's time to mobilize. Contact your district's board members to request that a financial literacy course be a high school graduation requirement. Canvas like-minded parents and have them do the same. Build a movement, and persist.

Set your sights higher by contacting your state's education department. Heck, send this copy of the book to the state board to demonstrate in black and white what some fortunate students in some high schools are learning.

You've always had the power to direct education policies and priorities. It's time to use it.

## *Help put this book on the map*

Dear reader, FinanciLit is self-published and will flourish or wither based on your support. If you have enjoyed this journey, learned a few things and gained new insights, please go online and leave a review to let others know. Then, pass this book on to someone who can benefit from it!

## *Take the conversation on line*

Throughout this book I've tried to approach each topic in a manner that addresses questions that commonly arise. There's no way, however, that I've addressed them all. Find me at FinanciaLit or Financialit_ on social media so we can continue the conversation. There are many questions I have for you, so I hope to see you on line!

## Closing

It recently occurred to me that the financial industry is waging a war to undermine the hard-won confidence we've built in our financial knowledge. It's a subtle but insidious affront. What do I mean? A typical article headline blares: "Beware These 10 Retirement Blunders!" Okay. Alright. It's advertising. It's meant to catch our eye. But, at some level we can't help but wonder what type of person would commit a blunder. Perhaps a fool. Maybe a dunce. Possibly a buffoon. We pray we're none of these things, muster up some courage and then click on the article. Before long, there it is in black and white, a passage that warns against making a financial decision we were sure was sound and were just about to carry out. The condemnation hits us like a hammer blow. As panic rushes in, we freeze. We question everything. We wonder if we're in way over our heads. We wonder if maybe we were just kidding ourselves the whole time, that maybe we should have turned our money and decision making over to that persuasive financial advisor we met a while back.

Haters reside in every facet of society. Why should the finance discipline be any different? Name a company, an investment or a strategy, and I'll find you a financial expert who hates it.

Here's what I can confidently declare: If you understand what you've read in these pages, then you are FinanciaLit! Never forget it and never doubt it. From your strong foundation, you are ready to converse with HR departments, banks, insurance companies, investment firms and the like as you turn your financial plans into reality. Should you encounter a specialist who is unable or unwilling to abandon industry jargon and speak to you in plain English, recognize that this is a reflection of him or her. You deserve to work with people who fully respect you, your time, your money and your objectives. Accept nothing less.

# NOTES

i. Halah Touryalai, "Work Until You Die? More Middle Class Americans Say They Can Never Retire," October 25, 2013, *Forbes*, http://www.forbes.com/sites/halahtouryalai/2013/10/25/work-until-you-die-more-middle-class-americans-say-they-can-never-retire/.

ii. "Jim Simons," *Forbes*, May 21, 2020, http://www.forbes.com/profile/james-simons/.

iii. "James Harris Simons: biography," *FamPeople.com*, May 18, 2019, www.fampeople.com/cat-james-harris-simons_2.

iv. David K. Li, "Surgeon Jumps from Bridge after Divorce from TV Personality Wife," *New York Post*, February 13, 2017, http://nypost.com/2017/02/12/surgeon-jumps-from-bridge-after-divorce-from-tv-personality-wife/.

v. Ben Brantley, "A Master of Mass Flirtation," *The New York Times*, November 11, 2011, http://www.nytimes.com/2011/11/11/theater/reviews/hugh-jackman-back-on-broadway-at-broadhurst-review.html.

vi. Peter Marks, "Hugh Jackman, Back? He IS Broadway," *The Washington Post*, November 11, 2011, https://www.washingtonpost.com/lifestyle/style/hugh-jackman-back-he-is-broadway/2011/11/10/gIQATWsh9M_story.html.

vii. "Hugh Jackman Net Worth," *Celebrity Net Worth*, August 6, 2015, http://www.celebritynetworth.com/richest-celebrities/actors/hugh-jackman-net-worth/.

viii. John Breech, "Vontae Davis Explains Why He Retired from the NFL in the Middle of a Bills Game," *CBSSports.com*, September 19, 2018, www.cbssports.com/nfl/news/vontag-davis-explains-why-he-retired-from-the-nfl-in-the-middle-of-a-bills-game/.

ix. Department of Labor, Bureau of Labor Statistics, *Consumer Price Index*, last modified May 22, 2020, https://www.bls.gov/cpi/home.htm.

x. Danielle Kurtzleben, "CHARTS: Just How Fast Has College

Tuition Grown?" *U.S News & World Report*, October 23, 2013, https://www.usnews.com/news/articles/2013/10/23/charts-just-how-fast-has-college-tuition-grown.

xi. Drew DeSilver, "For Most U.S. Workers, Real Wages Have Barely Budged in Decades," *FactTank News In The Numbers*, Pew Research Center, August 7, 2018, https://www.pewresearch.org/fact-tank/2018/08/07/for-most-us-workers-real-wages-have-barely-budged-for-decades/.

xii. Kathryn Vasel, "39 Million Households Are Paying More For Housing than They Can Afford," *CNNMoney*, Cable News Network, June 16, 2017, https://money.cnn.com/2017/06/16/real_estate/rising-home-costs-affordability-harvard/index.html.

xiii. Drew Lindsay, "Share of Americans Who Give to Charity Shrinks, Chronicle Data Shows," *The Chronicle of Philanthropy*, October 3, 2017, https://www.philanthropy.com/article/Share-of-Americans-Who-Give-to/241345.

xiv. Amanda Dixon, "Historical CD Interest Rates 1984-2020," *Bankrate*, last modified May 12, 2020, https://www.bankrate.com/banking/cds/historical-cd-interest-rates-1984-2020/.

xv. Federal Trade Commission, Consumer Financial Protection Bureau, How Long Does It Take to Pay off a Student Loan? last modified August 7, 2017, https://www.consumerfinance.gov/ask-cfpb/how-long-does-it-take-to-pay-off-a-student-loan-en-621/.

xvi. Zack Friedman, "Student Loan Debt Statistics In 2018: A $1.5 Trillion Crisis," Forbes, October 14, 2019, https://www.forbes.com/sites/zackfriedman/2018/06/13/student-loan-debt-statistics-2018/#74caaa6a73.

xvii. John W. Schoen, "The Real Reasons a College Degree Costs So Much," CNBC, last modified December 8, 2016, https://www.cnbc.com/2015/06/16/why-college-costs-are-so-high-and-rising.html.

xviii. U.S. Department of Transportation, Federal Highway Administration, Average Annual Miles per Driver by Age Group, last modified March 29, 2018, https://www.fhwa.dot.gov/ohim/onh00/bar8.htm.

xix. Federal Trade Commission, Consumer Financial Protection Bureau, What Is a Grace Period for a Credit Card? last modified July 6, 2017, https://www.consumerfinance.gov/ask-cfpb/what-is-a-grace-period-for-a-credit-card-en-47/.

xx. Amelia Josephson, "The Average Credit Card Limit," Smartasset, August 20, 2018, https://smartasset.com/credit-cards/the-average-credit-card-limit.

xxi. Don Reisinger, "The Average American Household Has $8,284 in Credit Card Debt," *Fortune* December 10, 2018, https://fortune.com/2018/12/10/american-household-credit-card-debt/.

xxii. Kelly Dilworth, "2019 Retail Store Card Survey: APRs rise, Despite the Fed's Recent Rate Cuts, "*Creditcards.com,* last modified October 10, 2019, www.creditcards.com/credit-card-news/retail-store-credit-card-survey.php.

xxiii. Alex Van Abbema, "Target Among Retailers Pushing for the Right to Reject Certain Rewards Credit Cards," *Minneapolis/St. Paul Business Journal*, The Business Journals, last modified September 26, 2018, https://www.bizjournals.com/twincities/news/2018/09/26/target-among-retailers-pushing-for-the-right-to.html.

xxiv. Dilworth, Kelly, "Your Rights Under the Fair Credit Billing Act," *Creditcards.com*, June 5, 2015, https://www.creditcards.com/credit-card-news/fair-credit-billing-act-1282.php.

xxv. Board of Governors of the Federal Reserve, *Regulation II (Debit Card Interchange Fees and Routing)*, Washington, DC: GPO, 2017, https://www.federalreserve.gov/paymentsystems/regii-about.htm.

xxvi. "World Debit Mastercard Comfortably in Command," *Mastercard*, accessed September 14, 2019, https://www.mastercard.us/en-us/consumers/find-card-products/debit-cards/world.html.

xxvii. "What's Not in My FICO Scores," *MyFICO*, accessed September 30, 2019, https://www.myfico.com/resources/credit-education/credit-scores/whats-not-in-your-credit-score.

xviii. "What Is a Good Credit Score?" *Experian* (blog), accessed September 30, 2019, https://www.experian.com/blogs/ask-experian/credit-education/score-basics/what-is-a-good-credit-score/.

xxix. "Home Purchase Center," *MyFICO*, last modified May 22, 2020, https://www.myfico.com/loan-center/home-mortgage-rate-comparison/default.aspx.

xxx. Elizabeth Weise and Nathan Bomey, "Equifax Had Patch 2 Months Before Hack and Didn't Install It, Security Group Says," *USA Today*, September 14, 2017, https://www.usatoday.com/story/money/2017/09/14/equifax-identity-theft-hackers-apache-struts/665100001/.

xxxi. Federal Trade Commission, Consumer Financial Protection Bureau, "A Summary of Your Rights Under the Fair Credit Reporting Act," Washington, DC: GPO, accessed September 30, 2019, https://www.consumer.ftc.gov/articles/pdf-0096-fair-credit-reporting-act.pdf.

xxxii. Cara O'Neill, "An Overview of Chapter 13 Bankruptcy," *NOLO*, accessed October 27, 2019, https://www.nolo.com/legal-encyclopedia/chapter-13-bankruptcy-overview-30099.html.

xxxiii. Kathleen Michon, "A Chapter 7 Bankruptcy Overview," *NOLO*, accessed October 27, 2019, www.nolo.com/legal-encyclopedia/chapter-7-bankruptcy-overview-29571.html.

xxxiv. Cara O'Neill, "Nondischargeable Debts in Chapter 7 Bankruptcy," *NOLO*, last modified March 28. 2019, https://www.nolo.com/legal-encyclopedia/nondischargeable-debts-chapter-7-bankruptcy.html.

xxxv. Lucy Lazarony, "What Happens to Your Credit Score After Bankruptcy?" *Credit.com*, March 10, 2020, https://www.credit.com/credit-scores/3-things-bankruptcy-does-to-your-credit-score/.

xxxvi. Kimberly Amadeo, "Bankruptcy Abuse Prevention and Consumer Protection Act," *The Balance*, last modified May 30, 2019, https://www.thebalance.com/bankruptcy-abuse-prevention-and-consumer-protection-act-3305555.

xxxvii. Lorie Konish, "This Is the Real Reason Most Americans File for Bankruptcy," *CNBC*, last modified February 11, 2019, https://www.cnbc.com/2019/02/11/this-is-the-real-reason-most-americans-file-for-bankruptcy.html.

xxxviii. Mark P. Cussen, "Top 5 Reasons Why People Go Bankrupt," *Investopedia*, last modified February 24, 2020, https://www.investopedia.com/financial-edge/0310/top-5-reasons-people-go-bankrupt.aspx.

xxxix. Mark Matousek, "One of NYC's Most Important Landmarks Is Set for a Five-Year, $364 Million Repair Project – Here's How It Forever Changed The City's Traffic Patterns," *Business Insider*, March 3, 2018, https://www.businessinsider.com/holland-tunnel-new-york-traffic-repair-project-history-2018-3.

xl. Port Authority NY NJ, *2019 Monthly Traffic and Percent of E-ZPass Usage*, accessed October 5, 2019, https://www.panynj.gov/bridges-tunnels/pdf/traffic-e-zpass-usage-2019.pdf.

xli. Port Authority NY NJ, Bridges and Tunnels, *Tolls*, accessed October 5, 2019, http://www.panynj.gov/bridges-tunnels/tolls.html.

xlii. Jerry Adler, "The History of the Verrazano-Narrows Bridge, 50 Years After Its Construction," *Smithsonian Magazine*, November 2014, https://www.smithsonianmag.com/history/history-verrazano-narrows-bridge-50-years-after-its-construction-180953032/#BmLbDjtU8MT8xOcl.99.

xliii. Tamar Lapin, "Verrazzano-Narrows Bridge Is Now Most Expensive Toll In US," *New York Post*, last modified March 31, 2019, https://nypost.com/2019/03/31/verrazzano-narrows-bridge-is-now-most-expensive-toll-in-us/.

xliv. New York State, Department of Motor Vehicles, *Passenger Vehicle Registration Fees, Use Taxes and Supplemental Fees*, accessed October 5, 2019, https://dmv.ny.gov/registration/registration-fees-use-taxes-and-supplemental-fees-passenger-vehicles.

xlv. Dave Merrell, "Pa. Turnpike to Become Most Expensive Long Toll Road in Nation," *The Philadelphia Inquirer*, July 28, 2010,

https://www.inquirer.com/philly/blogs/our-money/Pa_Turnpike_to_become_most_expensive_toll_road_in_nation.html.

xlvi. "Sales Tax Rates," *Sale-Tax.com*, accessed October 9, 2019, http://www.sale-tax.com/.

xlvii. New York State, Department of Taxation and Finance, *Quick Reference Guide for Taxable and Exempt Property and Services*, TB-ST-740, last modified February 1, 2019, https://www.tax.ny.gov/pubs_and_bulls/tg_bulletins/st/quick_reference_guide_for_taxable_and_exempt_property_and_services.htm.

xlviii. Eric Figueroa and Juliette Legendre, "States That Still Impose Sales Taxes on Groceries Should Consider Reducing or Eliminating Them," *Center on Budget and Policy Priorities*, last modified April 1, 2020, https://www.cbpp.org/research/state-budget-and-tax/which-states-tax-the-sale-of-food-for-home-consumption-in-2017.

xlix. Mark Faggiano, "Which States Require Sales Tax on Clothing?" *TaxJar* (blog), May 2, 2018, https://blog.taxjar.com/sales-tax-on-clothing/.

l. Department of Homeland Security, Transportation Security Administration, *Security Fees*, accessed October 12, 2019, https://www.tsa.gov/for-industry/security-fees.

li. Department of the Treasury, Internal Revenue Service, *Excise Taxes*, February 2020, Pub. 510, Washington DC: GPO, https://www.irs.gov/publications/p510.

lii. "California Cigarette and Fuel Excise Taxes," *Sales Tax Handbook*, accessed October 12, 2019, https://www.salestaxhandbook.com/california/gasoline-fuel.

liii. Janelle Cammenger, "State Gasoline Tax Rates as of July 2019," *Tax Foundation*, July 31, 2019, https://taxfoundation.org/state-gas-tax-rates-2019/.

liv. "Gas Prices," *AAA*, accessed Oct. 12, 2019, https://gasprices.aaa.com/state-gas-price-averages/.

lv. Janelle Cammenger, "How High Are Cigarette Taxes in Your State?" *Tax Foundation*, April 10, 2019, https://taxfoundation.org/2019-state-cigarette-tax-rankings/.

lvi. New York State, Department of Taxation and Finance, *Cigarette and Tobacco Products Tax*, accessed October 12, 2019, https://tax.ny.gov/bus/cig/cigidx.htm.

lvii. "Map of Cigarette Excise Taxes & Price Per Pack," *Sales Tax Handbook*, accessed October 12, 2019, https://www.salestaxhandbook.com/cigarette-tax-map.

lviii. Florida Department of Revenue, *Sales and Use Tax on Rental of Living or Sleeping Accommodations*, GT800034, October 2018, https://floridarevenue.com/Forms_library/current/gt800034.pdf.

lix. "Understanding Hotel Taxes, Resort Fees & Deposits for Incidentals," *Your Mileage May Vary*, August 26, 2018, https://yourmileagemayvary.net/2018/08/26/understanding-hotel-prices-hotel-taxes-resort-fees-deposits-for-incidentals/.

lx. City of Anaheim, California, Department of Planning and Building, *Transient Occupancy Tax*, accessed October 13, 2019, https://www.anaheim.net/575/Transient-Occupancy-Tax.

lxi. City of Anaheim, California, Department of Planning and Building, *Anaheim Tourism Improvement District (ATID)*, accessed October 13, 2019, http://www.anaheim.net/565/Anaheim-Tourism-Improvement-District-ATI

lxii. Carina Martinez-Gouhier and Kathleen Hunker, "The Hotel Occupancy Tax In Texas," *Texas Public Policy Foundation*, May 2018, https://files.texaspolicy.com/uploads/2018/08/16104507/2018-04-RR-Hotel-Occupancy-Tax-in-Texas-CEP-MartinezHunker.pdf.

lxiii. "Average New-Car Prices Up 2% Year-Over-Year for August 2019, According to Kelley Blue Book" *Kelley Blue Book*, September 4, 2019, https://mediaroom.kbb.com/2019-09-04-Average-New-Car-Prices-Up-2-Year-Over-Year-for-August-2019-According-to-Kelley-Blue-Book.

lxiv. John S. Kiernan, "Property Taxes By State," *WalletHub*, February 25, 2020, https://wallethub.com/edu/states-with-the-highest-and-lowest-property-taxes/11585/.

lxv. Nassau County, New York, Office of the Comptroller, *Cole Layer Trumble Company: Countywide Reassessment Project*, report prepared by John S. Kiernan, comptroller, FA03-03, May 13, 2003, https://www.nassaucountyny.gov/DocumentCenter/View/3357/0503ReassessmentAudit?bidId=.

lxvi. John S. Kiernan, "Property Taxes by State," *WalletHub*, February 25, 2020, https://wallethub.com/edu/states-with-the-highest-and-lowest-property-taxes/11585/.

lxvii. Nassau County, New York, Department of Assessment, *Glossary of Assessment Terms*, accessed October 27, 2019, https://www.nassaucountyny.gov/1505/Glossary-of-Assessment-Terms.

lxviii. *Encyclopedia Britannica Online*, s.v. "Sixteenth Amendment," by Brian P. Smentkowski,, accessed October 27, 2019, https://www.britannica.com/topic/Sixteenth-Amendment.

lxix. *Encyclopedia.com*, s.v. "Underwood Tariff Act," last modified April 15, 2020, https://www.encyclopedia.com/history/encyclopedias-almanacs-transcripts-and-maps/underwood-tariff-act.

lxx. "Briefing Book: A Citizen's Guide to the Fascinating (Though Often Complex) Elements of the US Tax System," *Urban Institute and Brooking Institution Tax Policy Center*, accessed October 28, 2019, https://www.taxpolicycenter.org/briefing-book/what-are-sources-revenue-federal-government.

lxxi. Dylan Matthews, "The Myth of the 70,000-Page Tax Code," *Vox*, March 29, 2017, https://www.vox.com/policy-and-politics/2017/3/29/15109214/tax-code-page-count-complexity-simplification-reform-ways-means.

lxxii. Department of the Treasury, Internal Revenue Service, *Child Tax Credit and Credit for Other Dependents at a Glance*, Washington, DC: GPO, accessed November 7, 2019, https://www.irs.gov/credits-deductions/child-tax-credit-and-credit-for-other-dependents-at-a-glance.

lxxiii. Department of Commerce, United States Census Bureau, *New Data Show Income Increased in 14 States and 10 of the Largest Metros*, report by Gloria Guzman, last modified October 29, 2019,

https://www.census.gov/library/stories/2019/09/us-median-household-income-up-in-2018-from-2017.html.

lxxiv. Quentin Fottrell, "More Than 44% of Americans Pay No Federal Income Tax," *MarketWatch*, February 26, 2019, https://www.marketwatch.com/story/81-million-americans-wont-pay-any-federal-income-taxes-this-year-heres-why-2018-04-16.

lxxv. "2020 Federal and State Income Tax Rates," *Tax-Brackets.org*, accessed November 9, 2019, https://www.tax-brackets.org/.

lxxvi. New York State, Department of Taxation and Finance, *Instructions for Form IT-201*, accessed November 9, 2019, https://www.tax.ny.gov/pdf/current_forms/it/it201i.pdf.

lxxvii. SJ Lynn, "Stephen A. Smith Becomes ESPN's Highest-Paid Sportscaster," *SportingNews*, November 10, 2019, https://www.sportingnews.com/us/nba/news/stephen-a-smith-becomes-espns-highest-paid-sportscaster/1c3ju2mr4jp191wcu0lppnpjia.

lxxviii. Jessica Bursztynsky, "Joe Rogan's Podcast Moves Exclusively to Spotify, Stock Soars," last modified May 19, 2020, https://www.cnbc.com/2020/05/19/spotify-lands-exclusive-rights-to-joe-rogan-podcast.html.

lxxix. Tina Orem, "2019-2020 Capital Gains Tax Rates — and How To Calculate Your Bill," *Nerdwallet* (blog), May 21, 2020, https://www.nerdwallet.com/blog/taxes/capital-gains-tax-rates/.

lxxx. Tina Orem, "Dividend Tax Rate 2020: Find Out What You'll Owe," *Nerdwallet* (blog), March 19, 2020, https://www.nerdwallet.com/blog/taxes/dividend-tax-rate/.

lxxxi. Department of the Treasury, Internal Revenue Service, *Topic No. 559 Net Investment Income Tax*," Washington, DC: GPO, last modified February 12, 2020, https://www.irs.gov/taxtopics/tc559.

lxxxii. Elizabeth McNichol, "State Taxes on Capital Gains," *Center on Budget and Policy Priorities*, December 11, 2018, https://www.cbpp.org/research/state-budget-and-tax/state-taxes-on-capital-gains.

lxxxiii. Alex Smith, "Warren Buffett Pays Less in Taxes Than Secretary," *Wealthy Diligence*, May 8, 2019, https://wealthydiligence.com/warren-buffett-pays-less-in-taxes-than-secretary/.

lxxxiv. Kathy Pickering, "How the Tax Cuts and Jobs Act Impacts U.S. Tax Returns, *H&R Block*, last modified October 24, 2018, https://www.hrblock.com/tax-center/irs/tax-reform/tax-cuts-and-jobs-act.

lxxxv. "Wealth Taxes," *Politico*, last modified February 26, 2020, https://www.politico.com/2020-election/candidates-views-on-the-issues/tax-reform/wealth-taxes/.

lxxxvi. Tucker Higgins, "Elizabeth Warren Would Double Her Proposed Billionaire Wealth Tax to Help Fund 'Medicare For All,'" *CNBC*, last modified November 4, 2019, https://www.cnbc.com/2019/11/01/elizabeth-warren-would-double-billionaire-wealth-tax-for-medicare-for-all-plan.html.

lxxxvii. United States Department of State, Bureau of the Comptroller and Global Financial Services, Office of Financial Policy, Reporting, and Analysis, *Fiscal Year 2018 Agency Financial Report*, Washington, DC: GOP, accessed November 11, 2019, https://www.state.gov/wp-content/uploads/2018/12/FY-2018-Agency-Financial-Report.pdf.

lxxxviii. United States Department of Defense, *FY 2018 Budget*, accessed November 11, 2019, https://dod.defense.gov/News/Special-Reports/0518_budget/.

lxxxix. Kimberly Amadeo, "Current U.S. Federal Government Spending," *The Balance*, last modified March 30, 2020, https://www.thebalance.com/current-u-s-federal-government-spending-3305763.

xc. Social Security Administration, *Understanding the Benefits*, 2020, Pub. 05-10024, ICN 454930, Washington, DC: GPO, 7-8, https://www.ssa.gov/pubs/EN-05-10024.pdf.

xci. Department of Health and Human Services, Centers for Medicare & Medicaid Services, *Fast Facts*, Washington, DC: GPO, 2020, https://www.cms.gov/fastfacts/.

xcii. Centers for Medicare & Medicare Services, *Fast Facts.*

xciii. Centers for Medicare & Medicare Services, *Fast Facts.*

xciv. Social Security Administration, *Contribution and Benefit Base*, Washington, DC: GPO, accessed November 11, 2019, https://www.ssa.gov/OACT/COLA/cbb.html.

xcv. Social Security Administration, *2020 Social Security Changes*, Washington, DC: GPO, 2020, https://www.ssa.gov/news/press/factsheets/colafacts2020.pdf.

xcvi. Social Security Administration, *Workers with Maximum-Taxable Earnings*, Washington, DC: GPO, accessed November 13, 2019, https://www.ssa.gov/oact/cola/examplemax.html.

xcvii. Social Security Administration, *Workers with Maximum-Taxable Earnings.*

xcviii. Social Security Administration, *Benefits Planner: Survivors | If You Are The Survivor,* Washington, DC: GPO, 2020, https://www.ssa.gov/planners/survivors/ifyou.html.

xcix. Social Security Administration, *Social Security History*, Washington, DC: GPO, accessed November 17, 2019, https://www.ssa.gov/history/lifeexpect.html

c. "Historical Social Security Tax Rates," *Tax Policy Center*, January 15, 2020, https://www.taxpolicycenter.org/sites/default/files/legacy/taxfacts/content/pdf/ssrate_historical.pdf.

ci. Social Security Administration, *Retirement Benefit: How It's Figured*, Jan. 2020, Pub. 05-10070, Washington, DC: GPO, 2020, https://www.ssa.gov/pubs/EN-05-10070.pdf.

cii. Michael Kitces, "When It Pays To Pay Social Security Taxes," *Kitces*, January 3, 2018, https://www.kitces.com/blog/social-security-fica-self-employment-taxes-return-on-investment-roi-irr/.

ciii. Ashlea Ebeling, "IRS Announces Higher 2019 Estate And Gift Tax Limits," *Forbes*, November 15, 2018, https://www.forbes.com/sites/ashleaebeling/2018/11/15/irs-announces-higher-2019-estate-and-gift-tax-limits/#38f6fcb84295.

civ. Department of Treasury, Internal Revenue Service, *The Estate Tax: Ninety Years and Counting*, report prepared by Darien B. Jacobson and Brian G. Raub and Barry W. Johnson, Washington, DC: GPO, 5, accessed November 27, 2019, https://www.irs.gov/pub/irs-soi/ninetyestate.pdf.

cv. Chye-Ching Huang and Chloe Cho, "Ten Facts You Should Know About the Federal Estate Tax," *Center On Budget And Policy Priorities*, last modified October 30, 2017, https://www.cbpp.org/research/federal-tax/ten-facts-you-should-know-about-the-federal-estate-tax.

cvi. Huang and Cho, "Ten Facts You Should Know About the Federal Estate Tax."

cvii. "State-By-State Estate and Inheritance Tax Rates," *Everplans*, accessed November 24, 2019, https://www.everplans.com/articles/state-by-state-estate-and-inheritance-tax-rates.

cviii. "Estate Planning Guide," *Smartasset*, accessed November 24, 2019, https://smartasset.com/estate-planning/.

cix. *Everplans*, "State-By-State Estate and Inheritance Tax Rates."

cx. "What Is Covered by Standard Homeowners Insurance?" *Insurance Information Institute*, accessed November 30, 2019, https://www.iii.org/article/what-covered-standard-homeowners-policy.

cxi. Pat Howard, "How Much Does Homeowners Insurance Cost," *Policygenius*, January 6, 2020, https://www.policygenius.com/homeowners-insurance/how-much-does-homeowners-insurance-cost/.

cxii. Marissa Perino and Dominic-Madori Davis, "Here's the Typical Home Price in Every State —and What You Can Actually Get For That Money," *Business Insider*, April 10, 2020, https://www.businessinsider.com/average-home-prices-in-every-state-washington-dc-2019-6.

cxiii. "Difference Between Med Pay and PIP Coverage," *Kemper Auto*, accessed December 1, 2019, https://www.infinityauto.com/

knowledge-center/understand-insurance/what-difference-between-med-pay-and-pip-coverage.

cxiv. Ava Lynch, "What Is PIP Insurance?" *The Zebra*, accessed December 1, 2019, https://www.thezebra.com/insurance-guide/pip-insurance/.

cxv. David Corum, "One In Eight Drivers Uninsured," *Insurance Research Council*, October 9, 2017, https://www.insurance-research.org/sites/default/files/downloads/UMNR1005.pdf.

cxvi. Kristen Hall-Geisler, "What Is Uninsured Motorist Car Insurance?" *U.S. News*, April 12, 2019, https://cars.usnews.com/cars-trucks/car-insurance/uninsured-motorist-car-insurance.

cxvii. State of Florida, Florida Highway Safety and Motor Vehicles, *Florida Insurance Requirements*, accessed December 1, 2019, https://www.flhsmv.gov/insurance/.

cxviii. Lisa Green, "Average Car Insurance Costs in 2020," *Nerdwallet*, January 29, 2020, https://www.nerdwallet.com/blog/insurance/car-insurance-basics/how-much-is-car-insurance/.

cxix. Lisa Rapaport, "U.S. Health Spending Twice Other Countries' With Worse Results," *Reuters*, March 13, 2018, https://www.reuters.com/article/us-health-spending-idUSKCN1GP2YN.

cxx. U.S. Department of Health and Human Services, The Center for Medicaid & CHIP Services, *November 2020 Medicaid & CHIP Enrollment Data Highlights*, accessed February 19, 2020, https://www.medicaid.gov/medicaid/program-information/medicaid-and-chip-enrollment-data/report-highlights/index.html.

cxxi. "How Many Americans Get Health Insurance from Their Employer?" *eHealth*, last modified December 6, 2019, https://www.medicaid.gov/medicaid/program-information/medicaid-and-chip-enrollment-data/report-highlights/index.html.

cxxii. "Average Cost of Employer-Sponsored Health Insurance," *eHealth*, last modified December 18, 2019,

https://www.ehealthinsurance.com/resources/small-business/average-cost-of-employer-sponsored-health-insurance.

cxxiii. Louise Norris, "The ACA's Cost-Sharing Subsidies," *Healthinsurance.org*, September 23, 2019, https://www.healthinsurance.org/obamacare/the-acas-cost-sharing-subsidies/.

cxxiv. Department of Health and Human Services, U.S. Centers for Medicare & Medicaid Services, *Out-of-Pocket Maximum/Limit, Healthcare.gov*, accessed February 20, 2020, https://www.healthcare.gov/glossary/out-of-pocket-maximum-limit/.

cxxv. Department of Commerce, United States Census Bureau, *Health Insurance Coverage in the United States: 2018*, reported by Edward R. Bercheck and Jessica C. Barnett and Rachel D. Upton, last modified November 8, 2019, Report P60-267 (RU), Washington, DC: GPO, https://www.census.gov/library/publications/2019/demo/p60-267.html.

cxxvi. "Chances of Disability: Me, Disabled?" *Council for Disability Awareness*, last modified March 28, 2018, https://disabilitycanhappen.org/disability-statistic/.

cxxvii. Social Security Administration, *Annual Statistical Report on the Social Security Disability Insurance Program, 2018*, Pub. 13-11826, Washington, DC: GPO, 2019, 25, https://www.ssa.gov/policy/docs/statcomps/di_asr/2018/di_asr18.pdf.

cxxviii. Adam Shell, "Buy Long-Term Care Insurance at the Right Age to Get the Best Value" *AARP*, December 20, 2019, https://www.aarp.org/caregiving/financial-legal/info-2019/when-to-buy-long-term-care-insurance.html.

cxxix. Shell, "Buy Long-Term Care Insurance at the Right Age."

cxxx. Gina Pogol, "Umbrella Insurance Policy: Because When It Rains, It Pours," *Insurance.com*, April 9, 2019. https://www.insurance.com/auto-insurance/coverage/umbrella-insurance-policy-guide.html.

cxxxi. Pogol, "Umbrella Insurance Policy."

cxxxii. Michael J. Mauboussin and Dan Callahan and Darius Majd, "The Incredible Shrinking Universe of Stocks: The Causes and Consequences of Fewer U.S. Equities," *Credit Suisse*, March 22, 2017, https://research-doc.credit-suisse.com/docView?language=ENG&format=PDF&sourceid=em&document_id=1072753661&serialid=h%2b%2fwLdU%2fTIaitAx1rnamfYsPRAuTFRGdTSF4HZIvTkA%3d.

cxxxiii. "Industry Classification Benchmark: Structural Enhancement to the Industry Categorization Framework," *FTSE Russell*, September 2017, https://content.ftserussell.com/sites/default/files/research/industry_classification_benchmark-final.pdf.

cxxxiv. "When Was the Dow Jones Industrial Average Created?" *Investopedia*, July 17, 2018, https://www.investopedia.com/ask/answers/100214/when-did-dow-jones-industrial-average-djia-begin.asp.

cxxxv. Caroline Valetkevitch, "Timeline: Key Dates and Milestones in the S&P 500's History," *Reuters*, March 28, 2013, https://www.reuters.com/article/us-usa-stocks-sp-timeline-idUSBRE92R11Z20130328.

cxxxvi. "History of S&P Global," *S&P Global*, accessed March 8, 2020, https://www.spglobal.com/en/who-we-are/our-history.

cxxxvii. James A. Barham, "The 100 Richest Universities: Their Generosity and Commitment to Research," *The Best Schools*, September 13, 2019, https://thebestschools.org/features/richest-universities-endowments-generosity-research/.

cxxxviii. Simon Moore, "6 Expert Investment Portfolios You Can Implement Today," *Forbes*, July 26, 2018, https://www.forbes.com/sites/simonmoore/2018/07/26/six-expert-investment-portfolios-you-can-implement-today/#5c72197974b2.

cxxxix. "Too Many Stocks Spoil The Portfolio," *Financial Times*, accessed March 18, 2020, https://www.ft.com/content/220c76fe-a1bd-11e2-ad0c-00144feabdc0.

cxl. Investment Company Institute, *2019 Investment Company Fact Book*, 59th ed., (Washington, DC: Investment Company Institute, 2019) 54-77, https://www.icifactbook.org/ch3/19_fb_ch3.

cxli. Investment Company Institute, *2019 Fact Book*, 30-53, https://www.icifactbook.org/ch2/19_fb_ch2.

cxlii. "Mutual Fund Screener," *MutualFunds.com*, accessed March 18, 2020, https://www.mutualfunds.com/screener/#tm=1-screener&r=Webpage%231068&only=meta%2Cdata&f_15=Fidelity%20Investments&f_14=Stock&tab=overview&page=1.

cxliii. "Mutual Fund Screener," *Zachs*, accessed March 19, 2020, https://www.zacks.com/screening/mutual-fund-screener.

cxliv. Aye M. Soe and Ryan Poirier, "SPIVA Scorecard," *S&P Global*, September 15, 2016, https://www.spglobal.com/en/research-insights/articles/SPIVA-US-Scorecard.

cxlv. "S&P 500 Historical Annual Returns," *Macrotrends*, last modified May 22, 2020, https://www.macrotrends.net/2526/sp-500-historical-annual-returns.

cxlvi. Brett Carson, "The Mutual Fund Fees We Don't Talk About," *U.S. News*, March 4, 2015, https://money.usnews.com/money/blogs/the-smarter-mutual-fund-investor/2015/03/04/the-mutual-fund-fees-we-dont-talk-about.

cxlvii. Kenneth Kim, "How Much Do Mutual Funds Really Cost?" *Forbes*, September 24, 2016, https://www.forbes.com/sites/kennethkim/2016/09/24/how-much-do-mutual-funds-really-cost/#1ca9b5cca527.

cxlviii. Craig L. Israelsen, "Get It Right When It Comes to Calculating Returns," *Financial Planning*, March 2, 2017, https://www.financial-planning.com/news/the-only-way-to-get-it-right-when-it-comes-to-calculating-returns.

cxlix. "John C. Bogle," *Vanguard*, accessed March 27, 2020, https://about.vanguard.com/who-we-are/a-remarkable-history/founder-Jack-Bogle-tribute/.

cl. "John Bogle," *Bogleheads® wiki*, accessed March 27, 2020, https://www.bogleheads.org/wiki/John_Bogle.

cli. "Compound Annual Growth Rate," *Moneychimp*, accessed March 27, 2020, http://moneychimp.com/features/market_cagr.htm.

clii. Michael Batnick, "Today in Market History, the First Index Fund" *The Irrelevant Investor*, August 31, 2017, https://theirrelevantinvestor.com/2017/08/31/today-in-market-history-the-first-index-fund/.

cliii. "Vanguard 500 Index Fund Investor Shares (VFINX)," *Yahoo!*, accessed March 27, 2020, https://finance.yahoo.com/quote/VFINX?p=VFINX&.tsrc=fin-srch.

cliv. "Fast Facts About Vanguard," *Vanguard*, accessed March 27 2020, https://about.vanguard.com/who-we-are/fast-facts/.

clv. John Gittelsohn, "End of Era: Passive Equity Funds Surpass Active in Epic Shift," *Bloomberg*, September 11, 2019, https://www.bloomberg.com/news/articles/2019-09-11/passive-u-s-equity-funds-eclipse-active-in-epic-industry-shift.

clvi. "Joint Life Probability Spreadsheet," *Financial Architects, LLC*, accessed April 4, 2020, https://www.financialarchitectsllc.com/resources.

clvii. Adam Grealish, "ETF Selection for Portfolio Construction: A Methodology," *Betterment*, August 27, 2014, https://www.betterment.com/resources/etf-portfolio-selection-methodology/.

clviii. Barbara A. Friedberg, "Robo-advisors With the Most Assets Under Management-2020," *Robo-Advisor Pros*, April 22, 2020, https://www.roboadvisorpros.com/robo-advisors-with-most-aum-assets-under-management/.

clix. United States, White House Archives, *The Effects of Conflicted Investment Advice On Retirement Savings,"* February 2015, Washington, DC: GPO, https://obamawhitehouse.archives.gov/sites/default/files/docs/cea_coi_report_final.pdf.\

clx. Scott Van Voorhis, "Personal Finances Are a Top Source of Stress for Americans," *TheStreet*, last modified December 29, 2019, https://www.thestreet.com/personal-finance/personal-finances-are-a-top-source-of-stress-for-americans-14795237.

clxi. Diana Divecha, "How Teens Today Are Different From Past Generations," *Greater Good Magazine*, October 20, 2017,

https://greatergood.berkeley.edu/article/item/how_teens_today_are_different_from_past_generations.

clxii. Hillary Hoffower and Libertina Brandt, "The Most Expensive and Affordable States to Buy a House, Ranked," *Business Insider*, July 5, 2019, https://www.businessinsider.com/cost-to-buy-a-house-in-every-state-ranked-2018-8?.

clxiii. Ellie Polack, "New Cigna Study Reveals Loneliness at Epidemic Levels in America," May 1, 2018, https://www.cigna.com/newsroom/news-releases/2018/new-cigna-study-reveals-loneliness-at-epidemic-levels-in-america.

clxiv. ATTOM Data Solutions, "Home Affordability Improves For Average U.S. Wage Earners To Best Level In Over Two Years," *Monterey County Weekly*, March 25, 2020, https://www.montereycountyweekly.com/news/state/home-affordability-improves-for-average-u-s-wage-earners-to/article_259bab7a-a165-5235-ae44-88610606c7ae.html.

clxv. Ellen Byron, "More Americans Are Living Solo, and Companies Want Their Business," *The Wall Street Journal*, June 2, 2019, https://www.wsj.com/articles/more-americans-are-living-solo-and-companies-want-their-business-11559497606.

clxvi. "Survey of the States," *Council for Economic Education*, February 2020, https://www.councilforeconed.org/wp-content/uploads/2020/02/2020-Survey-of-the-States.pdf.

clxvii. "2020 Best School Districts In America," *Niche*, accessed April 23, 2020, https://www.niche.com/k12/search/best-school-districts/.

Made in the USA
Las Vegas, NV
09 February 2022

43543051R00194